Praise for John Assaraf and Murray Smith's revolutionary book,

The Answer

"A brilliant formula for growing any business and living an extraordinary life—entrepreneurial wisdom embodied in a proactive, balanced approach to living. A must read!"

—Stephen R. Covey, author of
The 7 Habits of Highly Effective People

"Inspiring. . . . Motivates you to go after the grandest version of the greatest life and business you ever envisioned for yourself with the knowledge that it is absolutely possible. *The Answer* gives you the tools to change your life. This is one of the most exciting books I have ever read."

—Suzanne Somers

"*The Answer* is a book that could transform your life."

—Larry King, Emmy Award–winning host of
CNN's *Larry King Live*

"This book is a masterpiece! I couldn't stop reading it. It is by far the best book I have ever read on how to use the Law of Attraction and the latest breakthroughs in neuroscience to quantum leap the growth of any business. It is now required reading for all my staff and students."

—Jack Canfield, coauthor of *The Success Principles* and cocreator of the #1 *New York Times* bestselling Chicken Soup for the Soul® series

"In *The Answer*, the brilliant and wise John Assaraf and Murray Smith share their amazing breadth of experience and knowledge to unlock the secrets of success. Their comprehensive book informs, guides, and ultimately inspires you to take ownership not just of your business but your life."

—Debbie Ford, #1 *New York Times* bestselling author of
Why Good People Do Bad Things

"Everyone wants the answers to life's probing questions, particularly those of business, financial freedom, and how to make your life a masterpiece. John and Murray have made their lives masterpieces and share from deep profound insight how you can make yours the same or even better."
— Mark Victor Hansen, coauthor of *Cracking the Millionaire Code* and cocreator of the #1 *New York Times* bestselling Chicken Soup for the Soul® series

"If you really want to attract and make things happen faster in your business and life, read *The Answer* now! John Assaraf and Murray Smith will put you on the road to riches as fast as anyone I know. Read it and give a copy to your best friend."
— Bob Proctor, contributor to *The Secret* and author of *You Were Born Rich*

"*The Answer* brings the most advanced scientific research about the power of the mind and universe into cutting-edge business-growth strategies. This book will revolutionize personal and business growth."
— Jane Willhite, founder and CEO, PSI Seminars

"Step-by-step instructions, interaction, and learning abound here. You will have a clear road to your own success by the time you are finished and many 'Aha!' moments. Prepare to be astonished and build your new life!"
— Nan Shastry, CEO, Brainy Betty, Inc.

"John and Murray have packaged a lifetime of highly result-certain expertise into this content-rich book. . . . If your business isn't living up to your vision, this is the one book and philosophy of predictable, unstoppable growth that you need to read!"
— Jay Abraham, author of *Getting Everything You Can Out of All You've Got*

"A modern-day classic. A fascinating, breakthrough approach to business-booming based on hard science and real-world tests. I love it!"
— Joe Vitale, author of *The Attractor Factor*

"*The Answer* is a pragmatic and easy-to-use formula for building a solid entrepreneurial business. Read it, and most important, take action upon it!"

—James Arthur Ray, author of *Harmonic Wealth*®

"John Assaraf and Murray Smith have written a masterpiece on business strategy while connecting the heart and soul in the process. It is a must read for every business person and student alike. Great job!"

—Jim White, Ph.D., author of *What's My Purpose?*

"Enlightening! I have been reading business books, marketing books, and spiritual books for many years. This is the best book and easiest book that gives you a step-by-step process to make millions in your business."

—Steven E., author of the bestselling Wake Up . . . Live the Life You Love series

"A must read for any CEO serious about amassing a fortune."

—Chet Holmes, national bestselling author of *The Ultimate Sales Machine*

"There are great books on the unlimited power of our minds to cocreate the circumstances of our dreams. There are even more books on business development and the management of those dreams. What makes *The Answer* so remarkable is that finally both dimensions have been wonderfully explained and integrated into what is destined to be the 'how to' book of the century. Read and win!"

—Ian Percy, author of *The Profitable Power of Purpose*

"*The Answer* is absolutely a must read for anyone interested in a new and much higher level of prosperity. John and Murray have helped me more than triple my business income, and they can do the same for you. I highly recommend it."

—Dharma Singh Khalsa, M.D., America's #1 Brain Longevity Specialist

THE ANSWER

GROW ANY BUSINESS,

ACHIEVE FINANCIAL FREEDOM,

AND LIVE AN EXTRAORDINARY LIFE

JOHN ASSARAF and MURRAY SMITH

ATRIA PAPERBACK

NEW YORK LONDON TORONTO SYDNEY

ATRIA PAPERBACK
A Division of Simon & Schuster, Inc.
1230 Avenue of the Americas
New York, NY 10020

First Atria Paperback edition September 2009

ATRIA PAPERBACK and colophon are trademarks of Simon & Schuster, Inc.

For information about special discounts for bulk purchases,
please contact Simon & Schuster Special Sales at
1-866-506-1949 or business@simonandschuster.com.

The Simon & Schuster Speakers Bureau can bring authors to your live event.
For more information or to book an event, contact the Simon & Schuster Speakers
Bureau at 1-866-248-3049 or visit our website at www.simonspeakers.com.

Designed by Level C

Manufactured in the United States of America

10   9   8   7   6

The Library of Congress has cataloged the hardcover edition as follows:

Assaraf, John.
    The answer : grow any business, achieve financial freedom, and
live an extraordinary life / John Assaraf and Murray Smith.
       p.   cm.
    Includes bibliogaphical references.
    1. Success in business.   I. Smith, Murray.   II. Title.

HF5386.A795   2008
658.4'09—dc22   2008011886

ISBN: 978-1-4165-6199-6
ISBN: 978-1-4165-6200-9 (pbk)
ISBN: 978-1-4165-6205-4 (ebook)

To the Reader

You have dreams, big dreams.
Like most people, you also have questions.
And like most, you may have doubts.

We encourage you to set aside your doubts,
find answers to your questions,
and throw yourself headlong into the fulfillment
of your dreams.

We dedicate this book to you.

CONTENTS

Introduction: The Question   xi

1. Inside the Box: John's Story   1

2. The Search for How the World Works   9

3. The Law of Attraction   21

4. The Universe Inside Your Brain   35

5. How to Change Your Mind   55

6. Your Dream Business   73

7. The Neural Reconditioning Process™   103

8. Neural Reconditioning FAQs   139

9. The Important Things: Murray's Story   155

10. Vision, Focus, Action   163

11. Your Ideal Customer   173

12. Innovating Your Business   193

13. Finding Your Business's DNA   215

14. Reaching Your Ideal Customer   231

15. Big Thinking   251

     Conclusion: The Path   265

     Acknowledgments   269

     Appendix 1 Customer Survey Forms   273

     *Appendix 2 The Five Major Industries: Common
     Hot Buttons*   279

     *Appendix 3 Distribution Channels, Marketing
     Strategies, and Marketing Tactics*   288

     *Appendix 4 The Five Major Industries: Common
     Distribution Channels and Marketing Strategies*   296

     Resources   301

Introduction

Close your eyes for a moment and think about the greatest rewards you can imagine as you step into absolutely extraordinary levels of success. Whether it's an amazing lifestyle, the home of your dreams, financial freedom, charitable giving, or philanthropic work—whatever that dream looks like to you, picture yourself basking in it. Thank the pilot of your personal jet for waiting a few extra minutes while your family joins you on an exotic vacation; run your hands over the exquisite cabinetry in your vast, sunlit new kitchen; savor the feeling of knowing you'll always have enough money to pay the bills, no matter their size; graciously accept the gratitude of the international relief agency to which you have just contributed a gift of historic proportions.

Ahhh, that's the dream. Then there's the reality. Eyes back open now: What does your day-to-day life *really* look like? If what you see is worry, stress, or uncertainty, or if it simply isn't everything you want it to be, then this book is for you.

Maybe you're a small business owner who started a few years ago with big goals and bigger dreams, but now things seem to have stalled. Are you working harder and harder, but not really seeing results? If so, you're not the only one: In North America alone, there are more than twenty-five million small-business owners just like you, most of them facing a predicament just like yours.

Or perhaps you are an executive, department head, or manager for a company, corporation, or nonprofit looking for ways to grow your business unit out of a slump, to set yourself apart from the internal competition, or to take your own income to the next level. Perhaps you're that business's CEO or CFO, looking to make a major impact on the company's future.

Or you might be one of the 73 percent of Americans who want to start their own business but hesitate to take the plunge. You've heard that 95 percent of new businesses close their doors within five years, and you don't want to become another statistic. You're worried that you don't have what it takes, that the competition's too stiff and the risks too high, that you'll run out of money, that you'll find yourself in over your head.

Still, you don't want to let go of that dream of finally watching your business take off. Of being your own boss. Of changing lives for the better while generating big profits—doing well by doing good. Of being on the cover of *Fortune* magazine. Of having the corporate jet or limousine waiting to take you to your next client meeting. Of creating a foundation that will use your wealth to address the major problems in the world long after you're no longer with us.

There's the dream and then there's the reality—and for millions of people, the two just don't look like they'll ever match up. But they should, and they can. That's why we wrote *The Answer*.

Through the 2006 movie and book *The Secret*, millions of people were introduced to the concept of the Law of Attraction, the idea that by focusing our thoughts, we can actually attract those things we want most from life, turning even our wildest dreams into realities. One of the authors of this book, John Assaraf, was fortunate enough to be a teacher in *The Secret*. Since its release, many people have asked us, "How do I apply that idea, practically and specifically, to creating success in my work and business life?"

Having worked with thousands of businesspeople over the last few decades, we know the hopes and fears, aspirations, and anguish that lie behind those words. To us, the millions of business failures, bankruptcies, unemployed and underemployed across the land each year are not one-dimensional statistics, they are human stories with faces, names, and voices. We hear the question *behind* the question:

How can I access unlimited abundance?

The Answer does not come from experts with advanced degrees (neither of us has one of those) or an entrepreneurial upbringing (neither of us has one of those, either). We never went to college. We didn't come from money, and we didn't have successful business-owner parents to show us the ropes. In fact, growing up we both seemed pretty clearly destined to fail.

An immigrant from the Middle East living in a poor neighborhood in Canada, John Assaraf spent most of his teen years running with a group of kids who kept getting into trouble. In high school, he managed to find a path out of that directionless life to a promising career as a professional athlete—but that promise was soon cut short in a freak car accident that ended his prospects for pro basketball forever.

Murray Smith was labeled as learning disabled at a young age, pulled away from his classmates, and placed in a special school, on a voc-tech track headed for a life of factory work. His first job out of school had him cleaning sewers a hundred feet belowground.

Yet for some reason, we both found our way to success. How? Through trial and error, buoyed by sheer determination, we each happened to learn the fundamental laws that regulate the creation of business success, and we honed them into an approach that has worked again and again. For the past three decades, we have each been busy applying The Answer to building businesses, successful businesses, from scratch—eighteen of them, between the two of us. Yet all around us, we saw people failing. One thing we've learned is that success tastes that much sweeter when you have people to share it with. We wanted to share our experiences and the secrets to success we'd learned along the way with others—as many others as possible.

As best friends for all these years, we've built several of those successful businesses together. In 2005, we decided to come out of retirement and devote the rest of our lives to helping aspiring businesses around the world.

The Answer comes from a wide range of sources. In the course of this book, you'll learn about all sorts of things, from simple ways to redirect the power of your brain and how the universal laws of life can be used to succeed in business, to crafting a slam-dunk marketing message based on your company's unique value, to forming your own master-mind group and thinking like a multimillionaire. You'll learn the three critical questions that are responsible for driving growth in your business revenues, what your ideal customer looks like, and which are the crucial business activities, out of hundreds of possibilities, that you absolutely cannot afford to ignore.

All the answers that make up *The Answer* have come from hundreds of interviews with scientists and salespeople, business leaders and multimillionaires; they have emerged from our experiences working with thousands of clients and our in-the-trenches encounters with the ups and downs, trials and errors, failures and successes of the world of business, all of which provide critical elements of *The Answer*.

There is a principle in physics known as Heisenberg's uncertainty principle, which teaches us that when you change the way you look at something, *the thing you look at changes in response*. This is just as true of your life and your business as it is true of subatomic particles. *The Answer* is going to show you how to look at your business differently, whether you work within an organization or own your own business, so that your business will change in the way you've always dreamed it would. And as your business changes, so will your life.

The Answer is about taking ownership of your life and your business. It is about understanding how the principles of cause and effect operate in business, and how to design and execute your actions so that you are *the cause*, and not simply *the effect*. We'll show you how to build your dream business *from the inside*, by creating a picture within yourself of utter clarity and certainty. Then, we'll show you how to build that business by following battle-tested strategies for growing your business's revenues as large as you want.

Regardless of whether you are a solo entrepreneur or a business owner; a professional in private practice or an executive or manager running a department at a Fortune 500 corporation; someone about to start a business; or someone who wants to become irreplaceable in the business you're in: If you want to create financial freedom and live an extraordinary life, we wrote this book for you. We wrote it to inspire you with the confidence you need, the information you need, and the specific, step-by-step actions you need to take in order to build your dream business.

We'll share both our stories with you as we go, showing you how we came to the insights that contributed to *The Answer*, along with stories of other successful businesspeople we know who have applied these same ideas to create their own dream businesses.

The Answer has one purpose: to help you answer The Question — and not just answer it, but answer it with such clear, strong, and unshakable certainty that your life will never be the same. That your dream business will be not just possible, not just probable, but *unstoppable*.

How can I access unlimited abundance?

You'll find The Answer in these pages.

1

INSIDE THE BOX: JOHN'S STORY

One Tuesday morning in May 2000, my son Keenan and I opened a cardboard box that had been sealed for five years, and what we found inside changed my life forever.

I had no idea this was going to happen; in fact, I didn't know exactly what we were going to see when we opened that box. It had been five years, after all, and in those years we'd moved around quite a bit and seen a lot of change.

I began my career in business twenty years earlier, going to work as a real estate agent fresh out of high school. My dreams of professional basketball were long gone, and I had no idea what to do with my life. Real estate was the only thing I could think of that would keep me from working at a grocery store, and so, on June 20, 1980, this nineteen-year-old kid took his real estate exam and became a licensed Realtor. Within a few months, seminars and workshops on goal-setting were teaching me about some odd-sounding personal growth techniques they called *visualization* and *affirmations*.

I had been aware of the value of such practices, long before they had formal names. In my teens, I wanted more than anything to become a successful basketball star. In fact, I wanted to succeed in that career so badly that I constantly imagined myself winning championship games, sinking that winning shot as the clock ran out, running that movie in my head before I ever stepped onto the court. I literally went to sleep at night with a basketball next to me under the covers. And until I was injured, I was an impact player.

Now, however, winning on the court was no longer the issue. Now it was all about winning in business.

I started observing what the top achievers in my office were doing, watching them like a hawk, listening to them talk on the phone, even sitting in on meetings with them, just to hear exactly what they said and how they said it. I started reading voraciously, absorbing everything I could get my hands on that might give me clues as to how to become successful in my new career. I listened to audiotapes and attended live programs—and one of these was taught by a man whom I came to know as a friend, mentor, and business partner. His name is Bob Proctor.

In the early sixties, Bob had moved from his native Toronto to Chicago to work with a man named Earl Nightingale, who had launched the personal development industry a decade earlier. Nightingale's famous audio recording *The Strangest Secret* was the first recording in history outside of popular music to sell a million copies. Earl Nightingale, in turn, had learned his philosophy from Napoleon Hill, the author of what is probably the most well-known book in all of success literature, *Think and Grow Rich*.

From Napoleon Hill to Earl Nightingale to Bob Proctor, one theme ran through all their teachings: *The secret to our success lies in controlling our thoughts*. The only limitations on our accomplishments, these teachers were telling me, are those we place upon ourselves by our own self-limiting thoughts. What they said made complete sense to me; I didn't know how or why it worked, but to me the truth of it seemed self-evident.

Soon I was taking this business of writing down my goals very seriously. (In fact, I still have a copy of my carefully written-out goals from the summer of 1982.) I started writing affirmations and vivid word pictures of the kind of success I wanted to have, feeding my unconscious mind with new images of my goals, playing out new movies in my mind, movies of my triumphs as a serial entrepreneur.

That year, my first year in real estate, I earned about $30,000. Not bad for age twenty, I thought. My second year, my earnings totaled

$150,000. This goal setting, visualizing, affirmation repeating thing was working!

After that second year, I decided to take some time off to take stock and expand my horizons. I gathered my earnings and set off to travel around the world. My trip ended up lasting more than a year, as I circled the globe learning about other cultures and worldviews and expanding my sense of what was possible. In late 1984, I returned to Toronto and went back to work at my real estate office . . . but it was clear I wouldn't last there long. I was hungry to know more, to do more, and to *be* more.

A few years later, in late 1986, Walter Schneider and Frank Polzler, the two guys who owned the rights to the giant Realtor RE/MAX for eastern Canada, approached me with the news that the RE/MAX subfranchising rights for the state of Indiana had become available. (Today, Walter and Frank are the most successful subfranchisors in the world.) They knew I was itching to grow, and they had decided to offer me a partnership if I would move to Indiana to build the business there.

"John," they said, "would you like to move to Indiana?"

I said, "Absolutely! How soon do I leave?" and then added, "Where's that, again?" I hadn't even heard the "Indiana" part. I'd just heard "Would you like to move?" and I knew they were offering me an opportunity I couldn't possibly turn down.

My first week in Indiana, a reporter from the *Indianapolis Business Journal* came to ask about our plans. "In five years," I told him, "we'll be the biggest real estate company in Indiana—in fact, we will sell a billion dollars in real estate."

He scribbled all this down and then offhandedly asked, "So, have you talked with—" and he rattled off the names of the major owners of the largest real estate company in the area.

"Um, why?" I hedged.

He grinned. "I guess you probably already know this, but their firm has been here for about eighty years, and they control seventy percent of the real estate market in these parts."

I had no idea. I'd never even heard of the guys he was talking about. I knew nothing about Indiana real estate—and in fact, I knew nothing about how to run my own business, let alone how to build it to generate such massive sales. Let alone how to do it in the face of dominant, well-entrenched competition.

The reporter laughed. It was pretty clear that I'd stuck my foot so far down my mouth I might never get it out. Sure enough, a few days later, there was my picture in the paper, along with a story on me with the headline, "A Billion in Sales Within Five Years." I was the laughing-stock of the town.

That is, until five years later—when my company generated $1.2 billion in sales for the year.

This visualization and affirmations thing was *really* working. It was still a mystery to me exactly why or how it worked, but who cared—it worked!

In 1995, I started making what my mentors had called *vision boards*, cutting out pictures that represented the goals and dreams I aspired to achieve and pasting them onto bulletin boards; the idea was to create everyday reminders of my life's direction. I didn't yet grasp the full power of this exercise, but that would soon change.

By that time, I had run that RE/MAX region for a decade, growing it to over seventy-five offices and one thousand salespeople. I had also grown restless again; it was time to search for new and larger opportunities. I hired and trained a replacement, packed up my possessions and put them in storage, left Indiana, and moved back to Canada.

Over the next few years my family and I moved around, while I looked for the next big opportunity. I invested in a few companies and consulted for a few more, while we kept moving and looking. In late 1998, a friend named Len McCurdy invited me to come down to San Francisco to look at something his son Kevin and Kevin's friend Howard had developed.

"This program is amazing," Len told me. "It lets you do a virtual tour of a car or hotel property on the Internet, without any downloads or plug-ins. You've got to see it."

I admired Len and knew that working with him would provide me with an amazing opportunity to learn and grow. His last company had been worth a fortune before Len sold it to IBM. I flew to San Francisco and it didn't take much imagination to appreciate that this online application Kevin and Howard had developed would have fantastic applications in real estate, car sales, hotel room advertising, all sorts of areas. Len invited me to join him as senior vice president of sales and marketing for the new company, a position I accepted without hesitation. And then he said something that took me by surprise:

"Hey, why don't we take this thing public? And why not do it by this fall?"

He wanted to do an IPO—in *nine months*. Even in those heady dot-com-boom days, that was a pretty outrageous goal. But Len knew a lot about how to achieve extraordinary goals; he had read the same books and studied with some of the same people I had, and he knew that we are constrained only by the limitations we place upon our own thoughts.

I took a deep breath, and said, "Sure, let's do it!" We moved from Vancouver to Los Angeles, and I spent the next year or so flying back and forth between L.A. and San Francisco. My colleagues and I launched our new company in the beginning of 1999; nine months later we placed a successful IPO on NASDAQ, followed by a merger of equals with another company that left our new venture with a market valuation of $2.5 billion.

This whirlwind adventure had three results. It offered me the most vivid proof of the power of our thoughts that I had ever seen. It left me with the financial wherewithal to retire. And it found me once again wanting to move on and search for new horizons. It wasn't at all clear what those horizons would be, but there was absolutely no doubt as to where I wanted to live while I chased them: San Diego.

Living in San Diego had been a dream of mine for nearly twenty years. Way back in 1982, while traveling around the world, I had stopped over in San Diego and told myself, "Someday, when I can afford to live wherever I want, I'm going to live here."

Now, in the beginning of 2000, my family and I rented a house on the bluffs of San Diego and started house hunting. By April we had closed on an amazing property and I sent for our stuff, which had been languishing in storage back in Indiana for years.

A few weeks later, all my furniture arrived, along with dozens of cartons.

Which is how it happened that I was sitting in the study of my new home, early one beautiful Tuesday morning in May, surrounded by still-sealed boxes, catching up on my email. My six-year-old son, Keenan, sat on a carton near the door of the room, swinging his legs and banging them against the box. I said, "Honey, I'm trying to get something done here, do you mind not banging your legs like that? It's kind of distracting."

"What's in the box, Dad?" he said, as he continued banging his legs.

I peered at the Magic Marker scrawl on the box. "Those are my vision boards, from Indiana, remember Indiana?" Keenan had been a toddler when I had packed those boxes away.

"What's a vision board?"

I explained, as simply as I could, that this was something I made out of pictures of things I wanted to acquire or achieve in my business or in my life.

"Why do you do that?"

I was tempted to say "Just because," so we could close the conversation and I could get back to my email, but one glance at Keenan, who was obviously having a great time just hanging out in this exciting new home, made me change my mind.

As a kid, I'd promised myself that when I was old enough (and, hopefully, mature enough) to have kids of my own, I would never say "Just because." So I slit open the packing tape, opened the carton, and pulled out the first vision board. There was a picture of that Mercedes I'd wanted back then, which had since been purchased, driven, enjoyed, and sold. There was an image of a nice wristwatch, and next to it, a pair of alligator shoes. I gazed at the pictures for a moment, reminiscing, and then pulled out the second board—and we were staring at a picture of a huge, stunning, gorgeous house.

My first thought was, "Hey, how did *this* get in here?" Somehow, a real estate brochure must have fallen into the box when we were getting ready to move. . . . But no, how was that possible? The box had been sealed for years! I stared at the house in the picture. This was no brochure. The picture was glued to the board; it was *part* of the board.

And I started to cry.

There, on my vision board, was a picture I'd clipped five years earlier from an old copy of *Dream Homes* magazine. It was a unique house on six acres, with 188 windows, 320 orange trees, 2 lemon trees, and a slew of other special features. There was no mistaking it. It was a picture of the house that the two of us were sitting in at that very moment. Not *like* it. It was *this house*.

When I'd cut it out of that magazine, I hadn't even known where it was located or how much it cost. It was just a picture in a magazine.

My mind raced. What were the odds of my ending up buying that actual house? How would you even begin to calculate those odds?

And all at once, I knew what I was going to do with my life.

If you have seen the movie *The Secret*, you have heard me describe this scene. What we did not have the chance to describe in *The Secret* is what happened next. This event was a pivot point in my life, an epiphany that has driven everything in my life since then, and it had everything to do with the genesis of the book you hold in your hands. For twenty years I'd been engaged in the careful, consistent practice of affirmations, vivid goal setting, visualization, and meditation, and I had seen plenty of proof that it all worked. But I had never really known *why* it worked, nor, in truth, had I ever really cared. Now I *had to know*.

In 2000, I had just "retired," and had no business on the table at the moment, no immediate prospects for one, nor any pressing need to start one. I was in the incredibly fortunate position that we expect every reader of this book aspires to be in: a position of complete financial freedom. I didn't have to work.

So this became my work. That burning need to know how my house got inside that cardboard box became my full-time occupation.

I began by making a list of the top scientists in every field that seemed related to this quest, and then set out to read everything they had written. Soon I was flying around the country to hear them speak, and even calling them on the phone to talk with them. Over the following months and years, I communicated with some of the best and brightest minds in quantum physics, neuroscience, philosophy, and a host of related fields. What they told me blew my mind. It explained how I'd built one successful company after another—and it explained how we had ended up living in the dream home that lived inside that cardboard box.

In the next few chapters, we want to take you inside that box, too, and share with you some of the amazing things these scientists have shown us.

2

THE SEARCH FOR HOW THE WORLD WORKS

In 1633, an aging Italian astronomer named Galileo Galilei was taken before the Roman Inquisition, tried, convicted of heresy, and sentenced to spend the rest of his life in prison.

Galileo's crime? He endorsed the idea, proposed a century earlier by the great Catholic astronomer Nicolaus Copernicus, that the earth is not the center of the solar system. In fact, said Galileo, it is the other way around: The sun sits at the center, and the earth is simply one of a handful of planets that revolve around it.

This idea was judged as being diametrically opposed to the position taken by Holy Scripture. Galileo was forced to publicly recant his views, and his book containing the offending idea, *Dialogue Concerning the Two Chief World Systems*, was banned. The old man's sentence was later commuted to house arrest, and he lived out the rest of his days confined to his villa outside Florence, where he eventually went blind.

Still, Galileo's views persisted, and the meticulous experiments and mathematical models he used in his search to understand nature set the stage for all the developments of modern science that followed. Three centuries later, a German physicist named Albert Einstein called him "the father of modern science."

For more than a thousand years leading up to the time of Galileo, science had been more interested in creating intellectually satisfying descriptions of reality than in trying to see if those descriptions could be supported by proof. But with the age of Copernicus and Galileo, European scientists began the vigorous pursuit of empirical evidence. Thought experiments gave way to actual physical experiments, such as the famous moment when Galileo dropped two objects from the Leaning Tower of Pisa to test out Aristotle's assertion that heavier objects fall faster than lighter objects. (They don't.)

From Galileo's time onward, scientists' precise observations contributed to a picture of the world that looked very much like a massive piece of mechanical clockwork; they had little practical use for such ideas as soul, spirit, or consciousness. The French philosopher and mathematician René Descartes, a contemporary of Galileo's who is today regarded as "the father of modern philosophy," declared that the best way to understand how the world works would be to divide existence into two parts: the objective or material world, governed by the principles of science, and the subjective world of the mind and the soul, which would be the province of the church.

Descartes is especially famous for the statement *I think, therefore I am*. But the truth is, the *think* part of that declaration puzzled Descartes, much as it has puzzled scientists for centuries since. Just how *is* it that we think? Where do our thoughts come from? How do the bits of physical matter that constitute our brains generate consciousness? As contemporary physicist John Hagelin has said, "There is a deep philosophical problem surrounding how you get consciousness out of a hunk of meat."

Despite Descartes' neat division of reality, common sense suggested that our thoughts *must* be connected to the rest of existence somehow. But how, exactly? The answers to those questions open up a tremendous new world of possibility for what we can achieve in our lives, and they form a central part of *The Answer*.

A WORLD INSIDE THE ATOM

In the generations following Galileo and Descartes, Sir Isaac Newton took the idea of nature-as-machine much further, detailing the precise laws that govern how that machine operates. All of classical physics, and in fact, all of modern science, has been built upon the foundation created by Newton, who described a universe of empty, three-dimensional space, through which physical objects move according to immutable laws. These laws of motion made possible the advance of modern technology, from simple steam engines to the space probes that have analyzed soil samples on Mars.

What we have been able to accomplish by applying Newton's laws has been truly astonishing. But scientists eventually reached the limits of the Newtonian worldview. As their tools grew more sophisticated, their explorations of the physical world took them deep into the heart of the atom, where the nature of reality proved to be something quite different from anything Descartes or Newton ever imagined.

At the dawn of the twentieth century, the tidy, objective, mechanistic view of the world began to fall apart. With the discovery of radioactivity in the late 1890s, scientists began looking into the world within the atomic nucleus, and they were shocked to discover that on the subatomic level, the physical world did not behave at all the way Newton said it should. In fact, the "atom" itself turned out to be a sort of illusion: The closer scientists looked, the less it really appeared to be there.

Coined in ancient Greece, the term *atom* means "indivisible unit," and through the nineteenth century, scientists believed that our entire physical universe was composed of these elementary particles. But radioactivity showed us that the atom was divisible after all — in fact, there was a whole new world of phenomena inside the atom, waiting to be explored, measured, and described. And when our vision of the atom fractured, the foundation of classical physics fractured along with it. Our view of how the world works was in for a radical transformation.

EVERYTHING IS ENERGY

When we say the name *Albert Einstein*, what comes to mind? Perhaps you think of his wild mane of white hair, or that famous picture of the distinguished physicist sticking out his tongue. Or maybe you think simply, "Genius." But whatever picture you have, you will also probably come up with "$E=MC^2$." Why on earth would a mathematical equation for a sophisticated theory be so famous that even nonscientists recognize it immediately? Because with that simple equation, "Energy equals mass times the speed of light squared," Einstein shattered centuries of thinking and radically altered our view of how the world works.

In his effort to explain the puzzling behavior of light, Einstein found the only viable solution was to stop looking within the neat framework of Newtonian physics. Instead, he introduced his own picture of how the world works: the theory of relativity. One reason Einstein's idea was so transformative was that for the first time ever, it described how energy and matter are not only related, but can be *transformed back and forth into each other.* A chink had been found in the wall separating the worlds of matter and energy. Now the elegant, clear-cut world of classical, Newtonian physics would be forced to move over and make room for the fuzzy, strange, nearly unimaginable world of *quantum physics.*

Quantum physics is the study of how the world works on the smallest scale, at a level far smaller than the atom. And as scientists studied the nature of reality on a smaller and smaller scale, something strange began to happen: The deeper we went into reality, the more it seemed to dissolve from view. The search for the smallest known particle of matter had instead turned up distinct yet elusive little packets of energy, which physicists called *quanta.*

The Einstein breakthrough comes down to this: *Everything is energy.* A rock, a planet, a glass of water, your hand, everything you can touch, taste, or smell—it's all made of molecules, which are made of atoms, which are made of protons and electrons and neutrons, which are made of nothing but vibrating packets of energy.

This is where quantum physics intersects with what I found inside that cardboard box. What physicists found has everything to do with how you are going to create the life of your dreams by building your dream business. For once we know that everything is energy—that there is no absolute distinction between matter and energy—then the boundaries between the physical world and the world of our thoughts start to disappear as well.

READING THE MIND OF GOD

In the decades that followed Einstein's theory of relativity, the new quantum physics began to reveal some very strange things. The tiny packets of energy known as quanta exhibited some very peculiar behaviors, including an unexplainable ability to influence one another, a property called *entanglement*.

In his book *Science and the Akashic Field*, physicist Ervin Laszlo describes a series of experiments conducted by lie detector expert Cleve Backster. Backster took some white blood cells from the mouths of his subjects and cultured them in a test tube. He then moved the cultures to distant locations, more than seven miles away. He attached lie detectors to the cultures and then performed a series of experiments on his subjects.

In one of his tests, he showed his subject a television program depicting the Japanese attack on Pearl Harbor in 1941. This man was a former navy gunner who had actually been present at Pearl Harbor during the attack. When the face of a navy gunner appeared on the screen, the man's face betrayed an emotional reaction—and at that precise moment, the lie detector's needle seven and a half miles away jumped, *exactly as it would have had it been attached to the man himself*, and not just to a test tube of his cultured white blood cells miles away.

Subsequent experiments varied the circumstances and increased the distances involved to dozens and even hundreds of miles, with the same astonishing results.

How is such a thing possible? In the language of quantum physics, the particles of the gunner's body are still connected or "entangled" with one another, and no matter how far apart they are separated in space, they will continue to influence one another. In fact, this effect appears to occur at speeds faster than the speed of light, which violates one of Einstein's basic rules.

Scientists dubbed this mind-boggling capacity for instantaneous interconnection *nonlocality*. Einstein had a somewhat less technical term for it. He called it *spooky action at a distance*.

What could this force be? Could it be something even more basic than energy? The search was on for an underlying force that could bring together all the different kinds of energy we knew. This quest for a single mathematical equation that would account for the behavior of all the known forces in the universe—a unified field theory, or "theory of everything"—has become the holy grail of science. Some leading astrophysicists, such as Stephen Hawking, say that when we come up with this theory of everything, we will know the mind of God.

A BIZARRE DISCOVERY: THOUGHT INFLUENCES MATTER

Within twenty years of Einstein's radical work, another revolution in worldview occurred, just as cataclysmic as Einstein's. It started with two of the early pioneers of the quantum world, the Danish physicist Niels Bohr and his protégé Werner Heisenberg.

Bohr and Heisenberg studied the puzzling behaviors of these tiny subatomic particles and recognized that once you look deep within the heart of atoms, these "indivisible particles" are not at all like the neat little miniature solar systems of billiard balls everyone had expected, but were something far messier: They were something like tiny packets of *possibility*.

Each subatomic particle appeared to exist not as a solid, stable "thing," but as the *potential* of any one of its various possible selves. Heisenberg's uncertainty principle stated that it was not possible to measure all of a subatomic particle's properties at the same time. For example, if you record information about the location of a proton, you cannot pin down its speed or trajectory; if you figure out its speed, now its precise location eludes you.

Bohr and Heisenberg's work suggested that at its most basic level, physical matter isn't exactly *anything* yet. At the subatomic scale, according to this new understanding, reality was made not of solid substance but of fields of potentiality—more like a set of possible sketches or ideas of a thing than the thing itself. A particle would take on the specific character of a material "thing" (in the scientists' terms, its properties would collapse into a single state) only when it was measured or observed.

And that was the really strange thing: the discovery that the *act of observation* influenced these particles' behavior.

Every time the scientists looked for an electron, an electron would appear, right where they were expecting it. And it didn't matter if the person performing the observation was a scientist or a bus driver. In fact, even more bizarre, it was soon found that the mere *intention* of measuring particles, even without carrying out the actual act itself, would still affect the particles in question!

Suddenly subjectivity—the action of consciousness upon a piece of "matter"—had become an essential component in the very nature of reality.

THE ZERO-POINT FIELD

As scientists continued pursuing their explorations on staggeringly small scales, they eventually found themselves staring at something truly confounding. They termed it the *zero-point field* (ZPF), because at this most infinitesimal of levels, some sort of force appears to be present even at a temperature of absolute zero, when all known forms of energy vanish.

This is the place where the instantaneous connections of entanglement—those action-at-a-distance phenomena Einstein termed *spooky*—begin to make sense. Here, beneath the level of energy itself, exists a still more basic level. The field at this level is not exactly "energy" anymore, nor is it a field of empty space. It is best described, physicists realized, as a field of information.

To put it another way, the undifferentiated ocean out of which energy arises appears to be a sea of pure consciousness, from which matter emerges in clustered localities here and there. Consciousness is what the universe is *made* of; matter and energy are just two of the forms that consciousness takes.

Ervin Laszlo calls this field that underlies and connects all things the *A-field*, in deference to the ancient Vedic concept of the Akashic record, a nonphysical repository of all knowledge in the universe, including all human experience. The psychologist Carl Jung called it the *collective unconscious*; Teilhard de Chardin dubbed it the *noosphere*; Rupert Sheldrake refers to it as the *morphogenetic field*. It has been intuited and described for thousands of years and in a multitude of terms and images throughout human history. Only in the last few decades has science caught up to what we always sensed but could never fully explain.

Says Laszlo: "The ancients knew that space is not empty; it is the origin and memory of all things that exist and have ever existed. . . . [This insight] is now being rediscovered at the cutting edge of the sciences [and is emerging] as a main pillar of the scientific world's picture of the twenty-first century. This will profoundly change our concept of ourselves and of the world."[1]

In fact, it has already profoundly changed our picture of ourselves and our world—and it will radically change how you approach your business.

THOUGHT CREATES EVERYTHING

So what are we saying here, that everything that is, is made of thought? That *thought* creates the physical world? Yes, that is exactly what we're saying. Here, in a nutshell, is the conclusion so far of humanity's epic quest to understand the world:

Everything in the physical world is made out of atoms.
Atoms are made out of energy.
And energy is made out of consciousness.

Your thoughts not only matter, they *create* matter. Thought is where everything comes from. And your thoughts are where your business comes from.

If all this seems difficult to grasp or accept, imagine what it must have seemed like to the people of Galileo's time when they were asked to consider the proposition that the earth travels through space around the sun. To the ordinary citizen of the sixteenth or seventeenth century, it was so patently obvious that the earth stood still that the matter didn't even warrant serious discussion. After all, if we were shooting through space, why weren't we blasted by hurricane-force winds? "Besides, any

---

1. Ervin Laszlo, *Science and the Akashic Field* (Rochester, VT: Inner Traditions, 2004), 112–113.

fool can *see* that the earth isn't hurtling through space: We're just stand-ing right here!"

Or travel back a few thousand years further, to antiquity, when the world was generally perceived to be flat. "Of *course* the world is flat! I mean, aren't you going to believe the evidence of your own eyes?"

So it is with the discoveries of modern physicists. Anytime our view of the world shifts radically, things seem uncomfortable, strange, bi-zarre, surreal. Even impossible.

"The world, *round*?" "So you're saying the earth *moves*, that it orbits the sun—not the other way around?" "Matter and energy are actually the same thing? You mean, matter is *made of energy*?" "What, now you're saying that matter and energy and everything in our world is made of *thought*? And our thoughts actually influence the formation of matter?!"

Yes, indeed, this seems surreal. But to pre-Socratic philosophers, so did the idea of a spherical earth. The truth is, we don't see what is there. We see what we are prepared to see, what we are conditioned to see.

There is a story that when Magellan's expedition first arrived on the shores of Tierra del Fuego in 1520, the native canoe-going population didn't mount much of a response, because the vast European sailing vessels represented such an alien concept that they literally could not see them. Like Captain Kirk and Mr. Spock and the rest of the team of the USS *Enterprise* stepping out of their invisibility-cloaked spaceship, the foreigners seemed to the natives as though they stepped out into their smaller canoelike landing craft literally out of thin air.

You've heard the old expression "I'll believe it when I see it." But that's not really how it is. The truth is more like this: *You'll see it when you believe it*. In a very real, concrete sense, your beliefs don't simply *reflect* your reality, they *create* your reality—and that applies to the real-ity of massive success in business. In the chapters that follow, we're going to walk through the process, step by step, of building your dream business by first harnessing the most powerful force in the universe: your beliefs.

THE MOST POWERFUL FORCE IN THE UNIVERSE

If the idea that the universe is made of thought seems amazing, here is the truly amazing thing about it: The scale of power we're talking about here is staggering beyond comprehension.

The universe appears to be structured as a series of layers or levels, much like an onion or Russian nesting dolls: Inside of organisms, we find cells; inside cells, molecules, then "indivisible" atoms, then electrons and protons, then quarks, bosons, mesons, photons, leptons . . . and the smaller the world, the greater the amount of force we find wrapped inside it.

The deeper in nature you go, the more dynamic nature becomes. In other words, the more fundamental the level to which you penetrate, the greater the power you'll find.

For example, chemical power, the force of chemical interactions, operates at the level of molecules and atoms. Nuclear power operates at the level of the atomic nucleus, about a million times smaller—and it is a million times more powerful. Yet even the nuclear level pales in comparison to the deeper levels today's quantum physics is exploring. According to Laszlo, the zero-point field has an energy density of 10^{94} ergs per cubic centimeter—that's ten thousand billion, billion, billion, billion times *more* energy in a single cubic centimeter of "empty space" than you have in all the matter in the known universe.

And that's just one cc of empty space. Imagine what you'd have in a quart.

HOW QUANTUM SCIENCE HELPS YOU BUILD
YOUR DREAM BUSINESS

In 1902, two years after the physicist Max Planck first coined the term *quantum* to describe the core reality of light, a young British writer named James Allen penned a little book entitled *As a Man Thinketh*, which drew its title and its message from the biblical verse "As a man thinketh in his heart, so is he."[2] At the time, few would have associated the two men and their work, but with the hindsight of a century's dis-

---

2. Proverbs 23:7.

coveries, we can now see the connection. While scientists spent the rest of the century pursuing the horizon set by pioneers such as Planck, Einstein, Bohr, and Heisenberg, which would ultimately lead to the quantum vacuum, philosophers like Napoleon Hill, Earl Nightingale, and Bob Proctor worked to articulate its application to the practical world of human accomplishment.

This idea, that our thoughts have a direct, causal impact on our reality, has been observed, but it always seemed like something that rational people couldn't buy into, an idea that created more questions than answers. Now science has given us that set of answers.

Remember the mind-boggling amount of power in that cubic centimeter of "empty space," or consciousness? When Victor Hugo said, "There is nothing more powerful than an idea whose time has come," we now know that this was more than a metaphor. He may not have fully realized it at the time, but he was giving us a literal description of how reality works.

Thought is the most powerful force in the universe. Our thoughts are the controlling factor in what we manifest and create in our lives.

The idea precedes the thing.

That is at the heart of how my dream house showed up, as well as every business I've built, and the same thing happens to every businessperson who has a vision and applies these strategies and tactics. It started as a picture, an idea in my mind, and before I knew what had happened, I was living in it.

Science tells us that underlying what we know as the world is a field of pure consciousness, billions upon billions of times more powerful than any measurable energy, and that this field of absolute consciousness knows everything that happens, anywhere and everywhere in the universe, instantaneously and with absolute accuracy. This is not so different from the kind of descriptions people have given for millennia in their efforts to grasp the ultimate nature of our universal source, what some of us call God. Whatever you call it, the picture that emerges is of a world bounded by an infinitely large, omnipotent, omniscient intelligence, which lies behind everything in the phenomenal world as its source, author, and ultimate destination.

This is the dream world we live in, you and I, and it is the clay from which you will shape and give life to your dream business.

3

THE LAW OF ATTRACTION

We live in a universe of absolute laws, a world that operates on every level and in every detail with absolute precision. In the quantum universe, there may be random occurrences, but there are no accidents, no coincidences; every particle and every action is accounted for. The laws by which it operates are all as exacting as the calculations that place an astronaut on the moon and bring him home alive.

Descartes was wrong: The world of thoughts and ideas, of human ingenuity, creativity, and enterprise, is not separate from the world of chemistry and gravity and fields and forests. There are no separate rules—they all come from the same rulebook. The laws that govern the movement of subatomic particles and solar systems also govern our thoughts and feelings, families, and careers.

This fundamental truth is all too easy to forget as we go about our daily routines, because we seem to live in two worlds, the seen and the unseen, the world we can touch, taste, and see, and the intangible world that lies hidden away behind the curtain of our senses. The events and circumstances of your business take place in the seen world. But—and this is the key—that is not where they *originate*. Grasp this truth, and you have grasped the reason behind the success or failure of every business ever created.

As quantum physics has taught us, the unseen world is vastly more powerful than the seen world. It is the immense, hidden portion of the iceberg that most of us are unaware of 99 percent of the time, while the tangible, material world we think of as "real" is only the minuscule tip that juts above the surface of our conscious awareness. What sunk the *Titanic* was that hidden part of the iceberg that nobody saw coming, the part beneath the surface. And that is the part that sinks every business that ends up closing its doors.

As a result of the film *The Secret*, millions of people have become aware of the principle called the Law of Attraction, which explains the creative process through which the unseen world gives birth to the circumstances and events of our lives. As a result of *The Secret*, thousands of people from around the world have emailed, written, and called our offices to share stories about how knowing and applying this law has changed their lives. These stories are sometimes astonishing, often quite moving, and the range and variety of the circumstances involved is staggering.

There are actually a number of distinct laws or principles at work within what is called the Law of Attraction. In this chapter, we'll look at each of them and see how they work together, so that you can begin using the irresistible power of the unseen world to create your ideal life and business.

EVERYTHING STARTS AS AN IDEA

As Einstein's relativity revolution revealed, everything is made of energy. Cells, molecules, atoms, protons and neutrons, quarks, gluons, mesons, and bosons—they're all energy. The things that seem tangible to us, including ourselves, are simply energy slowed way down to a state that we recognize as "solid."

But what does that mean, exactly, "energy slowed way down"?

Take an ice cube: We can find out where it came from by speeding it up, that is, by adding energy to it to raise its vibrational state. When we apply heat to our ice cube, it soon reverts to a liquid. Continue speeding up its vibration, and that liquid soon evaporates to steam, and then further into water vapor. Continue accelerating its rate of vibration, and the elements that formed that ice cube will eventually revert to a state of pure energy, and beyond that, cross the Cartesian barrier to become what lies beyond energy, which is consciousness or information.

That's where the ice cube came from: *It was first an idea.*

In our daily lives, we often describe those rarefied, superenergized states we cannot see as "spiritual," and the slowed-down, more substantial states we can see as "physical," but science has now told us that this is an arbitrary distinction, just a convenience of language and perception. The truth is, water is water; it came from the idea or "quantum potential" of water through the states of vapor, steam, liquid, and ice. It's all water. But it starts with an idea.

Remember our summary of the history of humanity's quest to understand how the universe works?

Everything in the physical world is made out of atoms.
Atoms are made out of energy.
And energy is made out of consciousness.

In other words, everything in nature, every phenomenon in the universe, starts as an idea.

What does this have to do with your dream business? Everything. Because everything you manifest in your life follows the precise same pathway, from idea to physical form. We create from the nonphysical level, turning that which we can't see into that which we can.

CAUSE AND EFFECT

An important client says "Yes" or "No." A substantial investment comes through or falls through. Real estate prices rise sharply or fall unexpectedly. Markets shift, hurricanes blow through, and new developments surprise us. We see and react to all these events without realizing they are but the seen tip of the unseen iceberg, the physical end results of a nonphysical process of creation. We often respond to these events without realizing the role that we ourselves play in bringing them about.

We see the world of tangible phenomena; we don't see the vastly greater world that gives rise to it. That vastly greater world is the world of *cause.*

Newton used the principle of cause and effect as it operates in the physical, mechanical world as the basis of his law of thermodynamics:

Every action has an equal and opposite reaction. What the science of Newton's day did not yet grasp was that matter, energy, and consciousness are not distinct and separate domains, but are all simply different frequencies along the same continuum. What they did not fully grasp, but science has now shown us, is that the principle of cause and effect applies not simply to the mechanics of matter, but to the mechanics of everything, including our thoughts.

Every thought you form broadcasts a distinct and particular frequency, and that frequency elicits a response from the quantum universe as surely as a swinging hammer has an impact on the surface it strikes. Things don't arbitrarily happen *to* you. Events in your business are the reflection of your thoughts, the echo of your own actions and the thinking behind them. In the East this truth is reflected in the idea of karma, and in the West in the Golden Rule. The core of the principle is this: You are at cause in your life and in your business.

For many, this is a challenging principle because it puts you squarely in the driver's seat. Embracing this principle means you no longer have the luxury of blaming other people or external circumstances for the things that happen in your life. Here is the flip side of that equation: Embracing this principle also means you have far more capacity to create the events and circumstances in your life than you have ever imagined possible.

When we don't recognize this principle operating in our lives, it's easy to start seeing ourselves as being the *effect* of those events. Rather than seeing that we are making things happen, we start to believe that things are simply happening *to* us. This easily leads to what is often called *victim mentality*.

If you are someone who is growing a massively successful business, there is no place for victim mentality in your life. The two states of mind—victim thinking and entrepreneurship—are 100 percent incompatible and mutually exclusive. The word *entrepreneur* derives from the French word that refers to the source of the event, the one who initiates. Building and growing a successful business requires a commitment to being at cause, not at effect.

There are many things you need to know to successfully play the game of business. A great many of them you can learn as you go, and a great many skills and fields of expertise you can bring into your business by hiring or partnering with people who possess them. But there is one skill that you must have yourself, and it is the single most important skill of any successful businessperson, the one without which success is impossible: *You must be practiced at creating the thoughts that will serve your business.*

RESONANCE

Let's go back to that ice cube for a moment. We saw that it changes from ice to liquid to steam to vapor—but what exactly is the "it" that stays the same as it goes through all these transformations? Its form changes as its rate of vibration or energy level changes. But there is something about it that doesn't change, a basic waterness. What is that essence that stays constant, even while it changes all of its physical attributes?

In a word, *pattern*. There is an essential identity, a pattern or shape of vibrations that holds its integrity, no matter how much its physical form and medium might shift. You can see this principle operating with sound. Imagine you are walking down the street, and as you pass a certain house, you hear a singer practicing her music. You don't recognize the song, but the sound is captivating and you stop, entranced.

The sound your neighbor is making is created by the vibration of her vocal cords, but if that were the end of it, nobody would ever hear her sing. Those vibrating throat tissues impart the pattern of their vibration to the air inside the singer's throat and out into the air in the room where she is practicing her aria. But that doesn't really answer the question: How is it that you are hearing this? The windows are all closed. The air inside her room isn't pouring out of the house or coming anywhere near you.

No, the air isn't escaping the house—but the pattern is. When that vibrating air hits the windowpane, it imparts its waveform to the glass, which passes it on to the air outside the house, where it eventually reaches you. Entering your ear, it strikes the delicate membrane of your eardrum, passing that same waveshape into the interior of your ear, where it is then transferred through a series of tiny, delicate bones to become waves within the cochlear fluid, which transfers that same pattern of vibration to thousands of microscopic, hairlike filaments within the cochlear coil, which convert it to electrical impulses in the auditory nerve, through which it travels to your brain—where you finally hear it.

From vocal cords to air to glass to air to membranes and bones to fluid and filaments to nerves to brain—the harmonious pattern of vibrations of your neighbor's voice passes through many different physical media, just as the vibration called *water* passes through the dimensions of vapor, steam, liquid, and solid—but they are all recognizable as the *same thing*.

The transformation that occurs with the ice cube and the song also happens within you, from moment to moment without ceasing. Every second, about ten million of your trillions of cells die, and another ten million are created. Most of your tissues are replaced with new material in days; within a few months from now, hardly any of what is "you" today will still be here. But you will still be here. So, what is that "you"?

It is not what you're made of: It is the pattern that underlies your physical self.

Buckminster Fuller used to demonstrate this with a rope stitched together out of several smaller segments, one nylon, one cotton, and one silk. He would tie a slipknot in one end, and then slip it down along the entire length of the rope. Then he would turn to his audience and say, "Now, was the knot nylon, or cotton, or silk?" And the answer, of course, is, "All of the above"—or, depending on your point of view, "None of the above." The knot is the shape, regardless of the material through which it takes physical form. "And you," Fuller would then point out, "you are not your body—you are not the rope. You are the knot." You are the pattern that is taking this particular form, composed of this particular substance, at the moment.

Let's return to your neighbor. As you continue past her house, she hits a high note—and you hear a crash followed by a series of tinkling noises, coming not from her house but from the house next door. She didn't mean to do it, but the singer has broken her neighbor's chandelier. How? Through the phenomenon of *resonance*.

Resonance, from the Latin meaning "to sound again," is simply the transfer of vibration from one medium to another. Why did the singer's high note shatter the neighbor's glass? Here is a clue to the riddle: If you were to lightly strike that specific piece of that chandelier with a tiny hammer, it would ring out a tone: a tone with the same pitch as the singer's high note.

This is the principle of the tuning fork: Hold a tuning fork tuned to A440 near any musical instrument, play that same note, and the tuning fork will vibrate. Play a different note, and it won't vibrate. The piano's A-string and the tuning fork share the same waveform, as do the singer's high note and the chandelier, which is why they resonate.

You and your parents share patterns that are not identical but are strongly similar, enough so that you resonate. This is also true of you and your spouse, you and your best friends, you and your kids, even you and your dog. As we will explore in chapter 6, it is also true of you and your dream business. These are all things with which you reso-nate.

The way the right note, sung clearly and loudly enough, can cause a tuning fork to vibrate and even shatter glass, is the same way the right thought, held clearly and strongly enough, can cause events in the physical world to happen. A single thought, held clearly and firmly, can defeat an empire, as Gandhi demonstrated. And the right thoughts, held clearly and resolutely, can build your dream business.

The principle of resonance says that energy in a specific pattern or frequency will resonate with every other form of energy in a similar pattern. The Law of Attraction is simply the action of resonance to-gether with cause and effect. Thoughts create events and circumstances that have the same shape or pattern, and are thus resonant with those thoughts. Or as James Allen put it (quoting Proverbs), "As a man think-eth in his heart, so is he."

THE DREAM WITHIN THE SEED

Let's go back once again to your neighbor the singer. Did the strains of her song start with her? Probably not. More likely they were composed in another place and an earlier time. The song may even have traveled through centuries, and through countless media, forms, and dimen-sions before its sound reached your brain and caused your smile! The singer's voice and the smile on your face when you hear her sing are the fruit; it was the composer's imagination that created the seed.

Take an acorn in the palm of your hand and examine it. At this moment, where is the oak tree? Is it *in* the acorn? In other words, could you find it if you cracked the acorn open? No. All you'll find inside is a seed that contains the possibility of an oak tree, the *idea* of an oak tree. Yet if you plant that acorn in fertile soil, through the principle of resonance, those elements in its surroundings that resonate to that oak tree idea will be drawn to the seed. It will attract to itself all the nutrients, water, and sunlight that it needs to transform that invisible, immaterial idea into a fully formed tree.

So when you first planted that acorn, where *was* the oak tree? It was not in the acorn—it was scattered in pieces of *tree potential* throughout the acorn's environment. Successful businesses are created in exactly the same way. When you form the idea of a business, the actual, physical business is not inside you. But several years from now, your business will have hundreds or thousands of customers and dozens of employees. There will be thousands, hundreds of thousands, perhaps millions of dollars flowing through your business, and perhaps hundreds of thousands or millions more built into the substance of your business, in the form of product inventory, capital goods, buildings, or intellectual property, such as designs, patents, copyrighted words, and images.

Whatever the nature of your business, within a few years of its successful launch, it will be composed of a lot of *stuff*. Where is all that stuff right now? Where are the customers, the employees, the materials, the designs, the dollars? They all lie scattered in pieces throughout your environment, the water and nitrogen and sunlight of your tree. Everything you could possibly need to build your dream business, all the tools, resources, capital, people, ideas, expertise, everything, it all surrounds you today, right now—it just hasn't been gathered and assembled yet.

What force could possibly find all those disparate elements, extract them from where they are now, and bring them all together? To create your successful business, you need to start with the part nobody else sees, the hidden part of the iceberg: The seed of your business is the vision. This is the groundwork for every successful business that has ever been and ever will be: It starts with the power and precision of an idea. What you have to get good at doing is creating the seed of what you want with great precision. A vaguely formed, ambiguous seed will never sprout or take root. For a seed to flourish, it must be viable.

"Yes, but how?"

People tend to be focused on looking for the how, thinking that is where the answer lies. But it's not. Yes, you need to learn all sorts of hows, and in the second part of this book we'll show you which ones are crucial to the success of your business. But the real key to building your dream business lies in the clarity and strength of the idea—the seed. The how always comes *after* the vision and decision.

This is why "more capital" is rarely the answer to business start-up challenges. People often believe that lack of funding is one of a new business's major problems. It's not. In the same way that air, water, and sunlight are not hard to find, financing is not all that hard to find—if you have a compelling and clearly viable idea and strategic plan for growth. The world around you is absolutely flooded with money, ready to flow toward you and nourish your sprouting business. In chapter 6, we'll walk you through forming that seed, and in chapter 7, we'll walk you through how to plant it in nourishing soil so it will take root and grow.

THE LAW OF GESTATION

Ambitious businesspeople tend to be impatient. We are ambitious, we have big appetites for achievement, we like to think big and dream bigger. We want things to happen fast.

There is nothing wrong with that. In fact, a big appetite for achievement is pretty much a necessity for a successful business; dreaming big comes with the territory. But we have to be careful here. Ecclesiastes, Pete Seeger, and the Byrds had it right: There is "a time to plant, a time to reap . . . a time you may embrace, a time to refrain from embracing."[3] And when it comes to building your dream business, there is most definitely a time for patience.

---

3. "Turn! Turn! Turn! (To Everything There Is a Season)," music by Pete Seeger, text adapted from Ecclesiastes 3:1–8.

The Law of Gestation complements the Law of Attraction. It declares that for every seed, there is a set gestation or incubation period, a specific span of time that particular seed needs to establish itself before it can unfold from blueprint into fully realized physical form. This is true everywhere in nature, and your life is as much a part of nature as everything else. For example, a carrot seed takes about seventy days from the time you plant it until the time you have a fully grown carrot, ready for the eating. A lamb has a gestation period, from fertilization to birth, of about 145 days. For a human being, that period is about 280 days.

Every one of your clearly articulated, vividly formed goals is a seed in itself, and each has a gestation period, a set span of time from the moment you "plant" it to the point where it has fully grown into its physical form. How long is that gestation period? This is the hard part: We simply don't know.

How long does it take to attract the tools, resources, capital, and partners you need for a new business? How long will it take to attract the right soul mate for the relationship you envision? How long will it take for the world to wrap you in the right set of circumstances for you to step into that career or position that you see yourself occupying?

We have no idea. But what we do know is this: It will take some time. And we know this, too: If you keep digging up those seeds after you've planted them, you'll stop the process cold.

Imagine you are a waiter at a wonderful restaurant, waiting on your favorite customers, who have just ordered an exquisite meal. You take their order back to the kitchen and give it to the cook—and then, as he gets to work preparing the food, you stand there right behind him talking in his ear: "Is it ready yet? Is it ready yet? Is it ready yet? Is it ready yet? Is it . . . ? " You are not helping! In fact, if you keep it up, one of two things will probably happen: Either you will shatter the cook's concentration and ruin the meal, or you will be ejected from the kitchen.

When you create a picture of your dream business, you are both the diner and the waiter. After placing your order for this delicious meal, you take it back to the kitchen where all the preparation work is done that leads to the finished meal itself. Once you've delivered the order, you can't nag the chef. Restaurants don't work that way. You need to quietly exit the kitchen and leave the work to the kitchen staff.

The same holds true for the garden: If you are constantly digging up your seeds and poking through them, eagerly searching for any sign that they may have started to sprout, you can forget about ever growing anything at all. Gardens don't work that way. Neither do your life goals.

If you try to force an idea, it will never work. One of nature's laws is that force always negates. If you push on the process, it's going to push back. You have to allow an idea the time to germinate and grow, to take root and find its resources in its own time.

Let go of impatience. Instead, start putting your trust in your own resourcefulness and in the universe around you. Remember that the zero-point field, the quantum vacuum, is all-knowing, all-powerful, and all-capable. Understand that this universe is ready and willing to give you everything you want, once you are clear on what it is and patient enough to let it do its work.

THE LAW OF ACTION

There is one more ingredient in this process. For the plant to grow, it's not enough to simply plant it and wait. While you're letting it do its work, tucked away within the fertile soil, you have *your* work to do, too.

"Wait," we can hear you saying. "If everything starts from an idea, and creating a crystal clear picture of what I want kicks the Law of Attraction into gear, why would I need to work at all? Why not just visualize what I want and wait for the business to grow?" Because if all you do is sit around and visualize, the men in the overalls with the big trucks will come and take away your furniture.

The millions of people who have seen *The Secret* have become at least somewhat familiar with the Law of Attraction. But here is the part that so many people seem to have missed: The Law of Attraction cannot work effectively unless you also follow the Law of Action. Unless you get off your butt and *do* something, it's not realistic to expect that much will happen. The Quakers have an expression, "When you pray, move your feet." Another one we've heard goes like this: "If you're going to be praying for potatoes, you better have a hoe ready."

After you plant, you water; you weed; you take care of your garden. You can't do the seed's work for it: you don't *grow* the plant. But you do have your work to do to ensure that it has the environment and re-sources available to pull in what it needs.

So, what is "your work"? That's what we'll cover in the latter chap-ters of this book, where we'll walk you through what all that weeding and watering looks like in your dream business scenario. For now, the key point is to understand that these three laws work together: the Law of Attraction, the Law of Gestation, and the Law of Action. You might sum them up this way: *Be purposeful, Be patient,* and *Be active.* Learn to put all three of these laws to work, and you will save yourself years of heartache and trial and error. Instead, you will manifest what you want in your life and your business much faster than you've ever created anything before.

CLARITY AND FOCUS

We started this chapter by talking about the precise workings of the universe. Creating your dream business will require that you act with that same level of precision. This means your thinking and your vision for your dream business have to be clear in every detail—which brings us to the single most crucial concept that lies at the heart of the Law of Attraction: *focus.*

Imagine you're outside on a beautiful sunny day, and you have in one hand a magnifying glass and in the other a dried oak leaf. Hold the magnifying glass at a certain angle that focuses the sun's rays onto the leaf, and what happens? The leaf catches fire and burns. That's the power of focus.

Take that same energy and focus it even further, and you have a laser that will cut effortlessly through steel. That's the power you have at your command when you learn to focus your ideas and intention. This is the crucial importance of clarity. Sunlight diffused may cause the leaf to warm slightly; that same sunlight focused with a glass will make it burn. When your thought energy takes only vague form, without a crystal clear focus, it can do no more than warm the leaf slightly; it certainly cannot cause it to catch fire and burn. You need the clarity and focus of the magnifying glass.

We will return to clarity again and again. The more clarity you create around your business in every aspect, from its largest objectives to the particulars of your everyday actions, the more you harness the mind-boggling power of the quantum field to do your bidding and bring that idea into reality.

4

THE UNIVERSE INSIDE YOUR BRAIN

While physicists were plumbing the depths of the atom, another group of scientists was making equally startling discoveries about the universe that exists within the human skull. What they found has revolutionized our understanding of the human brain almost as dramatically as quantum physics has altered our picture of the world.

Until recently, the actual operation of this world within our brains was as much a mystery as the workings of the quantum world within the atom. Then, during the 1980s and 1990s, scientists made amazing strides in the development of a technique called *magnetic resonance imaging* (MRI), followed by newer and more precise brain-scanning technologies, including positron emission tomography (PET), single photon emission computed tomography (SPECT), and magnetoencephalography (MEG). With increasing sophistication, these instruments were able to map the brain's electrical activity in detail. For the first time since the dawn of science, researchers found themselves looking through a living, real-time window into the workings of the mysterious and remarkable human brain. They were able to actually *watch the brain think in real time*, and what they saw has turned the world of neuroscience upside down.

In fact, neuroscientists have estimated that 98 percent of what we know about the brain we have learned within the last decade. Even more startling, more than 80 percent of what we thought we knew about how the brain works has turned out to be false. In just the last decade, we have leaped from what was essentially a Newtonian model of the brain-as-machine to a quantum-universe, Akashic-field view of the brain.

With the new insights of neuroscience, we have a much clearer scientific understanding of how the brain operates—and this has illuminated a critical error in how we use our brains, an error that most of us are making, day after day. This critical error is what prevents most of us from achieving our dreams and keeps us in a prison of repeated failure. The purpose of this chapter is to explain what that error is, why we make it, and most important, how we can shift the way we approach our own brain so that we never make it again.

THE AMAZING BRAIN

The human brain is the most complex, powerful machine in the universe. Your brain contains a network of about 100,000 miles of blood vessels and 100,000,000,000 (one hundred billion) neurons, with the capacity to perform some ten quadrillion operations per second. Imagine the scope and complexity of every telephone system throughout the entire planet: Your brain embodies that same scale of complexity and capacity in *each individual brain cell.*

Imagine for a moment what is going on in your body right now, as you're reading this page. Every second, about ten million cells die off and another ten million new ones are created. Although you are completely unaware of it consciously, since you began reading this paragraph, your brain has overseen the decommissioning of some hundred million cells and the construction and installation of another hundred million replacements—without breaking a sweat. If you were to write out your brain's potential as expressed by the number of possible neural connections it could make, it would take you seventy-five years to write out all the zeros. That's the level of power and capacity you have at your disposal every moment of every day.

In other words, your potential to achieve what you want is essentially *without limit.*

The human body is designed to treat the brain like the king it is; there is no organ in the body that receives better or more elaborate care. Snugly encased in its protective bony shell, your brain weighs only two to three pounds, a mere 1 to 2 percent of your total body weight, yet it consumes 20 percent of the air you breathe, 25 percent of your total blood flow, 30 percent of the water you consume, and 40 percent of all the nutrients drawn from your bloodstream.

The brain is made up of progressive layers, each one tracing back to a different era and different stage of human evolution, from the simplest reflexive functions designed to ensure our physical survival, to the most advanced and sophisticated functions of imagination and intellectual analysis. The most primitive functions are controlled by those layers at the center of the brain, which were the earliest to develop. The most intellectually sophisticated and most recently developed functions are managed by areas toward the front and surface of the brain.

THE HUMAN BRAIN

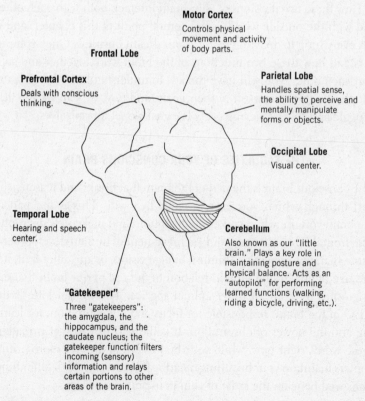

Motor Cortex
Controls physical movement and activity of body parts.

Frontal Lobe

Prefrontal Cortex
Deals with conscious thinking.

Parietal Lobe
Handles spatial sense, the ability to perceive and mentally manipulate forms or objects.

Occipital Lobe
Visual center.

Temporal Lobe
Hearing and speech center.

Cerebellum
Also known as our "little brain." Plays a key role in maintaining posture and physical balance. Acts as an "autopilot" for performing learned functions (walking, riding a bicycle, driving, etc.).

"Gatekeeper"
Three "gatekeepers": the amygdala, the hippocampus, and the caudate nucleus; the gatekeeper function filters incoming (sensory) information and relays certain portions to other areas of the brain.

The brain stem, also known as the "reptilian" brain because it is similar in structure and function to the brains of cold-blooded reptiles, controls many of your body's instinctive functions, such as heartbeat, respiration, and digestion. It operates by instinct and is responsible for keeping the organism alive. The "old mammalian" brain, similar in structure and function to the brains of other mammals, controls your emotions and sexuality and plays a key role in the regulation of memory. The most recent part of the human brain to be developed is the *frontal lobe*, or *neocortex*, which governs our conscious thoughts. The frontal lobe is where we create, speculate, learn, concentrate, and focus.

Don't worry about learning all these different distinctions. Here's what is crucial to understand: These various functions and aspects all fall into two larger, basic divisions of the brain: the *conscious* brain and *nonconscious* brain.

How these two divisions of your brain interact, both with each other and with the outside world, is the central point of this chapter, and it has everything to do with creating your dream business. Once you understand how these two functions of the brain work together and support each other, you will have the key to understanding why so many people struggle in pursuit of their goals, and how we can escape that struggle and start achieving every last goal we set for ourselves.

THE FACULTIES OF YOUR CONSCIOUS BRAIN

The conscious brain is the part of the brain that thinks and reasons, the part through which you exercise your free will. This is the part of the brain you use when you evaluate options and make new decisions. The frontal lobe is the crowning achievement of human development. More than our opposable thumbs, bifocal vision, or any other trait, it is the size of our frontal lobe in relation to the rest of our brain that distinguishes us from all other animal species. The frontal lobe is the CEO of the brain, responsible for focus and concentration, for learning and the power of observation. It is the part of you that is reading these words right now, while your brain stem and other more primal centers maintain your breathing, heartbeat, and a myriad of other functions well beneath the radar of your conscious awareness.

If your dream business is a ship, your frontal lobe is the captain. It decides where you want to go, charts the course, and gives the orders. And just as all ships' captains have distinct personalities, each of us has a prefrontal lobe that fulfills this commanding role in a unique and distinct way.

We tend to think of our conscious capacity narrowly, as if our intelligence were something that could be reduced to a number called *IQ*. In fact, our intelligence has a wide range of varying attributes and abilities. We can look at these functions as existing on a spectrum, like a color palette, ranging from lower to higher frequencies. None of these traits is "better" than any other, and none of us has just one or two of these abilities to the exclusion of any other. We each possess every single one of these abilities in ample supply, and it's a good thing we do, because in the course of building a business, they *all* come into play. Yet each of us will possess some of these more than others. This is one reason that various forms of partnership and teamwork are so critical in building a successful business.

From the lowest frequency to the highest, we call these different aspects of the conscious spectrum *will*, *memory*, *perception*, *reasoning*, *intuition*, and *imagination*.

Will

Almost by definition, all successful businesspeople tend to have a strong degree of will. This is the essential quality embodied in the phrase "If it's to be, it's up to me." Entrepreneurs don't wait for it to happen; they *make* it happen. Still, that doesn't mean this is necessarily your strongest conscious trait. Just as there are many styles of leadership, there are many styles of entrepreneurship.

Will is the conscious faculty involved when you make a decision to do something new or different. Will is what supplies the basic drive that catalyzes circumstances and moves the action forward. We often say, "If you're interested, you'll do what's convenient; if you're committed, you'll do whatever it takes." Will is the conscious exercise of that quality of commitment. A person with a "strong will" is someone who can dig down deep and do whatever it takes to get the thing into motion.

Courage, discipline, commitment, loyalty, perseverance—all of these traits are reflections or variations of this core conscious drive we call *will*.

Memory

Neuroscientists tell us that short-term memory is an electrical phenomenon, while long-term memory is chemical. However, memory itself is more than a simple mechanical action of data storage and retrieval. Memory is the capacity to use your conscious brain to search and pull together information relevant to the situation at hand. That can mean something as simple as recalling someone's name or phone number, and it can also mean an incredibly complex process of drawing on scores of different experiences and factors, all at the same time, and considering them to help make a difficult decision.

Having a "good memory" means having a well-developed faculty for tuning your brain to those specific stored experiences you need to draw on at the moment. In a way, it is a type of associative logic; as it turns out, the best techniques for improving memory typically use a process of associating one thing with another to make it more readily available to recall.

While conventional wisdom says our memories are stored in our brain, some researchers are now saying that some of our memories (or perhaps even *most* of our memories) are "stored" outside ourselves in the quantum field. That idea might seem like science fiction, but think about this the next time you're watching a show on television: Where was that program in the moments *before* you turned on the set? Was it *in* the set? No, it was swimming in the air all around you. In a similar way, scientists are now suggesting that once you have an experience or a thought, that experience or thought is broadcast out into the quantum field and resides there in wave form, potentially available to anyone. Of course it will be most readily accessible to you, because your brain is the one that first processed that experience—that is, your brain and that experience have unique resonance.

Grasp, perspective, insight, and *having a big view* are all different ways we have of describing this conscious function of memory.

Perception

If I ask you, "What do you see with?" you would probably say, "My eyes." But this isn't really true: You see *through* your eyes, just as, if you wear glasses or contacts, you see through those lenses. But you see *with* your brain. Because of this, what you see is based not on what the eye can detect, but on the neurological patterning in your brain.

This explains why perception is so individual, and so variable. You can have several people observe the same event, yet when you interview them carefully about what happened, you can get a completely different story from each one. It's not that only one is telling the truth: They may all be telling the truth. It's just that they all saw something different.

When your perception is different from somebody else's, the temptation is to dismiss their version as "wrong." Instead, ask them to show you how they see what they see. This allows you to have the benefit of their experiences and perspectives, and to add that to your own. Then, and only then, can you ask yourself, "Will their perception help me achieve my goals, or not?" When you learn how to take somebody else's perception and add it to yours, you significantly increase your own intelligence.

Reasoning

While will is related more to physical action and perception to the input of the senses, reasoning is where we start moving into the more cerebral activity we typically think of as *intelligence*. Reasoning is the capacity to connect the facts of a particular situation with larger principles, based on thousands of other experiences, even those far removed in time and space. There are two broad types of conscious action here, *deductive* and *inductive*. Deductive reasoning is the ability to logically examine available facts and arrive at a logical conclusion based on consistent principles. Inductive reasoning is taking the same process in the opposite direction: arriving at a principle or set of principles by extrapolating from observed facts.

In modern, literate societies, we tend to put reasoning on a bit of a pedestal. And there's no doubt about it, having a strong analytical capacity is a fantastic strength to have. At the same time, the world is full of remarkably successful businesspeople who are not particularly strong in this area. It is not a good or bad trait, but simply another color in the spectrum.

For example, between the two of us, Murray has an especially strong logical, analytical sense, which is why the second part of this book is authored primarily by Murray. On the other hand, while my sense of analytical logic is nowhere near as strong as Murray's, my sense of intuition is perhaps my most acute conscious attribute. This is one reason the two of us work so well together: We complement each other's strengths.

Intuition

Intuition is the faculty of *knowing before you think*. In business, you'll often hear people use other terms to describe this capacity, such as hunch, judgment, or instinct—"He has good instincts," or "She's got sharp judgment"—but none of these is really accurate. What we really mean is *intuition*.

The word *intuition* comes from the Latin *intueri*, which means "to look upon"; it refers to our ability to observe a situation instantaneously, without our sense perception or our logic acting as intermediary. It is closely related to that "action at a distance" that Einstein called *spooky*.

Have you ever walked into a room full of people and immediately known that something was wrong, even though nobody said anything or gave any outward indication? You didn't know how you knew—you just *knew*. That's intuition.

Imagine walking into a party and noticing a person across the room. He's not smiling, and you immediately pick up a strong sense of negativity—a "negative vibe." You might think "Jeez, what's his problem?" or perhaps conclude that you've done something that has offended him. Or, perhaps you just think "What a jerk," or whatever other interpretation you come up with to make sense of the situation. Then someone else whispers to you that earlier that day, this guy's dog was run over by a car. Suddenly you have a very different understanding of that "bad vibe" you'd picked up on, and what it actually means.

Here is what just happened: Your intuition read the information absolutely correctly—but your reasoning gave it the wrong interpretation. It was not your intuition that was at fault, it was the rational process of trying to understand it. The way to strengthen your intuition is to put complete faith and trust in it, and at the same time resist the temptation to attach meaning or interpretation to what you are sensing. Intuition is the direct perception of pure energy, and energy never lies.

Intuition is not the same thing as instinct. Instinct is a primal capacity of your nonconscious brain, something that dates from very early in the brain's development. Intuition, on the other hand, is a conscious function: It is a highly refined, high-vibration way you have of observing the world. In fact, it is one of the most powerful conscious gifts you have. It gives you the capacity to feel the energy within you and all around you.

There is no such thing as someone with "poor intuition" or "no intuition." We all have an acute intuitive capacity; we differ only in our ability to integrate that intuitive sense with the rest of our conscious functions. Often we let our other conscious functions get in the way and question what we're feeling. When we say someone has especially strong intuition, what we're really saying is that he has a particularly well-developed ability to be aware of his intuition and not drown it out with other conscious processes.

Imagination

The capacity to imagine is perhaps our most powerful conscious gift. In the context of business, this is the faculty that people typically call *vision*. Creativity, vision, imagination . . . They're all shades of the same color, and it is right at the top end of the spectrum of human consciousness.

Imagination means that we are able to create pictures in our minds out of images drawn from the quantum field of all possibilities, and make those pictures as vivid as if they were physically happening. And this has some very powerful implications. Imagination is where every single successful business is born. In chapters 6 and 7, we are going to be working with some very specific, practical techniques for unleashing your imagination and harnessing its amazing creative power to create the seeds that will grow your dream business.

Unfortunately, imagination is often a prime casualty of the process of growing up. For most of us, by the time we're in our midthirties, 95 percent of the creative-imagination neurons in our brains have atrophied from lack of use. Why? Because when we were kids we were told, "Hey, stop daydreaming—pay attention. Get your head out of the clouds!"

If you want to build your dream business and create the most wonderful life for yourself, then you need to get your head right back up there in those clouds and exercise your imagination to its fullest. Imagination is the seat of your capacity to create anything: a thrilling career, your dream business, a wonderful home, a fulfilling relationship, a magnificent life. Einstein put it well: "Imagination is more important than knowledge." Imagination is where every extraordinary achievement begins. In your imagination there are no limits, you can be completely free. It's crucial that you reawaken that faculty you had as a child and start to daydream again.

And here is the best part, the part that, if you're like most people, nobody told you when you were young: Once you have seen that vision in your imagination, you have all the faculties you need to bring that vision into physical reality, using the very same processes that turn an acorn into an oak tree.

Right about now, you might be saying, "But wait, guys! I *do* daydream about my business. In fact, I do it all the time. I have *big* dreams. It's just that they aren't turning into reality!"

We hear you, and you're right: Imagination alone doesn't cut it. In fact, having all six of these conscious traits going at full tilt still doesn't cut it. You can have the biggest, most wonderful dream in the world, and it won't do a lick of good if you're still falling prey to that grand fallacy that sabotages so many people's business dreams.

THE GRAND FALLACY

Six frogs sat on a lily pad. One decided to jump off. How many were left?

If you answered "five," congratulations! Your capacity for analytical reasoning is in good shape. Unfortunately, that is not the correct answer. The correct answer is "six."

That's right: *All six* frogs are still sitting on that lily pad. Why? Because one only *decided* to jump off—he didn't actually do any jumping.

This is exactly our grand fallacy. We think that because we have imagined something, understood something, figured something out, planned something, decided something, it's a foregone conclusion that we are going to do that something. But in most cases, we don't.

Because we so strongly tend to identify with our conscious thoughts, we naturally tend to think of our conscious thoughts as "me." We assume it is our conscious mind that is calling the shots, the one that is at the controls, that is in charge of what we actually do. But it's simply not true. In fact, the amazing thing is that we keep thinking this despite the wealth of evidence to the contrary!

Visit any health club in America in the middle of February and you'll see what has become of everyone's New Year's resolutions. It's barely six weeks into the New Year, and the place is like a ghost town. Or, go into your local bookstore and take a look at all the different titles in the Dieting section—as if lack of books on the subject were the reason the rate of obesity continues to climb. So many lily pads, so many excellent and worthy decisions . . . but no results.

In the Bible, the apostle Paul writes this wonderful statement that so beautifully captures the common frustration of the human experience: "For the good that I will to do, I do not do; but the evil I will not to do, that I practice."[4]

Here's the grand fallacy. We think that all our wonderful conscious functions control what we do. But they don't. For all its brilliance, the

---

4. Romans 7:19 (NKJV).

conscious mind has one huge handicap: It doesn't get things *done* in the long term. It may be the captain of the ship, but it's the guy in the engine room who actually makes the ship go, not the captain. In fact, here's how much control our conscious functions exert over what we actually do: *somewhere between 2 and 4 percent.* That's it.

THE INCREDIBLY LIMITED CONSCIOUS BRAIN

One reason we believe this grand fallacy of conscious control is that we are so acutely aware of that little bit of control that our conscious brain *does* exert. And make no mistake, even if that 2 to 4 percent is only a tiny bit, it's a critically important tiny bit. Our conscious brain, remember, is where imagination happens, where visions and dreams are born, where new paths are chosen, new risks taken, new initiatives explored. It is the conscious brain that takes control and gives new orders, and it's an exhilarating adventure when that happens.

It's just that it doesn't last. The conscious mind can exert a very exciting kind of control—but only for the short term. The *very* short term.

For all its brilliance, the conscious brain has severely limited processing ability. That's right: severely limited. This comes as a shock to most people, but it's not hard to see that it's true. How many numbers in a random sequence can you remember? Think about the last time you called directory assistance for a phone number. After you hung up, how long were you able to remember all ten digits without writing them down? Can you remember them now? (In fact, can you even remember the last time you called directory assistance?)

Our conscious brain has a very difficult time remembering more than six or seven digits or more than two or three events at a time. Let's try it right now:

492-625-35-86937-4

Now, quick! While you're reading this sentence, cover up that sequence of numbers with your hand. Can you remember the entire sequence without looking at it again? And if not, can you remember the first six numbers? The first three? (No cheating: Keep them covered!)

Okay: If you can't remember the numbers themselves, can you remember at least how many digits there were in the sequence?

If you can answer *any* of these questions, then your short-term memory is stronger than most people's. In fact, listen to this: The average person loses focus *every six to ten seconds.*

This, by the way, is why we keep breaking the lines of text in this book to make new paragraphs, and why every other book does the same thing, too. If we ran this entire chapter as one long paragraph, who would read it?

Now, aren't you glad that part of your brain isn't in charge of running all your biochemistry? Think about all those biochemical reactions going on inside you (the number, in case you forgot, is ten quadrillion reactions per second). If you had to do all that with your conscious brain, you would not last five seconds.

Yet that is the part of our brain that most of us are trusting with our most precious life goals.

That's the bad news. Here's the good news: While your conscious brain can't possibly keep track of all that, your nonconscious brain *can,* and it does, nonstop, twenty-four hours a day, every day of your life. If your conscious brain is a lot more limited than you realized, your nonconscious brain is vastly more powerful than you have ever imagined. If your conscious brain is the ship's captain, your nonconscious brain is the guy in the engine room, along with everyone else on board. It is the entire ship's crew, fulfilling every last function that makes the ship run, and doing it impeccably, perfectly, every moment.

Remember how often your conscious brain loses focus? Every six to ten seconds. Guess how often your nonconscious brain loses focus? Never. Not once. Not ever.

YOUR MAGNIFICENT NONCONSCIOUS BRAIN

The power center of the brain is nonconscious. This is where the great bulk of perception happens; it is where your habits reside, where your accomplishments and achievements take root. Your conscious mind is what you use to define, articulate, and set goals. But it's your nonconscious mind that follows through with all the dozens, hundreds, or millions of actions necessary to *achieve* those goals.

CONSCIOUS AND NONCONSCIOUS

	Conscious	Nonconscious
Brain mass	17%	83%
Speed of impulse	120–140 mph	over 100,000 mph
Bits per/second	2,000	400 billion
Control of perception and behavior	2–4%	96–98%
Function	volitional	servile
Time	past and future	present
Memory horizon	up to 20 seconds	forever

- The conscious brain occupies 17 percent of total brain mass (about one-sixth of the brain's weight), yet it controls only 2 to 4 percent of actual perceptions and behavior. The nonconscious brain occupies 83 percent (about five-sixths) of total brain mass and controls 96 to 98 percent of perception and behavior.

- Conscious impulses travel at speeds of 120 to 140 mph. Nonconscious impulses travel at speeds of more than 100,000 mph, or 800 times faster than conscious impulses.

- The conscious brain processes about 2,000 bits of information per second. The nonconscious brain processes about 400,000,000,000 (four hundred billion) bits of information per second.

- The conscious brain is *volitional*: It is the part you control by conscious will, the part that sets goals and judges results. The nonconscious brain is *servile*: It sets no goals of its own, but instead executes the goals it is provided with; it does not judge the merits or values of results, only whether or not they match the given goals.

- The conscious brain perceives past and future. The nonconscious brain has no perception of past or future; to the nonconscious brain, everything is happening now.

- The conscious brain operates with a very short-term memory span, generally limited to about twenty seconds. The nonconscious brain remembers everything it experiences forever.

It is staggering to contemplate even a fraction of what your nonconscious brain achieves every second of every day in your life—and all this happens without the faintest shred of conscious awareness on your part. Yet it would not be accurate to say it happens "without your knowing it," because there is an intelligence that manages all of this complex maze of biochemical activity, and that intelligence is also "you." Your nonconscious brain is also the repository of all your habits, both physical and mental. In other words, in addition to running your basic operating system, it also runs all your programmable software. This, too, proves to demand an absolutely staggering amount of moment-to-moment activity.

If you've ever observed an infant go through the process of learning how to walk, you have a sense of just how complex an activity this is. It has taken scientists decades to develop a robot that can walk naturally without losing its balance. Yet once we have studied this sequence, learned it, and mastered it, we do it all the time without giving it a thought. We walk, tie our shoes, speak in one or several languages, type on our computers, and drive our cars, all without thinking.

What's more, *habits* covers a good deal more ground than just these basic, physical routines. Have you ever had the experience of getting into your car, and the next thing you know, you're home, without any clear memory of having driven there because you were so lost in thought? If you were paying no attention, why didn't you crash the car? And how did you end up at the right house? You did it all through force of habit—a slightly more complex form of habit than tying your shoes, but a habit nonetheless.

What exactly is a habit? It is what you create when you do something over and over, to the point where you no longer need to think about it consciously in order to repeat the process perfectly. And this applies not only to things you do physically, but also to your thoughts.

When you think the same thing over and over, it eventually becomes a habit of thought. A habit of thought over time (and repetition) becomes an attitude or belief.

FORCE OF HABIT, FORCE OF BELIEF

Beliefs are not some special category of idea sitting at a higher station of truth than our ordinary, everyday mortal thoughts. Beliefs are not necessarily "the truth" at all. (Remember, there was a time when everyone believed the earth was flat.) Beliefs are nothing more than specific neural patterns in your brain, thoughts that are so ingrained they have become automatic. They are not there because they are "the truth," they have simply been handed down from generation to generation. They are there because someone *put* them there.

We are not talking here about your faith or religious views. We're not here to challenge your faith. We are talking here about your beliefs — your habits of thought, opinion, and attitude about the world around you, and especially your beliefs about *you*, about your life and your prospects for financial fulfillment.

By the time you're seventeen years old, you've heard "No, you can't," an average of 150,000 times. You've heard "Yes, you can," about 5,000 times. That's thirty nos for every yes. That makes for a powerful belief of "I can't."

Most people view their own goals in the form of hopes or wishes. "I hope I succeed in this business," or "I wish I would earn a million dollars . . ." Here is the rest of the unfinished thought, whether conscious or not, that usually lies after those three dots: ". . . *but I bet I won't.*" The biggest obstacle to most people's goals has nothing to do with any external conditions or factors. It is this: *They don't believe it will happen or that it can be done.* If you don't believe it will happen, it is almost guaranteed that it won't. You simply cannot achieve a goal that you do not believe you can achieve, because those beliefs live in that part of the brain that is running the show, even though we typically are not aware of it.

Let's say you love your family very much, you place a high value on family, and one of your biggest goals in life is to have a rich, full family life — yet you also have a belief that the only way you can be truly successful and earn enough income to provide for your family is to work really, really hard. So what happens? You find yourself working eighty hours a week and never see your family. Why, because you don't value them? No, you value them, all right, but your beliefs have you captive on that eighty-hour track, like a hamster on a wheel. Beliefs trump desires, every time.

If you have credit card debt and financial struggle in your life, lack of money is not the problem, it is only the symptom. Lack of money is simply the fruit. To find the cause, you need to look at the seed. The fruit will always match the seed. And the seed is your habits of thought.

Here's the problem: Beliefs tend to be self-fulfilling. This is because habits are thousands of times stronger than desires. That is worth restating: not twice as strong, not even three times as strong, but *thousands of times* stronger. You may have the desire to increase your income tenfold, but if your habits of thought do not expect anything like that to occur, it will be next to impossible for it to happen; you will take no lasting, productive action toward that goal. Why not? Because it is your habits, not your desires or other conscious thoughts, that run your actions.

This is one of the greatest discoveries of the past decade of neurological research: 96 to 98 percent of all your behaviors are automatic. This is why we *set* goals, but don't *reach* them. *Setting* them is a function of the conscious mind. *Reaching* them is a function of the nonconscious mind.

HOW TO TAP THE POWER OF THE QUANTUM UNIVERSE

Here is the critical question: If the beliefs you presently have are not serving you, how do you change them? How do you adopt new beliefs?

You could try using your willpower, and simply *decide* to have new beliefs. And that will probably work very well—for a few minutes, anyway. But conscious thoughts are hard to sustain, as we've seen. If you are going to change your habits and beliefs, you have to do it where they reside, which is in the nonconscious mind—the dog that wags the tail.

Your conscious mind is excellent at assessing the situation and formulating a plan. Your conscious mind is where you *design* your new beliefs—but it is not where you *hold* those beliefs. It is like a brilliant conductor: He understands the music perfectly and has a masterful sense of how it should sound, but he doesn't actually play any of the instruments. Unless he gets the members of the orchestra to actually play those instruments, the music remains nothing but an idea in his head—not a sound is heard. Which is exactly what happens to most people's goals.

Retraining this nonconscious part of your personality is a two-step process. First, using your conscious faculties, you choose the thoughts you want to have as your beliefs. Then, you systematically impress these thoughts on the nonconscious part of your brain.

Remember the analogy of placing your order at a restaurant? That's exactly what this is like. Choosing a thought from the universe of possibilities is like sitting down at a table in a restaurant and choosing a great selection from the menu. We can imagine that delicious meal, and we congratulate ourselves, knowing we have made an excellent choice. Our stomach rumbles. We can already taste this great dish. But there is a problem: No matter how much we look forward to this wonderful food, no matter how excellent a choice we have made, our plate continues to be empty. We tuck our napkin under our chin, hold our fork and knife ready in anticipation: Oh, boy! Still, no food.

What's missing? We *haven't actually placed the order*. The frog has only decided to jump off the lily pad—he hasn't actually jumped yet. Until we relay our order to the kitchen, nothing happens. We know what we want, but nothing's being cooked back there.

The glory of our conscious mind is that using the power of will and imagination, we can pluck an idea out of the quantum sea of possibilities. *We can choose what we think*. Our mistake is assuming that because we have that idea, we will act on it; we believe that because we *think* it, we will *do* it. But the odds are, we won't—not unless we take those conscious thoughts, buff them to impeccable clarity, and deliver them to our nonconscious faculties.

This is what makes the difference between setting goals and achieving goals. *Setting* goals is a conscious exercise; *achieving* goals is a spiritual and nonconscious exercise. To achieve our goals, to actually create and build our dream business, we need to become expert at using both parts of our brain. That is what most of us have never been taught to do. And that is exactly what we are going to learn over the next several chapters.

We'll start by using your conscious faculties—your imagination, intuition, reasoning, and the rest—to craft a crystal clear picture of your dream business: the perfect seed. Then, using a broad repertoire of simple imprinting techniques that mimic the way you first learned the beliefs you presently hold, you're going to learn how to plant that seed in the fertile soil of your nonconscious brain.

"You can't always get what you want," sang the Rolling Stones, and they were absolutely right, because what you want has very little to do with what you end up getting. Simply having the desire to achieve something does absolutely no good, in and of itself. You can want all you want, and nothing happens. But impress that desire onto the power center of your brain as a new set of instructions, and you can transform that desire into a habit of thought—a belief. And once you do that, no force in the world can *stop* it from happening.

HOW TO CHANGE YOUR MIND

Except for the fact that she is the lead singer for her high school choir, the girl on the stage seems just like any other sixteen-year-old. As the concert proceeds, Beth keeps close watch on the choir's conductor, intently picking up his every movement and gesture. Her voice is lovely, and her keen observation of the choirmaster, wedded to her innate musicality, makes for beautiful music indeed. But her musical sense is not the only thing that makes Beth special. She may seem like any other sixteen-year-old girl, but there is something about her that makes her different from all the other girls in the choir.

Beth is blind. In fact, she has been blind from birth.

How, one naturally wonders, is she able to so keenly observe the conductor? *She is watching him with her tongue.*

Beth is wearing a device designed by the late Paul Bach-y-Rita, a neuroscientist at the University of Wisconsin at Madison, who devoted much of his career to researching and demonstrating the proposition that all senses are created equal. And not just equal, but pretty much interchangeable.

The tongue, explained Bach-y-Rita, has more tactile nerve receptors than any other part of the body except for the lips, and is sometimes even referred to as *the curious organ*. (Think about how busily inquisitive your tongue was the last time you had dental work, and you'll see why the phrase makes sense.) So why not use the tongue to see?

Bach-y-Rita's device starts with a video camera strapped to the user's head that feeds video information to a laptop, which reduces the image to a 144-pixel signal that is then fed through electrodes to a grid that rests on the tongue, which reads the image as a sort of superlingual braille.[5]

At the time of his death in 2006, Bach-y-Rita was also working with the military's Navy SEALs on a system that would allow them to see infrared through their tongues. NASA had worked with him to develop sensors that let astronauts feel things on the outside of their space suits. He had hoped to develop a miniature version of his tongue-vision system that would fit into a wireless retainer and run off a tiny camera hidden in a pair of glasses.

"Anything that can be measured can be transported to the brain," said the scientist, "[and if] we can get it to the brain, the brain can learn how to use it."

And that last phrase is what holds the miraculous part of the entire thing: *The brain can learn how to use it.* Because if the brain can learn to see with the tongue and read with the fingertips, what other marvels might the brain learn to accomplish? The answer turns out to be, anything and everything.

NEUROPLASTICITY: THE DISCOVERY OF THE DECADE

In the last chapter, we said that neuroscience has taken a quantum-physics-like leap in the past decade, and the single most astonishing and revolutionary finding that embodies that leap can be summed up in one word: *neuroplasticity.*

Before the advent of real-time brain scans, scientists believed that the process of cell division that creates new brain cells, called *neurogenesis,* slows down early in life and stops altogether by the time we are into adolescence.

At about six months into embryonic development, brain cells start to divide and make connections. This process of building up crucial brain circuitry by establishing new connections continues actively until about the age of two, at which point we've more or less completed the

---

5. Michael Abrams, "Can You See with Your Tongue?" *Discover* (June 1, 2003).

nailing down of our basic genetic neurological heritage. This foundation makes up about 50 percent of the configuration of our adult brains; the other 50 percent is contributed by our experiences and observations from that point on.

Children's brains contain a significant number of a certain type of neuron called *mirror neurons*. Mirror neurons do exactly what their name implies: They help us mimic the behavior we observe around us. As children, we experience the events, behaviors, and emotions taking place in our environment, and by mirroring these, we fill out the balance of what becomes our own personality, complete with its unique profile of behaviors, feelings, attitudes, thoughts, and beliefs. As we grow older, in other words, we learn to behave the way we are taught to behave and to think the way we are taught to think. By the time we are adults, the cognitive filters through which we see the world are quite well established and solidly in place. Our brains are hardwired, so the scientists believed we are who we are, and how we see the world and our own place within it pretty much determines how we view any new experience . . .

Except that neuroplasticity changes all that.

This dramatic new finding, which more than any other single discovery has turned neuroscience upside down, is the observation that we are making new brain cells and new neural connections all the time. As it turns out, the process of neurogenesis does not stop with adolescence but continues throughout the human life span. No matter what your age, your brain is perfectly capable of creating entirely new neural pathways. Ten years ago, scientists didn't believe there was such a thing as brain plasticity. (In fact, even using the term *plasticity* in papers on neuroscience was taboo.) Not anymore. Which is why today, scientists like Paul Bach-y-Rita are being taken seriously—and why people much older than Beth have learned to see with their tongues, too. It turns out that every time you have a significantly new thought or experience, your brain is actually making new neural connections.

You already know this, because you've felt it. Think of a time when you've suddenly had a burst of inspiration, a revelation of some new truth that you had never grasped before, a sudden insight so palpable that you felt almost physically shaken by it. If this felt physical, it's because it was: You were carving out new pathways in your brain.

Yes, we are all shaped by our genetic heritage and upbringing, and if we do nothing significant to alter our existing wiring, we will continue to go through life with the same attitudes, perspectives, beliefs, and patterns of thinking we have always had. But these new findings in neuroscience tell us that we can override our own genetic code—that if we learn how to gain access to the power center of our brain, where those attitudes, beliefs, and established thought patterns are stored, we can actually *rewrite* our genetic code.

And we are not talking about only minor changes here. The number of potential connections your brain can make over your lifetime is about one followed by six million zeros. To put it another way, your brain has room to store more content than would fit into six million volumes of the *New York Times*, all of it with the nonconscious brain's capacity for instantaneous access and total recall. Not only *can* you change your brain dramatically, but it *is designed specifically* for you to be able to do exactly that. We are structured so that we can grow our creativity, intelligence, and capacity for achievement throughout our lives.

THE GUARD AT THE DOORWAY OF YOUR MIND

As you start learning the process for changing your mind, there are several crucial functions of the nonconscious brain that you need to become familiar with. Untended and left on their own, they can completely block that path between you and your goals—yet once you learn how they operate, they become magic genies that can help you achieve your heart's desire. The first of these two functions is a network of nerves that stands guard at the doorway of your mind.

Remember what it is you see with? Not with your eyes (and no, not with your tongue) but with your brain. Your sense organs simply convey data. Your brain is what turns that data into perception. And this is where it gets really interesting: What your conscious brain sees is not the same thing as what your nonconscious brain sees.

The brain processes over four hundred billion bits of information every second, yet we are aware of only about two thousand. In other words, for each bit of information you are aware of, there are about two hundred million bits that your brain processes behind the veil of your awareness. So what determines which bit we will "see" and which we will skip over? That all-important, life-shaping decision is made moment to moment, all the time, day or night, awake or asleep, by a part of your brain called the *reticular activating system* (RAS).

The RAS is the scientific term for a network of nerve pathways at the base of your brain that connects the spinal cord, cerebellum, and cerebrum and acts as a filter for all the sensory input your brain draws from your external world. (*Reticulum*, from the Latin for "little net," simply means a netlike structure.) Anything that you see, hear, feel, taste, or smell passes through this fine network, which then relays the signal or message on to the appropriate part of your brain for processing.

Your reticular formation stands guard at the doorway of your mind, sorting through the torrent of incoming information and searching for those specific bits that best match those information patterns already established in your brain. Your reticular formation picks up all the sensory input from your environment and, if it's important to you, sends a signal to your conscious brain to alert you that something important is going on. And it does this at a speed eight hundred times faster than your conscious brain cells operate.

This is why a mother standing outside a schoolroom will hear the undifferentiated stream of sound coming from fifty children, but the moment her own child cries or exclaims, she'll hear that child and *only* that child. Why? Because she recognizes that sound, and she has programmed herself to filter out all the rest.

In the film *West Side Story* there is a scene where the young lovers, Tony and Maria, meet for the first time. They are standing across the room from each other at a dance, when suddenly every other person in the room goes blurry, and from clear across the crowded dance floor they both become acutely aware of each other. It is as if nobody else in the room exists.

This is more than good storytelling. It's a vivid example of the reticular formation at work. Tony's nonconscious brain is fully programmed to search through his sensory environment for information that relates to his brain's picture of his "dream girl," and Maria's nonconscious brain is likewise conditioned with the specific neural pattern that says "dream guy." To each other, they both become that one bit of information out of four hundred billion that is critically relevant to the conscious brain.

You can think of this system as being something like Google. When you type a word or search string into Google, it scours the Internet for everything it can find that relates to that specific phrase, then retrieves it and presents it to you for your inspection, and it does all this in a matter of seconds. Your reticular formation does much the same thing, only it does its work not in seconds but in *thousandths* of a second. Your RAS works so rapidly and efficiently, it makes Google seem like carving a stone tablet.

Here is the most important thing about the reticular activating system: Just as with Google, you can enter whatever search string you want it to look for. When you program a specific idea or goal into your RAS, no matter whether you're asleep or awake, thinking about it or not, the RAS will do its job and sift through the entire ocean of information swirling about you at all times to find precisely what you've told it to find, picking out that one bit of crucial data for your awareness and editing out the other 399,999,999,999 bits of irrelevant data.

Imagine you're asleep, and you're in charge of your baby sleeping in the next room. Cars honk outside, a dog barks nearby, the guy next door comes home late and slams his car door, and the grandfather clock downstairs rings its gong every quarter hour—yet none of that rouses you from sleep. But when that baby in the next room starts to whimper, you're up and out of that bed in a flash. Your nonconscious brain heard all those other sounds perfectly, but only the sound of the baby managed to get through to your conscious awareness and wake you up. The reticular formation is the most intelligent and sophisticated alarm system in the universe.

When you create a clear, focused picture of what you want, this part of your brain kicks into high gear, and doesn't stop until it finds it for you. You may be at a party, standing in the middle of a noisy room, and suddenly pick up a snippet of conversation between two people standing thirty feet away, because one of them happens to mention something about short-term warehouse leasing—and it just so happens that you need to find a way to lease a warehouse facility for a few weeks. At that same moment there may be a dozen other conversations going on in your audible environment, some of them much closer and louder than this one. Yet you don't hear any of those. You hear just that one fragment of conversation that you *needed* to hear. That's your reticular activating system at work.

The reticular formation is part of the answer to why I ended up living in the very same house I had pasted onto my vision board years earlier. I had imprinted that house into my nonconscious mind and, years later, when I went real estate hunting in the area where that house happened to be, my reticular formation had its neurological radar out and picked up on that one house out of two hundred million.

YOU GET WHAT YOU'RE LOOKING FOR

This amazing ability to sort through an ocean of information and find the one droplet of water you're looking for can function as a blessing or as a curse, depending on what you've got entered into it as your search string. This is true for two reasons.

First, if your RAS is not programmed for what you really want, then no matter how diligently you pursue a goal, you'll miss all the cues in your environment and overlook all the resources, connections, and other pieces of the puzzle that might help you realize that goal.

Let's say you've been earning about $50,000 a year for a while, so that is what seems "normal" to you. This translates into a belief: "I am worth $50,000 a year, that's my normal income level." Because your nonconscious mind is holding tightly to that picture of you earning $50,000 per year, even if a million-dollar idea comes along, your RAS will filter it right out so that you never even become aware of it. Rather than being routed to your conscious brain, that information is shuffled off to a closet in your nonconscious brain. The neurological term for this is *scotoma*, which is Greek for "blind spot." The answer could be literally right under your nose, but you don't see it.

Here's the second way your RAS can work against you: If you program it with what you *don't* want, then that is precisely what you *will* find, and you'll keep finding it. This is why so many people seem to make the same mistakes over and over in life, whether it's in business, in love, in health, or anything else. How do you program your RAS with what you don't want? Simply by focusing on it, thereby creating a habit of thought around that thing.

When you focus on what's *not* working in your life, or on those things you are unhappy about, you are entering those problems as a search string into your reticular activating system, and like the good little search engine it is, those problems are exactly what it will go looking for. And remember, the brain is really, really good at what it does. If you unwittingly tell it to go searching for trouble, heartbreak, or disappointment, it will absolutely find it, guaranteed, every time.

This means that when you're focused on the ten pounds you want to lose, on that twenty-thousand-dollar debt you wish you didn't have, on your worries that your new business might not make it past its first year, your own brain stem network goes diligently to work, humming and buzzing away, digging through the morass of sensory input to find those ideas, opinions, snippets of overheard conversation, and other bits and pieces of evidence—and only those bits and pieces of evidence—that support *precisely those things you don't want.*

Why? Because you told it to.

What's more, your RAS will dutifully ignore everything else. Which means that all the evidence, resources, ideas, or other useful information that might actually help you lose those pounds, dissolve that debt, or successfully build that business will be discarded by your RAS as irrelevant.

Let's say, for example, that you're in a new relationship. And let's say, further, that because of all that you witnessed around you while you were growing up, you have a belief that relationships that start out looking happy eventually turn sour and break apart. Now, while you love this person and the two of you seem very happy together, you are secretly worried that it won't last. Maybe you haven't told anyone about this, maybe you haven't even voiced those worries out loud to yourself. But to your nonconscious, there are no secrets. That worry isn't simply gnawing at you, it's taking center stage as the search string in your RAS.

Here's what happens: You could be surrounded by all the evidence in the world that your relationship is solid, secure, and as healthy as can be, with everyone around you seeing the two of you as perfect for each other, and everything in both your lives pointing to that same sweet conclusion—but none of that evidence will make any difference, because your RAS will edit it all out. If even a wisp of pessimism arises—say, a cynical comment from an acquaintance who secretly envies your happiness—your well-trained reticular formation will ignore the two hundred million pieces of positive evidence and rush in to deliver to your awareness that single negative perspective. As it joins with your already-established belief, your worry that this relationship is doomed moves closer to becoming a conviction. And because beliefs and habits are thousands of times stronger than desires, that conviction becomes a self-fulfilling prophecy: If you believe the relationship is doomed, then it *is* doomed.

And the same thing happens in your financial and business life. Your reticular formation goes on the hunt for supporting evidence and resources to bolster whatever viewpoints have been programmed into it. And if that viewpoint is negative, that's exactly the evidence and "reality" you'll find, reinforce, and amplify.

Worry is a prayer for what you don't want.

This is why it's so critical that you learn how to consciously direct your reticular activating system, and why neuroplasticity is so life-changing.

The process we call *neural reconditioning*, which we'll walk you through in detail in chapter 7, is designed to write a new search string into your nonconscious neurological search engine. Through neural reconditioning, you can train your RAS to direct its amazing capacity to focus on what you *do* want, not what you *don't* want—on the solution, not the problem. Now it can sort for the excitement, fulfillment, and satisfaction evoked by reaching your goals, not the worry, doubt, or fears about whether you will reach them.

In the film *My Big Fat Greek Wedding*, Toula complains to her mother about her father and how autocratic he is: "Ma," she says, "Dad is so stubborn! What he says goes. Ah, he says, the man is the head of the house!" Her mother looks at her, nods wisely, and in a confidential voice replies, "Let me tell you something, Toula: He is the head—but I am the neck. And I can turn him any way I want."

Using the simple techniques of neural reconditioning, you can be the neck that turns your nonconscious brain and points it in whatever direction you want.

GORDON'S DILEMMA

Along with resetting your RAS to search out the new information you want from your environment, you will also want to recalibrate your brain so that it will accept this new information and not reject it as a threat. To do that, we need to look at the second crucial nonconscious function, sometimes called the set point. To explain how it works, let's look at Gordon's dilemma.

One day Gordon takes his friends fishing in the brand-new boat he has just bought. After heading due west about a mile out to sea, he and his friends start fishing. They fish for hours, but with no luck. His friends beg Gordon to change course and head south, where they've heard the fishing is better.

Gordon is anxious for his friends to have a great time, so he heads to the front of the boat, grabs the wheel, and brings it about a good ninety degrees port, now headed due south, and then he goes back to rejoin his friends. After an hour goes by without a catch, one of Gordon's friends glances up at the sky and says, "Gordon! We're still headed due west!"

Mortified, Gordon realizes it's true. He goes back up to the helm and this time, just to make sure, he steers the boat way past 90 degrees to 135 degrees, heading south*east*, before returning to his friends. After another hour of no results, they realize that, once again, they are still headed due west! Frustrated and embarrassed, Gordon now rushes to the helm and pulls the vessel clear around, 180 degrees, setting it on a course due east, headed back for home. Yet fifteen minutes later, they are mysteriously headed due west again! Gordon is ready to tear his hair out, when one of his friends says, "Hey, Gordon . . . you know about the automatic pilot, right?"

Gordon doesn't know what to say. The automatic *what*? He didn't know the boat had one of those.

Does Gordon's dilemma sound at all familiar? Most of us have had experiences like this in our lives. After the third failed relationship, or the fourth failed business effort, the seventh time losing our temper when we swore we weren't going to, or the eighth (or eighteenth) time we "forget" to stay on our diet or exercise routine, we say, "Why does this keep happening to me?"

It could simply be that, like Gordon, you've never given your auto-pilot a thought because you didn't even know it existed. Because it isn't just boats that have them. We have one, too, and it's called the psycho-cybernetic mechanism.

THE THERMOSTAT IN YOUR BRAIN

The term *cybernetic* refers to a control-and-response mechanism in organisms and some machines.[6] A thermostat is a simple example. When you program the thermostat in your home to a specific tempera-ture, it will control the activity of your heating-and-cooling system to maintain that temperature, regardless of fluctuations in the exter-nal climate. If a current of cold air enters the room and lowers the temperature, the thermostat will activate the heating system to raise it back to the set temperature. Likewise, if the July sun baking your house raises the building's internal temperature, the thermostat will prompt the air conditioner to kick in and restore the temperature you had set.

The term *set point* is often used to describe a physiological version of that same mechanism that controls our body temperature, weight, or any one of many other types of bodily homeostasis.

In the 1950s, a plastic surgeon named Maxwell Maltz made a bewil-dering discovery. He found that even after significant facial plastic sur-gery, many of his patients didn't see any changes when they looked at themselves in the mirror. He was fascinated. How could this possibly be? Dr. Maltz studied the dynamics of self-image and discovered an internal self-corrective process he dubbed the psycho-cybernetic mech-anism.

According to Maltz, any change that we make in our lives—whether in our finances, health, spiritual connectedness, relationships, or ca-reer—that takes us out of our comfort zone, sends a chemical signal to the rest of our nervous system. Our brain picks up that signal as doubt,

6. The term was coined by Norbert Weiner in the 1940s and popularized through his book *Cybernetics: or Control and Communication in the Animal and the Machine* (1948). The word itself is derived from the Greek *kybernetes*, meaning "pilot" or "rudder."

fear, or anxiety, and automatically interprets that feeling as a danger signal, prompting us to make whatever adjustments necessary to return us to our previous state — just like a thermostat.

But what if you *want* to deviate from your set path?

For sheer survival, the psycho-cybernetic mechanism is brilliant: A jolt of epinephrine triggered by a signal from the brain will cause you to jump back off the street and onto the sidewalk without even the glimmer of a conscious thought, and quite possibly save your life in the process. However, in a world where our day-to-day survival is seldom threatened, this same life-saving mechanism can cripple our efforts to grow and change, both in our life and in our business.

The problem is not the mechanism itself but our interpretation of that chemical signal as "danger." The fact is, risk and the sense of stretching oneself that goes with it are part and parcel of the entrepreneurial experience. In fact, they are an integral part of *any* sort of genuine growth.

Here's what we need to understand: That psycho-cybernetic alert signal does not literally mean "danger," it simply means "Hey, you're stepping out of the normal range and moving into uncharted territory, are you aware of this? Are you sure this is what you want to be doing?"

The psycho-cybernetic mechanism is an autopilot that will *always* kick in and attempt to steer your ship back on whatever course it has programmed into its neural circuits. Just as with Gordon and his ill-fated attempts to change his boat's course, your willpower and conscious effort may have an impact on your course, but only for short bursts, never for the long term. That is the great flaw in all behavior modification programs: They are conscious efforts, and the conscious brain is simply not very effective at modifying our habits. To have an impact at the level of cause, we need to address these habits where they live: in our nonconscious brains.

CHANGING YOUR FINANCIAL SET POINT

Last chapter, we said that even if you want to increase your income level tenfold, unless you impress that intention upon your nonconscious brain, the wish will remain nothing but a wish. Gordon's dilemma is the reason why—because you also have a *financial* set point. Before you can significantly increase your income, you need to recalibrate that financial set point, because if you don't, every time you start taking any significant action that might result in your income substantially increasing, your psycho-cybernetic mechanism will kick in, flood your brain with epinephrine and cortisol, and cause you to jump back up onto the curb and get back on course!

So, just how do you go about recalibrating that thermostat? Let us illustrate with a story.

Two weeks before John Assaraf's son Keenan started kindergarten, John took Keenan up to the kindergarten building and looked through the window with him. John told his son all sorts of stories about what a blast John had had when he first went to kindergarten, how the classroom had all kinds of toys and other kids who liked doing all the same stuff he liked to do, how cool it was for John, and what a great time it was going to be for Keenan.

By the time his first day of school arrived, Keenan was completely psyched. As John and he walked up the steps together to enter the building for the first time, John could barely keep him from running in there ahead of him. It was a brand-new experience, but Keenan was totally ready for it. He had recalibrated his psycho-cybernetic mechanism.

John noticed another dad bringing his son in, too, only the scene with them was very different. While Keenan rushed into the room eagerly, this boy hung on to his dad's leg for dear life; his lip was trembling and he clearly looked like he was about to cry. It wasn't hard to read the expression on his young face: This was way, way out of his comfort zone, and he didn't want any part of it. His psycho-cybernetic mechanism was going off like a firehouse alarm, dumping chemicals into his blood that were screaming, "Stop! Danger! Turn around! Run!"

The boy's dad was being great; he was clearly being very kind and supportive, yet at the same time firm in his resolve that his son was going to find the courage it would take to let go and enter the classroom. He urged, explained, coached, calmed, and assured—but it seemed that no matter what he said or did, nothing made any difference. Why not? Because at that point, it was too late. Everything the dad could do was happening at the conscious level.

And whenever you have a contest between the conscious and non-conscious mind, the nonconscious will win out—hands down, no contest, every time.

Remember, your psycho-cybernetic mechanism is doing exactly what it's supposed to do: keep you feeling *safe*. If you haven't been taught how to analyze these feelings, you'll do what everybody else does, which is to retreat to the safety of your comfort zone. You'll sabotage any success you might begin to have in the pursuit of your goals—in most cases, completely without being aware of doing so—in order to return to your preset homeostasis.

And by the way, this has nothing to do with happiness. You could be miserable, and delivering an equally miserable performance at work, but if that's what you've established as normal, your psycho-cybernetic mechanism will obediently manage all of your nonconscious habits, modes of thought and action, every mechanism, to keep you safely in that miserable place.

Let's take a closer look for a moment at what happened with my son. I helped him formulate new neural connections, which caused him to feel comfortable with the new surroundings. He became acclimated to a new experience—in his case, the kindergarten environment—by creating that experience internally. And the nonconscious mind cannot distinguish between an external experience in the physical world, as conveyed to the brain by our senses, and that same experience conveyed to the brain purely by our imagination. For all its awesome power, this is the critical limitation of our nonconscious mind, its magnificent blind spot. And this plays beautifully into the hands of the magnificent strength of our conscious mind. While it has only an insignificantly tiny amount of horsepower, compared with the awesome power of the nonconscious, our conscious brain has an amazing capacity to create pictures through imagination—pictures that the powerhouse of our nonconscious cannot distinguish from the "real" thing.

When my son was imagining himself having all sorts of fun in that classroom with new friends and fabulous toys, none of that was actually happening in a physical sense. But his nonconscious didn't know that, and it didn't care. To his nonconscious, the experience was just as real, in that moment, as it would be two weeks later when he physically stepped into the room.

What I did with my son is exactly what you're going to do with yourself and your dream business: create it first, as a vivid, genuine experience in your nonconscious mind. This will recalibrate the mechanisms of your brain so that when you actually go to work on building that business, instead of rejecting it the way your immune system rejects a hostile virus, your nonconscious will welcome the new situation with open arms, just like my son on his first day of school.

The key is to feel the fear, feel the doubt, know there's going to be uncertainty, and do it anyway. Successful entrepreneurs don't have fewer chemical alerts than everyone else; they just interpret those alerts differently. They have learned how to recognize that feeling and use it to move forward instead of reacting protectively to it—that is, to interpret it as a sign that a breakthrough is in the offing rather than seeing it as a threat.

Think back to anything you've ever done that was thrilling: stepping off a chairlift at the top of a ski slope, preparing to dive off a high diving board, asking your future spouse on that first date, writing out that terrifyingly large check for a down payment on your first home. That's the adrenaline rush that tells you that you're up to something great. Think of that feeling, and remember it when your business breaks into new and thrilling levels of success—because it is the same thing.

This capacity is no different from a muscle: The more you work it, the stronger it gets. When you start having doubts or an edgy feeling of nervousness about your goals, pay attention—and take control. Ask yourself, "Is this a genuine danger? Is this really something that can hurt me, or is it part of my natural growth process as I achieve my goals?"

Anytime you learn something new, whether it's riding a bicycle, making more money than you have ever made before, entering a brand-new relationship, or starting your first day of kindergarten, there's going to be a point of resistance, a point of fear where you will feel discomfort. Here's what that means: You're growing.

THE AMAZING PROCESS OF REWIRING YOUR BRAIN

As you start reprogramming your reticular activating system and recalibrating your psycho-cybernetic mechanism, realize what it is you are actually doing: You are overriding your genetic programming and your upbringing, with all its years of ingrained habit.

You aren't simply entertaining a new thought in your imagination, a new thought that will last no longer than a New Year's decision to join the gym or cut out excess carbs. No, you are fundamentally changing how your brain works by physically forging new neural pathways within the tissues of your brain. There is no more fundamental change you can possibly make in your life than this. You are changing the definition of *you*.

Imagine deciding to go on a hike through a stretch of wild forest, a tract that hasn't been traveled for centuries. You have to knock tree limbs out of the way, treading plants and grasses underfoot. As you retrace your steps on the way back later that day, you can just make out the path you traveled a few hours earlier: a broken limb here, flattened grasses there—but it takes an acute eye.

The next day, you make the trek again, following the same path, only this time the trail you blazed the day before is easier to follow.

Every day you repeat your journey, widening the trail and eventually creating an obvious, comfortable pathway through the forest.

This is what happens when you create new neural pathways. It may take an incredible act of will and imagination to have a new thought, to forge that new pathway in your brain. It can take a similar leap of faith, courage, and imagination to picture yourself building your dream business and creating a personal net worth of millions. You're cutting a new path through thickets of habitual thoughts, which can be one stubborn, overgrown forest indeed. But you make the leap and slice through the underbrush with your new thought, and in the process, you start laying down a new trail.

Neurologically, here's what's happening: Your thought is carried along a series of electrical impulses, moving from neuron to neuron by leaping across the gaps, or *synapses*, in between. For that thought's electrical charge to leap the synaptic chasm, a certain electrical threshold must be reached and exceeded. And with that leap, something fascinating happens: You begin ever so slightly to *lower* that threshold. The next time you evoke that same thought, there is a tiny bit less electrical resistance to that same synaptic leap. Over time, as you repeat the thought over and over, the threshold gets lower and lower, making it easier and easier to pass along those electrical charges, easier to have the thought. You are bushwhacking a new pathway with your thoughts.

Neuroscientists have an expression: "Neurons that fire together wire together." As your new thought pattern is repeated over and over, the new neural patterns in your brain literally wire themselves together, creating a brand-new network of neurons. In time, your new path becomes a superhighway, across which the constant traffic of your new beliefs and new identity drive effortlessly and automatically.

Changing from the inside out, you have paved the way for your dream business.

6

YOUR DREAM BUSINESS

In a recent study, five thousand successful businesspeople were interviewed to see what traits, characteristics, or attributes they shared. Not surprisingly, they varied enormously. Successful people come in all imaginable shapes, sizes, backgrounds, histories, skill sets, and personalities. There is no single "entrepreneurial type." This was as varied and colorful a group of humanity as one could imagine. But the researchers did find one trait in common: All the subjects had an intense passion for what they were doing.

There is a difference between being *committed* to your success and being *interested* in your success. If you are interested, you will do what's convenient. If you are committed, you will do whatever it takes—and doing whatever it takes is what you need to succeed in business, no matter who or where you are. It's no longer possible (if it ever was) to get by with a halfhearted approach.

"Yes," you might say, "but let's keep this in perspective. I mean, it's not like we're trying to change the world here, right?"

Actually, it's exactly like that. The truth is, successful businesspeople are driven by the idea of changing the world around them. They want to leave their imprint.

Of course, part of that passion is financial. When you're in business, it's natural to focus on money. Money, after all, is the medium of business; it's how you measure the relative success of what you're doing.

But here is something that too many businesspeople never realize and are never taught: It's difficult to be genuinely passionate about money, because money has no intrinsic character.

There are two types of income. One is monetary income, and it's great to have the comfortable or even luxurious lifestyle it can provide. But in order to be genuinely happy and fulfilled, to be truly successful, you also need a healthy flow of *psychic income*. Psychic income is the feeling that comes from the sense that your contribution matters, that you are making a positive difference in the world. There is no better feeling than knowing your life and your business have purpose and meaning. This is the ultimate goal of a successful business.

For example, here is the stated purpose for one of our businesses:

We are changing the world by helping at least a million people build the businesses of their dreams—which will have a ripple effect that makes a tangible difference to hundreds of millions of people worldwide.

Now *that* gets us out of bed in the morning!

Scale and size are not the issue here: impact is. It doesn't matter whether your business is a multinational nonprofit that feeds, clothes, and shelters hundreds of thousands of disadvantaged people, a printing company that makes brochures and signs, or an auto body shop that serves your neighborhood. We've seen people who are responsible for putting a little plastic piece on the end of a shoelace be passionate about what they do—because they can visualize the safely tied shoes of children, athletes, students, firefighters, hospital workers, the elderly . . . they can see their shoelaces *having an impact on the world*. From coffee shops to software giants, any business can make a contribution to other people's lives. Every time either of us has been a part of creating or building any business, for us that business has been like working on a cure for cancer. Successful businesspeople truly do want to change the world.

The United States today is buried under a staggering mountain of debt—trillions of dollars' worth. How will this country ever be able to get out from under? There is one and only one way that will ever happen: through the efforts of creative and passionate people building the businesses of their dreams.

The planet's ecology is also facing some serious threats right now. How will we ever be able to solve our worldwide energy needs without ruining the planet in the process? There is one and only one way: through the ingenuity and passion of entrepreneurs.

People like you don't just *want* to change the world: You *are* changing the world. This group of people is going to rewrite the future. It's not about governments, corporations, and organizations anymore. In the twenty-first century, it's the individual man and woman passionately in pursuit of their business dreams who will have a positive, transformative impact on everyone's lives.

LIVING A LIFE OF PASSION

There is a difference between being passionate and being obsessed. We're not saying that in order to build a successful business, you have to live and breathe that business every second of the day while ignoring the other dimensions of your life. It's vitally important to learn to live with a sense of balance between work and home, between business and personal life, including your relationships, physiological and spiritual health, personal development, and more. But if you want to accelerate your growth and sustain it, if you want to create your dream business, that business needs to be an expression of your passion.

It often amazes us that anyone would consider getting into a business doing something they were *not* passionate about. But it happens all the time—you've seen it, too. All too often, people don't believe that they can follow their passions and still make enough money to achieve their goals and dreams. In a word, they settle, not because they want to, but because they simply don't believe they have a choice. But they do, and so do you. Making that choice, and becoming crystal clear about it, is what this chapter is all about.

Is it possible to grow a successful business based on a concept or industry that's *not* your passion? Yes, it's possible—but it's not sustainable. Let's have no illusions here, building a hugely successful business is not easy. It takes discipline and work and involves a lot of challenges.

It's not about convenience or waiting for opportunity to knock on your door. It's about meeting those challenges, persevering through your dream business's gestation, and seeing it through to the point where you start reaping the rewards. It requires your being willing to *do whatever it takes*. And the only way you're going to do that is if you are in love with what you're doing.

Besides, if you're not passionate about it, why bother? Why settle for something less than a business that will absolutely thrill you? There is a reason you want abundance: That's what you are designed for. It makes no sense to have so much potential within you and not do something that will bring it to the surface and realize it in abundant terms, in a form that makes you feel your life is complete and all the challenge is worthwhile.

Rather than ask, "Am I worthy of my goals?" we encourage you to reverse that question and ask, "Are my goals worthy of me?" When you are finished creating a vision for your dream business, you should be able to look at what you've written, ask yourself that question again, and answer with a resounding "Absolutely!"

WHY ARE YOU IN BUSINESS?

Let's start by asking a fundamental question: Why? *Why* are you in business? Why are you doing what you're doing?

People talk about motivation, but motivation—at least the way we usually interpret the word—is fairly ineffective. Getting pumped up because someone else has cheered you on or whipped up your enthusiasm is all very well, but typically it doesn't last more than a few hours or days. Here's what does last, for months, years, a lifetime: your *motive*.

Big goals, in and of themselves, do not create great accomplishment. What creates great accomplishment is what lies behind the big goals: your own personal motive, the force that drives you. It may have to do with other people; perhaps somebody else is relying on you—your children, your spouse, your business partners. It may be that you've made a commitment to yourself. Whatever it is, that motive is what we call your *why*. Clearly knowing *why* you want to achieve your goals will play a major role in your achieving them.

Remember the power of the seed, the power that enables that tiny acorn to pull in everything it needs from its environment? Your dream business is also formed around a seed, and your why is what lies at the core of that seed. On the days you don't feel like doing what it takes, the days when the obstacles seem bigger than the possibilities, it is that irresistible force within you that will provide everything you need.

The first step in the process of growing your dream business is creating the right seed—not just a strong seed, but the *perfect* seed. In other words, creating a picture of the end result with as much clarity and emotional meaning as possible.

HOW TO GET THE MOST VALUE FROM THIS BOOK

Up to this point, we've been sharing information and insights; this is where we shift gears and *The Answer* becomes a more interactive process.

From this point on, we will periodically ask you to stop reading and *do* something. In most cases, this will mean writing down *your* answers. As you can see, there is a bit of lined space here for your writing, but you might also take a blank notebook of lined paper, title it "My Answers," and keep it as your personal companion volume to this book, using it to write out your thoughts and conclusions every time we come to a point like this one.

Here's our promise: If you take action and do what we're suggesting, as much value as we hope you'll find in *The Answer*, you'll find even more value in that companion notebook and *your own answers.*

Take a moment now to consider the following questions:

What does success look like to me?
To me, success means:

_____

_____

_____

_____

_____

_____

What is it I love to do that lies at the heart of my dream business?
My dream business is a vehicle that allows me to do:

_____

_____

_____

_____

_____

What feelings do I want to experience as a result of my dream business?
Because of my dream business, I get to feel:

_____

_____

_____

_____

Because of my dream business, I arrive at the end of every day feeling:

_____

_____

_____

_____

Each of us has a purpose that we are here to serve. Purpose is that which gives our life meaning; it is our reason for living, and when we have a strong sense of what that purpose is, we tend to be not only far happier but also far more effective at whatever we're doing.

Your dream profession or business is an expression of your purpose, which these questions are designed to help define.

THE POWER OF GOALS

Equally as important as defining your purpose is defining your career or business *goals.* What's the difference? The simplest way to say it is this: You *achieve* goals; you *live* purpose. In other words, your purpose is something ongoing and never-ending; it's not something you ever "finish."

Your purpose is a description of what living your ideal life looks like. Goals, on the other hand, are concrete and finite; they are something that you most definitely can finish, and should. And when you do, you'll then set new goals, and complete those as well, leading to still newer ones, and so on. Goals are mileposts along the road of life; purpose is the direction the road takes.

Practically speaking, goals in business come down to numbers. Creating a set of definite, concrete numbers is critical. Trying to grow your business without a concrete number as a target is like saying you'll meet a friend, but neglecting to set a time or place for the meeting: How will either of you know where to go, or when?

Setting numeric targets is the pivotal first step in taking an idea from the abstract dimension to the realm of physical reality. Without a set of clear numbers to which you commit yourself, you will wander forever like Alice in Wonderland, as illustrated in her conversation with the Cheshire Cat:

> "Would you tell me, please, which way I ought to go from here?"
>
> "That depends a good deal on where you want to get to," said the Cat.
>
> "I don't much care where—" said Alice.

"Then it doesn't matter which way you go," said the Cat.

"—so long as I get *somewhere*," Alice added as an explanation.

"Oh, you're sure to do that," said the Cat, "if you only walk long enough."

—Lewis Carroll, *Alice's Adventures in Wonderland*

Without a set of clear numbers, you're sure to get *somewhere* . . . but who knows where? If it's your dream business you want to build, then you're going to need to supply the coordinates!

So which numbers are crucial? There are all sorts of numbers that might be relevant to your business, or to your position in a company. For example, you might set goals in terms of:

- Size of market

- Number of territories served

- Number of items sold

- Number of customers served (think McDonald's!)

- Ranking in industry (think GM—no, Toyota!)

- Annual sales volume

- Growth in sales

- Net worth

- Dollar value of receivables

- Net income

- Stock value

- Distribution to investors

- And more

There are literally hundreds of numbers that might be relevant goals for your business, or the business you generate. For the sake of simplicity, we will focus here on three that are not your business's numbers but your own personal numbers:

1. Your net worth

2. Your annual gross income

3. Your annual contribution

CREATING POWERFUL FINANCIAL GOALS

Why these three numbers? They are three critical dimensions of your financial state. Your net worth defines your present position in financial space; your annual income defines the level at which you are presently playing the game of business; and your annual contribution defines the scale at which you are giving to causes you believe in, which is another way of saying, the financial impact you are having on the world around you.

Money is like water: It is a universal solvent, capable of flowing anywhere, nourishing anything, and wearing down even the hardest stone. And like water, it becomes stagnant and even poisonous if it is prevented from flowing freely. The first two numbers measure the force and volume of your money; the third number is a measure of its *flow*.

When projecting financial goals, here's what most people do: They take a number that represents what they *think* they can earn, and add just a little more, perhaps 10 percent—as if that represented a "hope" factor. But hope is not a business strategy.

You are capable of earning *any amount of income* you truly want to earn. Income is exactly like the sunshine, air, water, and minerals that come to an acorn to grow an oak tree. It is available all around you, in abundance. How much you draw all begins with the seed you plant.

When you write out your goals, don't write what you think you can achieve. Write what you *want*. The word *desire* has a wonderful derivation: It comes from the Latin *de sidere*, which means literally "from the stars." What you want in life is something that arises in you from the infinite ocean of intelligence that is the source of all energy and matter. Your desires are an expression of the universe seeking realization and manifestation through the unique vehicle that is you. If your social conditioning tells you that your desires are somehow unworthy, don't believe it! Don't be intimidated or skeptical of your true desires: acknowledge them; honor them. They come from the stars.

GIVE IT MEANING

Finally, there is a third crucial ingredient to goals: what those numbers *mean*. Remember, money has no intrinsic value, which is to say that these numbers have no meaning in and of themselves. This is where people often miss the critical connection that makes written goals an effective and powerful force.

Suppose you set a goal of having a $500,000 net worth and annual gross income of $200,000. What does that actually mean? The truth is, it means nothing—that is, until you *give* it a meaning. And you do that with a very simple question: *What will that provide?*

When you reach your target of an annual income of $50,000, or $500,000, or $5,000,000, what will that *provide* you? It may be a new home, an education for your child, financial security for your golden years, or setting your spouse free from the job he or she hates.

If you are a wholesale ceramic tile salesman in Brooklyn, New York, it may even be a dream vacation home in Italy.

CASE STUDY: MEROLA TILE

Merola Tile is a Brooklyn, New York–based wholesale ceramics supplier to all two thousand Home Depot stores and about two thousand other retail outlets. Kevin Merola started Merola Tile in 1988 as a one-man operation. By the time I (John) visited Kevin's facility to do a one-day training for his sales force in 2005, Kevin had built the business to an annual sales of about $13 million.

Kevin has his company's vision and purpose emblazoned right on their website:

Vision: *We Are the Leaders in the Ceramic Tile Industry Transforming Living Spaces Across America.*

Mission [i.e., purpose]: *To make our customers feel like they are the most important people in the world, because to us, they are. We accomplish this by delivering exceptional service, going the extra mile, and doing whatever it takes to go above and beyond our customers' expectations.*

But it's one thing for the founder to set a vision for his company. What would it be like if *everyone* in the business operated out of their own equally compelling sense of vision?

"John Assaraf taught us how to focus on what we really want," says Kevin, "and not just what I want, or what Cono Tavolaro, my sales manager, wants, but what we *all* want."

Kevin has always been a big believer in setting ambitious goals and committing to play full out to hit those numbers. One thing we did a little differently was to have each person in the company set his own goals and define his own dreams.

"We'd always set goals as a company," says Cono Tavolaro, "but now we started having each guy put down his own number. If we could get them to put down their own thoughts and ambitions and dreams, then it all starts becoming more real. John had everyone there write down what they wanted, both for their careers and their personal goals. Whatever it was, no matter how outrageous—you want to have your own personal jet someday? Put it down! And there were definitely some ambitious goals on those pages. We had people talking about having vacation homes in Italy—and for a tile salesman, that's pretty ambitious. But you know what? If you want it bad enough, it's doable."

What we did that day was to make Merola Tile not just Kevin's dream company, but the dream company for everyone on his team, too.

In the year since we worked together, Merola Tile has grown from $13 million to $20 million. "And hang on," adds Kevin, "'cause we're just getting started."

YOUR DREAM BUSINESS, ONE YEAR FROM TODAY

Now it's your turn. Take a moment below and fill in a description of your goals. Imagine that it is now one year from today, and that you are describing your dream business and your own position within it, including your financial state, from that vantage point.

Don't worry about making this perfect; just let it rip. Creating goals is always a work in progress. In fact, we strongly recommend returning to this exercise regularly—not just once a year, but once a season, once a month, even once a week. As you grow, so will your goals.

MY ONE-YEAR GOALS

Today is (one year from today) _____, and I need to take a moment out of my busy day to reflect on all the amazing things that have happened over the past year, and to note the amazing place at which I have arrived:

1. PURPOSE
My dream business or career is making a huge difference in the world around me, because through it:

_____

_____

_____

_____

_____

2. NUMERIC TARGETS
I now have a net worth of $_____,
an annual gross income of $_____,
and I am giving $_____ to (church, charity, or other recipient).

3. MEANING
As a result of this extraordinary financial abundance, I now have and feel:

_____

_____

_____

_____

_____

YOUR UNIQUE STRENGTHS

Now let's take a closer look at how you go about realizing those goals through your business by seeing just what is inside that business.

A successful business is always the expression of a successful person. Your dream business is just one manifestation of your dream *life*. In other words, at heart, your business is really an extension of you. To get a clear picture of your business, we need to take a closer look at you.

Many of us were given all sorts of messages about ourselves while growing up that left us with a very skewed sense of our true strengths and value. For example, how intelligent are you? Wait—before you answer that question, let's talk about what *intelligent* means.

When John Assaraf was a child, he was told that if he didn't do well in school, he wouldn't be able to take care of a family and wouldn't amount to much. Murray didn't even get that far. He was placed in a school for kids with "special needs." Both of us were given the clear message that we just didn't cut it: We were not smart enough or good enough to make it in the real world. John started hanging out with a rough crowd, heading down the path toward a life of petty crime; Murray found himself cleaning out sewers for a living.

Yet within just a few years, we had both carved out very successful careers as self-made millionaires who were—wonder of wonders— pretty savvy in business. How was this possible?

For one thing, it was possible because the definitions people were using when they labeled us were useless for predicting true potential for success. Today, new information tells us that intelligence is not a single, one-dimensional trait, but is expressed in many different ways.

For example, your brain has two hemispheres connected by a sheaf of fibers called the *corpus callosum*, which allows communication between the two. You're probably already familiar, to some extent, with the distinct nature of the functions of these two hemispheres. If you are more left-brained, you'll tend to be more analytical, more structured and organized in your thinking. More right-brained people tend to be more creative or arts-oriented, more rhythmic and free-flowing in their thinking. IQ testing and the traditional "three Rs" approach to education tend to place far more value on left-brain capacities than on those of the right brain.

TWO HEMISPHERES OF INTELLIGENCE

Left Brain	Right Brain
Words	Rhyme
Sequence	Rhythm
Numbers	Pictures
Mathematics	Music
Logic	Imagination

While we all have abilities that emanate from both brain hemispheres, each of us also tends to emphasize one side more than the other. Are you more organized, methodical, analytical, and structured? Are you more creative, more into the free flow of life? Neither side of the brain is better or worse than the other, and both can be helpful when it comes to achieving success in business. The point is simply that we are all unique, and those traits and characteristics that make you unique are what make you shine. What you need to discover is which talents are special to you.

There are many, many ways of measuring intelligence beyond the classic intelligence quotient (IQ) that used to be considered the be-all and end-all. As it turns out, IQ is a fairly narrow measure of certain specific intellectual capacities. For example, in his bestselling book *Emotional Intelligence*, science writer and *New York Times* bestselling author Daniel Goleman, Ph.D., writes about a quality he terms *emotional intelligence* (EQ); elsewhere he has written about further levels of ability he calls *social intelligence*. In her coauthored book *SQ*, physicist Danah Zohar explores a capacity she identifies as *spiritual intelligence*.

There are multiple facets of our innate human intelligence; no one type or number can hope to represent the complexity of the human mind. Some of these types are still in the process of being named and described by contemporary researchers, and it is very likely that there are many that yet lie over the horizon. Below, you'll find some of the variations we now know something about. Which type or types of intelligence resonate most with you?

THE MANY TYPES OF INTELLIGENCE

Verbal-Linguistic Intelligence

Exhibits sensitivity to the sound, meaning, and order of words. Loves to read, talk, listen, and write. Writers, speakers, and linguists draw on this type of intelligence.

Logical-Mathematical Intelligence

Demonstrates ability in mathematics and other logic systems. Loves to solve problems, reason things out, and think sequentially. Computer designers and technicians, engineers, and scientists draw on this type of intelligence.

Musical-Rhythmic Intelligence

Has an innate grasp and appreciation of music. Loves to sing, hum, tap, or move to music. Musicians, composers and songwriters, and dancers show a heightened musical intelligence.

Visual-Spatial Intelligence

Has the ability to perceive the visual world accurately and create art. Designers, architects, and graphic artists all work from this sphere of intelligence.

Bodily-Kinesthetic Intelligence

Uses one's body in a skilled way, for self-expression, goal attainment, or entertainment. Athletes, dancers, and actors are skilled in this intelligence.

Interpersonal Intelligence

Perceives and understands other people, their moods, feelings, desires, and motivations. Loves to communicate, listen, persuade, and negotiate. People richly endowed with this kind of intelligence include business leaders, politicians, salespeople, facilitators, and therapists.

Intrapersonal Intelligence

Understands one's own emotions, values, and personal philosophy. Loves to be alone, thinking thoughts through and working with internal processes and development. Counselors, inventors, religious leaders, and introspective writers are strong in this form of intelligence.

Naturalistic Intelligence

Recognizes flora and fauna, makes distinctions in the natural world, and uses this ability productively. Is especially attuned to nature. Perceives connections and patterns in the world, including in the plant and animal kingdoms. Biologists, botanists, farmers, and explorers often place an emphasis on naturalistic intelligence.

By identifying the unique emphasis of your intelligence and finding your unique mix of abilities and passions, you open up a pathway to express yourself in way that is extraordinary. Every one of us has this reservoir of talents we can tap into, and developing a stronger awareness of our unique gifts and leanings will help us achieve our goals and our dreams.

TAKING INVENTORY

One way to help you recognize your own strengths and capacities more objectively is to do a thorough inventory of your past business accomplishments.

As you do this exercise, don't focus purely on your biggest achievements or only those that came with a title, award, or other external form of recognition. In fact, let's take this out of the realm of business for a moment. Think of something you did, some moment in your past when you experienced a moment of absolute triumph. It could be something public that hundreds of people witnessed, or a private moment that nobody knows about but you. The first time you rode a bike; that time you got over your shyness and asked a date to the dance; the paper for school that you struggled with but finally completed; an athletic victory, mastering a musical instrument, throwing a beautiful piece of pottery, the birth of your first child, mustering the courage to quit a job you hated—triumphs come in all shapes, sizes, and colors.

SAMPLE LIST OF ACHIEVEMENTS

- Graduated from high school

- Graduated from college

- Was completely debt free within three years of finishing college

- Ran a marathon

- Fathered and helped raise two wonderful children

- Have been happily married for five years to the love of my life

- Grew my annual income from $30,000 to $50,000 in one year

- Made All-Conference team in high school soccer

- Got my driver's license

- Helped my aunt through a critical illness

- Learned to play the guitar (and sounded pretty good!)

- Became a successful consultant

Now it's your turn. Starting back as early in your life as you can, jot down a list of all the achievements you can think of that relate in any way to business, or to any of the skills you want to use in your business.

MY INVENTORY OF ACHIEVEMENTS SO FAR

_____

_____

_____

_____

_____

_____

_____

_____

_____

Now let's add to this picture. Think back to the many different types of intelligence we just looked at, and take an inventory of your core strengths and unique abilities. A core strength might be your capacity for deductive reasoning, or your intuition; your capacity for kindness, or the fact that you are a straight shooter people can always count on to tell it like it is.

SAMPLE LIST OF PERSONAL STRENGTHS AND ABILITIES

- Optimistic
- Friendly
- Compassionate
- Determined
- Purpose-driven
- Honest

- Loves to learn

- Adaptable

- Genuine

- Maintains a positive attitude no matter what

- Excellent student

- Can make people laugh

- Great communicator

- Patient with others

- Terrific mediator

- Strong sense of the natural world

- Expresses appreciation

Now take a few moments to list some of your greatest strengths and abilities.

MY INVENTORY OF STRENGTHS AND ABILITIES

_____

_____

_____

_____

_____

_____

_____

_____

_____

WHY IT'S CRITICAL TO IDENTIFY YOUR WEAKNESSES

When we were young, we were taught, "Identify your weaknesses, then go to work to strengthen them so you'll become a well-rounded person." We think that's a colossal waste of time, and that the myth of the "well-rounded person" is one of the most destructive educational fallacies there is. Please, don't give up a moment of your precious life struggling to strengthen yourself in those areas where you are weak!

Nevertheless, it's very important to take yourself through this self-inventory process to identify which pieces of your business you are especially well suited to and which ones you should not take on yourself. This is crucial. Most entrepreneurs and business owners never take the time to think this through; they start out with a passion and then turn that into a full-fledged business without first completing this part of the picture. And this can be a fatal omission.

For example, let's say you're a beautician. You have a full calendar of happy clients who love your work, and now you want to open up your own shop, where you can bring in a few other beauticians and build your practice into something really substantial.

This sounds exciting. But if you first sit down and take a careful inventory of your core strengths and unique abilities, you may realize that there are a few crucial skills your business is going to need that are *not* on that list. Perhaps you have a great artistic sense, a natural feel for how to do makeup and hair so that it perfectly complements each individual client; and further, let's say you are very personable and love people. Your clients love you, and they love your work. But you may have absolutely no affinity for logical or mathematical thinking. Accounting and bookkeeping may be a painful chore to you, and the more methodical, analytical aspects of solving logistic problems and managing a growing business may feel like a foreign language you've never studied.

Being a successful beautician is one thing. Being a successful beauty shop owner is another thing entirely! Going from the one to the other is like going from being a surgeon to owning a hospital. You need some very different skill sets to make that work. Identifying those traits and strengths you don't have tells you where you need to bring other people into the equation.

FIND PEOPLE WHOSE PLAY IS YOUR WORK

Be clear on this: A weakness is not a negative, it's just an indication of strengths you'll need to look for in other people. Your strengths, passions, and unique abilities are your most precious asset, and the second-most precious asset you have will be your associations and working relationships with people who embody all those complementary strengths, passions, interests, and abilities you do *not* have.

Each one of us has to do it alone, but we can't do it by ourselves. We need one another. Being the Lone Ranger is a tough way to go, and even he had Tonto to lean on. One of the secrets to achieving your goals is knowing how to ask for help from people who have those skills you don't possess. In return, you offer them the skills you have, which will often turn out to be just what they need to achieve *their* goals. Complementary skills serve everyone involved.

Do you have a passion for numbers? Could you spend contented hours playing with columns of numbers and exploring the accounting dimensions of your business? If you say, "Ha! Are you kidding?" we have a message for you: No, we're not! There are people who love numbers, and you're going to want to get to know some of them.

There are people who love standing up in front of a crowd and speaking, and people who would rather have a root canal without novocaine than speak to a group. There are people who absolutely hate to sell—and people who absolutely love the thrill of getting to a "Yes." There are people who love to work with words but have absolutely no feeling for numbers, and people who are the complete reverse. There are "people people" who seem to be able to hit it off with anyone—and there are people who love their solitude and for whom having to provide hours of customer service every day would be a punishment more cruel than public flogging.

One of the biggest secrets there is to being successful in business, and one of the most commonly ignored, is this: Find people who *play* at those things that for you are *work*.

The two of us are a good example. One reason we work so well together is that we are very different. John is a voracious student and reader, and has been learning about the Law of Attraction, visualization and affirmations, and the science of achieving goals, for years.

Murray is the complete opposite. He was initially very skeptical about the personal development industry, and focused instead on honing his keen analytical skills. We were so different, yet we complemented each other like a left hand and a right hand.

"Work on your weaknesses" makes absolutely no sense to us. Here's what does: Discover those areas where you are strong, those areas where you have keen intelligence, and focus on those. Discover what it is you are uniquely gifted to be and to do, then build your business and your life in ways that take maximum advantage of those aspects of yourself. That's when life flows. That's when goals come easily.

Take the gifts you have and make those your pillars. Then, find other people who have other intelligences, other gifts, and help them become your allies. Make it your goal to share your gifts with the world. Your journey will be so much more enjoyable when you focus on what you love to do, when you focus on how spectacular you are rather than on what you're not good at and what you're not here to do.

Know this: You have within you, right now, everything you need to achieve your goals. To unleash those resources, you may need to effect some changes in your beliefs and habits of thought, and you may need to collaborate with people who are strong in areas where you are weak, people who play at what to you seems like work. But just as an acorn pulls in the sunlight, water, nitrogen, and minerals it needs from its environment, you have within you the capacity to attract and secure every one of the traits, people, resources, and elements you need to create your fully realized dream business and a happy, purposeful, fulfilling life.

WHY EXTRAORDINARY IS MANDATORY

Is your business a purple cow? In his amazing book *Purple Cow*, marketing master Seth Godin writes:

> Cows, after you've seen them for a while, are boring. They may be perfect cows, attractive cows, cows with great personalities, cows lit by beautiful light, but they're still boring.
>
> A Purple Cow, though. Now *that* would be interesting.

He goes on to explain that to be a truly successful business, it's no longer enough to be good: You must be extraordinary. Good is common; good is boring. Good (as author Jim Collins says in *Good to Great*) is the *enemy* of great.

If you want to put yourself into the millionaire category and create a key role for yourself in a business that is massively successful, you have to strive for excellence in what you do. And today, when there is such a range and diversity of businesses in the world and the Internet has made information about all of them available to everyone, even excellence is no longer sufficient. Today, to be massively successful, you *have* to be extraordinary. This is not an option; it's a necessity.

Later on, in chapter 12, we're going to introduce you to a methodical process for finding innovations that will take your business from good to great to extraordinary. For now, let's just take a moment to look at your dream business from the outside in—that is, from your customers' point of view. Because while your business is an expression of you, it is also an expression of your customers.

What does your dream business provide for your customers?

What kinds of experiences do you see your customers having as they interact with your business? When they do business with you, use your products or your services, what kinds of feelings does that elicit in them?

How does it change their lives?

In chapters 11, 12, and 13, we will define your ideal customer and explore what your business offers from the customer's point of view. For now, we just want to introduce the idea that when you are defining your dream business, you want to look at it from both points of view: yours, and everyone else's. As you saw in the example of Merola Tile, that includes not only your customers' experience of your business, but also your employees' experience. It also includes the experience of investors, partners, and anyone else who in any way comes into contact with your business.

You want your dream business to make a memorable footprint—an extraordinary impact that nobody will forget.

CASE STUDY: YOUR ENTITY SOLUTION

In early 2005, Wendy Byford and her husband, Gary Bauer, launched a consulting business helping other small businesses to incorporate. After its first year of business, Your Entity Solution had a small staff and a solid foundation but lacked profitability.

"We were meeting our day-to-day expenses, but any capital expenditures still had to come out of our pockets. There was no room to expand our business—and we weren't paying ourselves. We thought that we knew the answer: increase the number of clients coming through our doors and start generating a profit through sheer volume."

Wendy and Gary sought us out for marketing help to bring in more clients. Instead, we took them through a careful process of examining their business and asked them: "What is extraordinary about your business? What unique value do you bring to the table?"

"We really didn't know how to answer those questions," says Wendy. "So we took a long look at what was really at the heart of our business."

They had planned to create a back-office system for CPAs and attorneys who didn't want to do incorporations themselves. By automating certain aspects of their work and selling that as a system, they could increase volume and reach profitability—theoretically. But as they began defining their own core strengths and unique abilities, it was soon clear that this was *not* the answer.

"Our strength is that we're coaches," explains Wendy. "We understand the fears and frustration people face in putting together a company—we've been there ourselves. Our value is in being able to put our arms around the client and say, 'Take a deep breath. You can do this, and we'll show you how.'"

But there is a limit to how many clients one can work with in that thorough, personal way. If they had gone for volume, they would have been forced to stop doing what they do best. Their proposed growth strategy would have *eliminated* their unique value.

"Once we realized this," says Wendy, "we looked closely at our fee structure—and we realized that we weren't charging enough for our services. We had inherited a price from a partner when we started the business. It was time to look at it fresh."

They knew their client base was very happy with their work, so they took the plunge and raised their prices. From a fee structure of $695 and $795 (for two different groups of clients), they increased their rates to $983 and $1,350.

"It was like someone had flipped a switch," says Wendy. "Suddenly we started making money. We made enough to pay ourselves back for our capital investment, to pay Gary a salary, to make distributions to our partners, and pay a larger staff."

They began working with us in July of 2006. They made the price change effective November 15, and by the end of the year, they were profitable.

CREATING A VISION FOR YOUR BUSINESS

Now let's wrap together all the elements we've looked at, including your purpose, your numeric goals and what they provide you, your unique strengths and abilities and how they express themselves through your dream business, and combine all this information into a statement that expresses your vision for your business.

What does it look like when you have everything in place that you want to have, when your business is bringing you everything that you want it to, fully drawing on your greatest passions and strengths, and making the right kind of contribution to the world?

Again, this is not about getting this perfect; you can always refine and revise it later. Start by just observing and recording some glimpses of this picture. Just make sure that what you're seeing excites you, stirs your soul, and sets your imagination on fire.

A few guidelines:

1. Put it in the present tense.

Your nonconscious brain perceives everything as "now." It doesn't operate with a concept of future turning into present—it's *all* present. Therefore, if you tell yourself, "My business is *going to* serve millions of people . . ." to your nonconscious, it will *always* be "going to." Make sure you put your statements of visualization in the present tense: "My business *is* serving millions of people . . ."

2. Make it vivid and emotional.

The more vivid this picture is, the more real it feels, the faster you will attract what you need to manifest it as a physical reality. *Manifest*, by the way, comes from the Latin *manus*, for "hand": It means "placed in your hand."

3. Aim for the bleachers!

Don't skimp on your dream. You've heard the expression "The sky's the limit." Even that is not big enough to describe the possibilities. The *universe* is the limit.

As you start describing this picture, ask yourself these questions:

"Does it express my core strengths, unique abilities, and interests?"

"Does it honor my values and fulfill my purpose?"

"Is it the most exciting expression of me that I can imagine?"

"Is it unique? Is it a purple cow? Will people talk about it to others because of the unique and satisfying experience they've had with my business?"

Once you've gotten some of your thoughts and ideas down on paper, work with them. Read them out loud to yourself: Do they really say exactly what you want to say? Put all these pieces together into one paragraph that you can really hang your hat on, a description that thrills you.

Before you go on to the next chapter, take a moment to describe what your dream business looks like.

MY BUSINESS VISION

Use the space below (or your own personal "My Answers" notebook) to write out your vision for your dream business.

_____

_____

_____

_____

_____

_____

_____

_____

_____

_____

It's fascinating to consider what it is you're actually doing here as you put words together to draw this verbal picture of your dream business. You are using the magnifying glass of your brain's frontal lobe, like focusing those sun's rays to burn an oak leaf. You've pulled ideas from the quantum field of all possible thoughts and focused them like a laser with the conscious powers of your imagination. As you sift through them and get them onto paper in a way that is meaningful to you, you are using every other conscious faculty as well—your intuition, logical reasoning, memory, perception, and will.

By bringing these ideas into crystal clear focus and committing them to paper, you are also directly invoking some of the most powerful laws of the universe. You are declaring your intentions to the zero-point field, which is tantamount to hurling a stone into a still pond—you are creating ripples with far-reaching consequences.

In addition to making a declaration to the universe at large, clarifying your goals by writing them down makes a declaration to yourself. By doing so, you are creating a set of very specific instructions that you can then give to your nonconscious brain, which is exactly what we'll be considering in the next chapter.

BUT WHAT ABOUT "HOW"?

Most people, when first tackling the process of writing out goals and aspirations, don't come up with what they really want, because they can't see how they would be able to get it. They've been conditioned from childhood to think you've got to know *how* you're going to get something, or else, forget it. As kids, when we got excited about something, we went to our parents and said, "Hey, I want to get this cool bike!" or "I want to go on this great trip!" And in most cases, the first thing our parents said back was, "Well, how are you going to get it?"

Don't worry about the *how* right now. In fact, don't even let yourself think about it. Later on we'll talk about the how of your business. For now, remember the Law of Gestation: Create the right seed and give it time to take root. If the seed is right and you plant it well, the how will unfold.

In chapter 4 we mentioned two of your nonconscious brain's functions: It runs all the vast complexity of processes required to keep your organism alive—that is, your "operating system"—and it also runs your programmable software—that is, your routines, habits, and beliefs. But there is also a third major function of the nonconscious brain: *It connects you with the quantum field of infinite intelligence.*

THE THREE ROLES OF THE NONCONSCIOUS BRAIN

The nonconscious brain:

- runs your personal biochemical operating system;

- runs your programmable software: your habits, routines, attitudes, beliefs, etc.;

- connects you with the quantum field of infinite intelligence.

Remember, we live in two worlds: the seen and the unseen. The brain is an electromagnetic switching station—the most complex such device known—and it connects us to and allows us to interact with both the seen and the unseen world.

In the 1860s, the German chemist August Kekulé was absorbed in trying to puzzle out the mystery of the structure of benzene. One day, gazing into the fireplace as he thought about the problem, he drifted off and had a half-sleeping daydream in which he imagined he saw a snake eating its own tail. As he shook himself out of his reverie, he realized that in that image lay the secret of the benzene molecule: It was formed in the shape of a ring. In an address he gave many years later, he recounted this experience, and then added, "Let us learn to dream, gentlemen, and then perhaps we may find the truth."

At almost the exact same time that Kekulé was working out the mysteries of the benzene ring, a brilliant Russian chemist named Dmitry Mendeleyev was trying to come up with a rational way to categorize the chemical elements. "I saw in a dream a table where all the elements fell into place as required," he later reported. "Awakening, I immediately wrote it down on a piece of paper. Only in one place did a correction later seem necessary." The result of this dream was what is now known as the periodic table of the elements.

And remember the French mathematician René Descartes? On November 10, 1619, he had a dream during which he discovered the foundation of what would become analytic geometry.

These are just a few examples of discoveries that first reached their discoverer through the nonconscious brain, and only then percolated into consciousness. Thomas Edison would purposely put himself into a light sleep in order to solve intractable problems with whatever invention he was working on at the time. And it isn't only famous inventors and scientists who can do this. The quantum soup of infinite possibility is available to everyone.

The truth is, your nonconscious brain has access to all knowledge. No matter what the problem, challenge, or need, it knows where to find the answers. What it doesn't know is which answers you want. It has to be *told*. You have unlimited access to a five-star kitchen that can prepare any meal under the sun, but someone has to place the order. That is the purpose of your conscious mind.

THE FIVE MUSTS

Creating a clear business vision is the critical first step to your success, but it is just that: the first step. No matter how crystal clear it is, simply having a goal doesn't make it happen. All the years we've watched people writing down their goals only to see none of them come to pass have shown us that.

If you truly, passionately, want to create huge success on every level, if you want to earn major income and create financial freedom for yourself *and* live a hugely happy and fulfilled life at the same time, five key elements have to be in place. We call them the "Five Musts" of major success:

- You must find something that stirs your soul.

- You must become excellent at it.

- You must recondition your mind to believe you can have it and achieve it.

- You must understand how to make money at it.

- You must take daily action.

This chapter has been all about the first two musts: identifying what it is that stirs your soul, and making sure you have designed it so that it is something you either are excellent at doing or are willing to *become* excellent at doing. The next chapter is all about the third must: reconditioning your nonconscious brain to embrace and pursue your new business vision.

Now we come face-to-face with the wall into which most people's goals, hopes, and dreams slam, never to go further—the reason so many people *set* goals but never *reach* them. When it comes to imagining and articulating a vision of your dream business, the conscious brain is brilliant. But for that vision to turn into reality, it has to be imprinted as a new set of instructions onto the nonconscious brain.

What you've done is create a strong, viable seed. Now you need to plant that seed in good soil.

7

THE NEURAL
RECONDITIONING PROCESS™

Years ago, NASA designed a fascinating experiment to test the physiological and psychological impact of spatial disorientation, the kind that astronauts might experience during extended time in a weightless environment. NASA outfitted a group of astronaut candidates with convex goggles that flipped everything in their field of vision 180 degrees, so that the world they saw was completely upside down. The test subjects wore these glasses twenty-four hours a day, even while asleep. Then the scientists sat back to observe what happened.

At first, the extreme stress and anxiety were obvious, as reflected in the astronauts' blood pressure and other vital signs. The astronauts gradually adapted to this new level of stress, but it still didn't dissipate altogether. After all, their entire world was upside down! But twenty-six days after the experiment began, something amazing happened to one astronaut: His world turned right-side up again. The goggles hadn't changed, and he was still wearing them continuously. *But now he was able to see everything around him as normal.* Within the next several days, all the other astronauts followed suit.

What had happened? After twenty-six to thirty days of this constant stream of strange new input, the men's brains had created enough new neural connections to completely rewire their brains, so that their visual and spatial perception worked at 180 degrees opposite from the way the brain normally works.

In repeated trials, the researchers also discovered that if the goggles were removed during this three-to-four-week period, even for short times, the neural adaptation would not occur. In other words, it took about twenty-five to thirty days of uninterrupted, consistent input of new perceptual (conscious) information for the nonconscious brain to accept that it had to adjust to this new information and regard it as normal.

Our conclusion? It takes about thirty days of consistently applying neural reconditioning techniques for your nonconscious brain to absorb a new orientation. And our experience with thousands of clients over the past twenty years confirms this.

OVERVIEW OF THE NEURAL RECONDITIONING PROCESS

Imagine you have decided you want to run a marathon. Whether or not you've ever actually run a marathon before, you probably have a pretty good idea of what it takes to get in shape for something like this. It's not something you can just decide one day and do the next, and preparing for it is not something you can accomplish over a weekend. It takes time and consistent, methodical effort. You need to work out daily, breaking in your system bit by bit, toning and strengthening your muscles, training your lungs and heart, gradually acclimating your entire system to new habits of activity.

This is exactly what you're going to do with your brain. We're going to show you how to recondition and tone the neural networks in your brain so that they establish new habits that match up with new beliefs, so that your success happens naturally and organically, from the inside out, as opposed to your struggling to make it happen from the outside in. We've developed a process called *neural reconditioning* that will help you take those goals and dreams and turn them into neural patterns in your nonconscious brain, as opposed to simply writing them down for your conscious brain and then forgetting about them.

Just like when you're getting ready to run a marathon, this process will condition and tone your neural system to do what it takes to achieve your dream business. And just like getting ready to run a marathon, this conditioning process is something that takes consistent, daily effort. It is not a huge task; in fact, it is almost ridiculously easy to do. It's just that most people don't do it. But you will—and that will make all the difference.

THE 6 STEPS OF NEURAL RECONDITIONING

Step 1. Create a new vision of your financial and business success. Make it emotionally rich and crystal clear.

Step 2. Create powerful declarations and affirmations that support that new vision.

Step 3. Develop emotional anchors for neural linking.

Step 4. Prepare a portfolio of imprinting material, which may include written, auditory, visual, and subliminal pieces.

Step 5. Maintain a brief daily routine of reconditioning techniques, three times a day (on waking, midday, before bed).

Step 6. Employ various forms of neurotechnology to reinforce these images throughout the day.

First, you create the vision or goals that you want to achieve; we laid the foundation for this in the last chapter by developing a clear, written vision for your business. Next, we'll add to that some written declarations to create the beliefs you need to support that vision. We'll also practice playing that vision on the screen of your mind, like a mental movie—in other words, turning that written vision into a living visualization. We will also explore a technique called *neural linking*, creating emotional anchors based on your past experience that will add power and impact to your new beliefs.

Then, we'll learn how to translate your new vision and affirmations into physical materials that you can use to play them to yourself over and over, materials such as typed and laminated statements, audio recordings, bulletin-board collages or vision boards (like the one I described in chapter 1), and others.

Finally, you'll establish a brief daily routine for playing those materials back to yourself in such a way that their content sinks into your nonconscious. We'll explore a simple form of meditation as the foundation of this brief daily routine. And we'll introduce you to some simple forms of neurotechnology that you can use throughout the day to further reinforce the process.

As you repeat this process over time—again, just as the NASA experiment showed, this will start to have an effect in as little as three to four weeks—the nonconscious experience of these new pictures you're playing for yourself will become habits of thought, carving an entirely new set of neural pathways in your brain. Far beyond being simply wishful thoughts, nice ideas, or hopeful goals, these new pictures will become ingrained in your nonconscious brain as *inevitable*, resetting your reticular activating system to be on high alert for any resources or input from your environment that might reinforce or support those new realities, and recalibrating your psycho-cybernetic mechanism to accept these goals as your new "normal."

DON'T STRESS ABOUT PERFECTION

One of the great things about this neural reconditioning process is that it's a very forgiving system. There's no need to stress about doing every part of the process perfectly. In fact, there's no need to stress about any part of the process, period. We'll offer you a variety of things you can do; you don't need to enact each and every element of the plan, or follow this like a recipe or "program."

It's just like physical exercise. Does following a carefully designed workout program get great results? Yes. Must you do so in order to get in shape? Not at all. Most of us get so little exercise that simply taking a brisk fifteen-minute walk every day would make a world of difference. Of course, a fifteen-minute walk won't win you the Olympic gold medal. But that's not what most of us are after.

It comes down to this: The more you do, the better results you'll see. If you do it all, fantastic. But the key is, do *something*.

The most important thing to note here is that none of this is complicated or difficult, and none of it is very time-consuming. Once you've completed your initial preparation (refining your completed vision and affirmative declarations, and preparing the materials you'll use), the actual neural reconditioning routine is something you can complete in just minutes every day.

The keys to its effectiveness are clarity and consistency.

Make your statements clear and vivid, and take as much time as you need to refine them until you are confident they represent exactly what it is you want to achieve.

And then, engage yourself in the process *every day*.

If you maintain clarity and consistency, you will get results. It's that simple. And over time, the results will astonish you.

STEP ONE: CREATE A NEW VISION

First, create a powerful financial vision for your life, including the three numbers we looked at in chapter 6: net worth, annual income, and annual contribution.

You have to be 100 percent clear on what you want to achieve. There is no ambiguity involved in the way the quantum universe works, and there can be no ambiguity in the seed you create for your business. There is also no ambiguity about how the reticular activating system and psycho-cybernetic system work. You have to give them very clear and precise instructions, so that they know exactly what they're looking for as they go about matching up what's out there with what's in here.

Your nonconscious brain retains the memory of everything you have ever witnessed or experienced; what's more, it retains the memory of everything you have ever *imagined*. Remember, your nonconscious brain does not distinguish between experiences that are "real" and events that happened only in your mind. When you imagine a vivid experience, in neurological terms it has taken place, and your brain views it as every bit as real as your hand or the chair you're sitting in.

It was only natural that I would end up living in that house in San Diego, because as far as my nonconscious brain was concerned, after gazing at the photo on that vision board thousands of times, I had *already* bought it and moved in. The belief center of my brain saw this as my house, and it made sure my senses and conscious mind picked up on whatever actions it would take to put me there physically.

While your nonconscious brain does not distinguish between whether an event is externally real or imagined as real, what it does distinguish is *how strongly it is imprinted*. Memories that have carved a deeper channel in your brain, regardless of whether they are of actual or imagined events, have a greater influence than those of lesser imprint.

What determines the strength of imprint? The same two factors that dictate the power of any memory: *repetition* and *impact*—that is, emotional content. Both factors are crucial.

Repetition

Repetition is simple: You don't create a habit by doing something once; you create a habit by doing that same thing over and over. This is how you learned to walk, to talk, and to do your multiplication tables. Repetition creates habit, and this is also true for your habits of thought.

This is one major reason why people so often fail to achieve the goals they set. You can sit in a seminar and declare a goal, or take pen to paper on January 1 and write down a New Year's resolution—but doing that once means next to nothing. The only way it stands the slightest chance of coming true is if it becomes a habit of thought—and the only way that stands the slightest chance of happening is if you repeat it, over and over, dozens of times, *hundreds* of times. This is why the real power of neural reconditioning lies not so much in exactly *how* you do it, but *that* you do it every day, day after day, for weeks on end.

Impact

Repetition will create habit, even if there is no great emotion involved, but without the factor of emotional impact, the habit may be fairly shallow and not have much staying power. The reason for this is that there is a strong interaction between emotion and memory. Events that occur with a powerful emotional charge attached—say, a time of great elation such as the birth of a child, or a traumatic car accident—have far more impact in the brain than the unexceptional lunch you had six months ago.

Can you recall where you were and what you were doing on January 8, 2002? Probably not, unless that happens to be your birthday. Does it help if we tell you that particular day was a Tuesday? Again, probably not. What if we go back to another Tuesday, about four months earlier—say, to September 11, 2001? Now you probably remember exactly where you were and what you were doing.

Why is this? Chances are good that unless you were directly involved in the attacks in New York City and Washington, D.C., your own circumstances on that day were really not much different from your circumstances on January 8, seventeen Tuesdays later. But you remember the details of that particular Tuesday because the events of that day had great emotional impact.

In the same way, an especially positive experience makes a deep imprint. The first kiss, the wedding proposal, the graduation, the winning of a prestigious athletic event, the birth of a child, the first meal in the first home you ever bought—the details of these events tend to stay with us, right down to the smells, the sounds, and the music that was playing.

Repetition + Impact = New Reality

Let's say your goal is to win a gold medal at the Olympics. Here's what you do: Create a vivid picture in your imagination of what that experience would be like—the feeling of standing up there on the podium with your national anthem playing, the crowd roaring their enthusiasm, the feeling of the blood pumping in your veins, the thrill and rush as the Olympic official reaches up and hangs the medal around your neck. Can you feel it?

When you imagine all that in such vivid detail, you are evoking that experience and exposing it to your nonconscious mind just as effectively as if you were actually standing on that podium with the whole world watching and that medal hanging around your neck.

Repeat this vividly and consistently enough, and pretty soon you aren't just *imagining* you are an Olympic gold medalist; on a very real, visceral level, you *are becoming* a gold medalist. And because you are, you'll start doing what a gold medalist does, taking the actions a gold medalist takes, living the way a gold medalist lives, and attracting those circumstances that a gold medalist attracts.

If this at all sounds esoteric, all you have to do is ask any Olympic gold medalist if they ever spent any time visualizing themselves taking that top medal. You better believe they have—every single one of them, over and over, every day, for years. It's a recipe for outstanding achievement that every top athlete, every award-winning musician, actor, or dancer, every famous speaker, president, CEO, or supersuccessful businessperson knows.

When you visualize something, you are literally creating a neural network or pattern within your brain that corresponds to what it is you want to achieve. You're creating the seed that is required to start attracting those resonant resources necessary to allow that blueprint to unfold into its physical manifestation.

It's as simple as this: No seed, no tree. You want a tree? Visualization is how you create the right seed.

VISUALIZATION IS NOT NECESSARILY VISUAL

Visual images don't come with the same ease to everyone. We are all different. For you, there may be specific sounds, tactile feelings, or even smells that can evoke the moment you want to create more powerfully than just seeing it. Or perhaps for you, "visualizing" might include the full spectrum of your senses.

What we want to do is get you into the feeling of having your dream business be a living, thriving, active experience. Whatever that looks like, sounds like, feels like, that's the experience you want to evoke and imagine, as vividly and descriptively as you can.

EXAMPLE: MY ONE-YEAR GOALS AND VISION

I am happily building my business into the #1 small-business franchise company and business community in the world. I am thrilled to hear and read all the incredible stories of people whose businesses, jobs, and lives have changed. People love the experience of working with us, and they tell us this every day with emails and letters that pour into our office from around the globe. We have fans all over the world who recommend us to all their friends and associates.

Today my net worth is $_____, I am now earning $_____ a year from my investments and the businesses I own, and I am saving $_____ per year after taxes. Money is flowing to me in abundance. I am joyfully giving 10 percent of my income to my favorite charities. Life at the summit is sweet and satisfying.

I am living the life of my dreams. Love, laughter, and unbridled passion fuel my life and turn my dreams into reality. I am grateful for my vibrant health and high energy, and for the health and happiness of my wife and children. My family and I grow closer and wiser every day, sharing joy and possibility with all those we love and care for. My heart and my head are soaring with possibility and opportunity. I am blessed and grateful for my whole life and everything in it.

CASE STUDY: RE/MAX

When I purchased the franchising rights for RE/MAX of Indiana in November 1986, RE/MAX had already failed twice before in that state. When I arrived there, I found that everyone who was in real estate had a clear, firm belief that RE/MAX would not work there—and it would have been really easy for me to succumb to that belief, too. But I didn't. I knew enough at that point about how to create a clear vision and to build for myself an unshakable belief that I would succeed. I'd been a RE/MAX agent in Toronto and had done well there. Why shouldn't I do well here, too?

So I set a goal of doing a billion dollars in sales and becoming the largest real estate company in the state—and I not only set the goal, I put it out there for all to see. As I said in the introduction, I was the laughingstock of the town. But that didn't deter my belief, nor did the fact (which others were quick to point out) that I had absolutely no experience recruiting, hiring and firing, or managing a business. But I had my vision, and the way I acted, spoke, planned, and went about doing everything I did reflected that vision.

I went and talked with the owners of other real estate companies, and they laughed me out of their offices. Then I went to talk with their managers and shared my vision with them. As we talked, they could see their dreams within my vision; when I told them about what I saw for myself, they could see the financial freedom and the extraordinary lives they wanted for themselves. One by one, they left where they were and came to join me at RE/MAX.

Soon we had twenty-seven people; then it was suddenly sixty, and then a hundred. Within five years, we were the largest real estate company in Indiana, and doing a billion dollars in sales. Today we have 1,700 salespeople, and we are at $6 billion and growing.

STEP TWO: CREATE POWERFUL AFFIRMATIONS

Now that you have your crystal clear vision in place, you need to ensure that your everyday, moment-to-moment beliefs are in line with what you say you want to achieve. This step is critical. Why? Because if you try to realize a new vision while maintaining old beliefs that do not support that vision, you've got a classic case of mixed messages.

You may have heard it said that your words make up only 7 percent of the impact of your communication, while the rest is conveyed by your facial expression, tone of voice, and body language. This is a common urban legend of the personal development field, and in fact, it isn't true at all. It is based on a distortion of research findings by UCLA social psychologist Albert Mehrabian, published in his book *Silent Messages* (1971). However, what those findings *do* reveal is fascinating, and it has tremendous relevance here.

Under normal circumstances, our words carry far more weight than 7 percent. (If that weren't true, it would hardly matter what we say!) However, Mehrabian was not studying ordinary circumstances, he was studying what happens when someone you know gives you mixed messages. If the words you are hearing are at odds with the person's gestures or tone of voice, which one do you believe?

For example, when a mother says "Come here, I love you," but her arms are folded and there is clearly anger or irritation in her voice, which message does the child receive? (Hint: It's not the words.) That's right: When your words don't match your actions, feelings, moods, beliefs, the nonverbal will win out, every time.

This is exactly how it is with the conscious (verbal) and nonconscious (nonverbal) brain: When the message your conscious brain puts out (such as your written goals) competes with a message your nonconscious brain holds to be true (your beliefs, even if they are unstated), guess which one will win out? You already know the answer.

In other words, you may say, "I want to quadruple my business, from $250,000 per year to a million a year," but if your nonconscious mind is still set on a quarter-million-dollar picture, then it's like saying "I love you," with your arms crossed and a scowl on your face. Again, whenever there's a conflict between conscious and nonconscious, the nonconscious will always win. *Always.*

So let's take a closer look at your underlying beliefs.

YOUR PRESENT BELIEFS

How do you know what your present beliefs are? This can be a tricky thing, because our beliefs tend to be so much a part of us that we often aren't even aware of them. There is a wonderful ancient Hindu expression: "There are three mysteries in the world: the air to the bird, the water to the fish, and man to himself." Fish aren't aware of water: It's what they swim in all the time, so they don't think about it. Same with birds and the air: It's their normal environment. And that's how our beliefs are: We swim in them all the time, so much so that they are typically invisible to us.

So how do you know what you believe? The answer turns out to be incredibly simple: *Just look at your life.* What do you see? Whatever you find, there's the evidence of your beliefs. Your current life—your relationships, your health, your income, your lifestyle, where you live, where you work, where you play, what you do every day, *all* of it—is an accurate reading of the picture you've been holding in your nonconscious brain.

If you are broke, then your belief is, "I'm broke: That's how and who I am." Or, "I don't deserve to have a lot of money."

If you are stressed out, pressured, never have enough time, then welcome to your belief, "There is never enough time."

If you feel like your life is okay overall, but there's never quite enough time to do what you really want to do and never quite enough money to do what you want to do, then guess what belief you are holding?

"There is never quite enough." And if you are thinking, "Well, no, not right now, but there *will* be, soon, eventually, someday"—then we have some bad news for you: No, there won't. To your nonconscious, there is no past and future, only the present moment, right now! And your nonconscious brain will keep you forever trapped in "someday" like a fly in amber.

The first step is to accept the fact that you are in the driver's seat: *Your life is your creation*, and the principal tool you have used to create it is your beliefs. If you want to change things, then decide what beliefs you *want* to have.

CASE STUDY: MY TREASURES & ME

Virginia Chong Kun runs an import business called My Treasures & Me on the little island of Mauritius. For the last five years, her business had been stuck on a plateau. She went looking for some outside support, and found us on the internet. Despite the eleven-hour time difference, she began working with us, voraciously devouring all our course material and conference calls.

Right away, Virginia realized that it was her own limiting belief that was holding her business back.

"Living on a little island where the population is limited and the people are quite poor," says Virginia, "it's easy to fall into the belief that you can do only so much and no more. The business was working, but I wasn't seeing any possibility of taking it to the next level, even though that's what I *wanted* to do."

Once she had identified that belief, she designed a radically different belief and began imprinting it daily through neural reconditioning—and results came almost immediately.

"Within less than a month," reports Virginia, "I became connected to a mining house in Africa that deals in semiprecious stones. They flew to Mauritius to meet me and appointed me as their international agent. We are now marketing and receiving orders for containerloads of gemstones from other countries as well.

"I've been in marketing for years," she adds, "and I know how hard you have work to close a deal, or even just to get your foot in the door. But suddenly, it's no longer hard. Every day now, some new opportunity comes up out of nowhere. I will meet people in town who are visiting from other parts of the world, and by the time our conversation is over, we've made a plan to do business together."

Within thirty days after beginning her work with us, Virginia's business had tripled its revenues. Within another thirty days, she had finalized a substantial deal, and her monthly sales had equaled the previous year's *annual* sales.

CREATING YOUR AFFIRMATIONS

The key to writing effective affirmations is that they must be bold, clear, positive, and stated in the present tense.

We've explored the problem posed by the fact that people often articulate their goals in negative terms. In other words, rather than focusing on what they *want*, they focus on what they *don't want*. "I want to be in a fulfilling, lifelong relationship" and "I really don't want to end up sad and alone" might seem like two ways of saying the same thing. They're not. To your nonconscious brain, they are saying the opposite. Your nonconscious doesn't know the difference between "I want" and "I don't want." It just hears "lifelong, fulfilling relationship" or "sad and lonely."

Your conscious brain puts things in logical, linear sequences. It has to: It can't focus on more than one or two things at a time. But your nonconscious can focus on a million things at once. It doesn't need to think, "First this, then that, then eventually . . ." While your conscious brain might read a story from beginning to end, your nonconscious brain just sucks up the entire story as one impression, like a big neurological slurp of Jell-O. You can see this with kids, especially young kids, who have had less time to develop sophisticated filters and defenses and often reveal the truth of their thought process far more innocently and openly than adults or older kids do. If you tell a child not to do something, what will he be drawn to do? Exactly what you told him not to do!

Let's say you want your child to get through a meal without spilling his milk. If you say, "Hey, make sure you don't spill your milk," have you decreased the chances that milk is going to spill? No; in fact, chances are good you've actually *increased* them.

The same is true for the things we say to ourselves—in fact it is hundreds of times *more* true. Why? Because you might tell your child not to spill his milk at most, what, once or twice a day? Three times? But if you're giving yourself a similar warning—"Whatever you do, don't get nervous"—how often will you repeat that to yourself in a single day? Easily hundreds of times. The things we say to ourselves, we say over and over, dozens, hundreds, thousands, tens of thousands of times. The one person you have by far the most influence over is you—because nobody whispers in your ear even a tiny fraction of the amount that you do yourself.

CASE STUDY: JOHN ASSARAF

Growing up, I developed the belief that I was not very good at achieving worthwhile things in life. As I mentioned in the introduction, I soon started running around with a crowd of kids who were up to no good, and seemed destined for a life of failure. When I first began creating goals and visions for myself in business, it was critical that I create new beliefs around my abilities as a businessperson—otherwise my existing beliefs would end up sabotaging every new goal I set for myself.

I wrote a statement for myself that was in such stark contrast to what I had grown up believing, it still resonates with huge impact to this day:

I am a brilliant and savvy businessman.

Mind you, when I wrote this, I didn't *believe* it. Not one bit. And there was a very good reason: *It wasn't true.* At least not yet. But I decided that I would *like* it to be true. That is who I wanted to become. And the only way that would happen would be if I designed that new belief and entrained it into my brain. And that is exactly what I did.

Over the years, I have added to the list and redesigned the statements I tell myself; it's a constantly changing, evolving thing. Here is a current list of declarations and affirmations I use with myself.

- I am a genius and I use my wisdom daily.

- I give myself permission to be powerful.

- I have absolute certainty in my ability to generate any amount of income I choose.

- Money is flowing to me from both expected and unexpected sources.

- I consistently attract all the right people to help me grow my business.

- I am a brilliant and savvy businessman and I have everything it takes right now to grow my business to a billion-dollar company.

- I have all the talent, intelligence, and money I need to create this new masterpiece.

- I am always calm, succinct, happy, and outstanding when being interviewed or presenting a seminar or keynote.

- I am a master presenter and persuader on and off the platform. It is so much fun!

If you look at these carefully, you can probably figure out certain beliefs that I *used* to have and wanted to change. For example, "I am always calm, succinct, happy . . ." Do you think that I have always been a calm and happy person? One who expressed himself succinctly, with elegance and brevity? Far from it! *Calm* is definitely not a description I would have applied to myself many years ago. In fact, virtually all of these positive traits are qualities that I perceived myself at one time as not having, and that I have worked to develop in myself by designing those statements and using them to carve brand-new neural pathways in my nonconscious brain.

Or, take this one: "I consistently attract all the right people to help me grow my business." If you're like me (and a lot of us), you know what it's like to feel, "If you want it done right, you have to do it yourself." But it's just not true. We can't create large, successful businesses all by ourselves; none of us can. There was a time when I worried about whether I would find the right people to help me — in fact, when I really had a belief that I would *not* find the right people.

That belief didn't serve me. This new one does. It's that simple.

CASE STUDY: TAYLORMADE MARKETING

When Scott Taylor came to us for coaching, he was hitting a wall of frustration. After more than a decade in business, the design company he and his wife, Laurie, had started, TaylorMade Marketing, was stuck. They'd grown into a full-service creative agency, doing Web design, press releases, search engine optimization, and sales consulting. But no matter how hard they worked, they weren't getting any closer to their goals.

Scott soon realized that the biggest factor stopping their growth was his own beliefs. He knew he was good at what he did, and that he could help his clients become wealthy—but he didn't believe that he could charge the fees commensurate with that level of success.

"I was helping my clients become millionaires," says Scott, "and I could barely keep up with my own expenses."

Scott immersed himself in the neural reconditioning process and began creatively bombarding his nonconscious brain with visualizations and affirmations. One of his affirmations was geared toward the idea of participating more in the fruits of the successes he was creating for his clients:

I am working with more partners and owning much more of the projects I work on.

Scott began repeating this affirmation every morning as part of his neural reconditioning routine. Here's what happened:

"After only two weeks, one of my clients approached me, and out of the blue, asked me to join him and take a third of his business!"

The client had loved the rollout Scott and Laurie had just done for them, and they figured giving him a share of the business would provide the incentive to keep providing them with work of that same quality.

But that wasn't the end of it. Two days later, as he was still reeling from that first offer, Scott got a call from another client. "I hope you don't think I'm being odd," said this client, "but I just want you to know that I like working with you . . . and, well, I'm wondering if you'd like to join me as a partner and take a piece of the business."

What both clients said was so precisely in line with what he'd written in his affirmation, Scott was flabbergasted. And this was in a matter of *fourteen days*. That's the power of a clearly stated, positive belief, neurally imprinted into your nonconscious brain.

YOUR AFFIRMATIONS

Now it's your turn. Using the space here, or using a page in your notebook, take a few minutes and write out affirmative declarations that represent the beliefs you want and need to have to support your powerful vision.

EXAMPLES OF AFFIRMATIONS

- I live each day with passion and purpose.

- I am a success in all that I do.

- I respect my abilities and I always fulfill my potential.

- I always have enough money for all that I need.

- My business is now filled with prosperity and abundance.

- I easily achieve all my goals and dreams.

- I am totally confident.

- I am an excellent businessperson.

- I am wealthy and successful, every day, in all that I do.

- I use my wealth and prosperity very wisely.

- I now have all the resources necessary to fulfill any and all of my business goals and dreams.

- Making money excites me and energizes me.

- I am a powerful and resourceful creator.

- I have absolute certainty in my ability to generate any amount of income I choose.

- I have all the resources I need right now to become a multimillionaire.

- I have great abundance flowing into my business, which affords every luxury that I desire.

- I am an organized, proactive, disciplined, talented, innovative, and intelligent businessperson applying sound and honest business practices.

- I am a powerful and resourceful creator attracting all the wealth and opportunities I need for me to meet my financial success.

- I have all the skills, intelligence, contacts, and money I need right now to create an incredible masterpiece with my business.

- I deserve to earn money easily and in abundance and to live totally paid in full and on time on all accounts. I am completely paid in full on all accounts and money is flowing to me from expected and unexpected sources.

- I deserve happiness, abundance, and prosperity.

- I accomplish my financial goals with ease.

- I have complete freedom over my time.

- I am a genius and I use my wisdom every moment.

- Day by day, in every way, I am better and better.

- I am inquisitive, creative, fun-loving, and adventurous.

- I have the extraordinary ability to accomplish everything I choose and want.

- I am committed, determined, and passionate about what I do.

- I am very focused and persistent.

- I have tremendous energy and focus for achieving all my business goals.

- My business is a masterpiece.

- I meditate daily and stay in constant sync with the vibration of abundance and success.

- I visualize all that I desire and I have complete control over manifesting it all.

- I feel happy and at peace with myself.

- I give myself permission to be powerful.

- I have absolute certainty about my ability to generate any amount of income I choose.

- I consistently attract all the right people to help me grow my business.

- I am a brilliant and savvy businessperson.

- I have all the talent, intelligence, and money I need.

- I am a master at what I do.

As with your vision, your set of affirmations is something you'll want to take time with, to edit, alter, and refine, until you have a finished set of crystal clear, powerful statements that articulate exactly what you want to say.

In the list above, we've provided some more examples of affirmations, just to help jog your creative process. If you see one or two there that really speak to you, go ahead and put them on your list. But don't feel you need to use these; they are simply examples. The most powerful statements will likely be those you craft yourself. Nobody knows you better than you do.

MY AFFIRMATIONS

_____

_____

_____

_____

_____

_____

_____

_____

_____

STEP THREE:
CREATE EMOTIONAL ANCHORS FOR NEURAL LINKING

Remember the example we used above of remembering two different Tuesdays? If you try to remember where you were and what you were doing on September 11, 2001, and January 8, 2002, you find that your memories from one of those Tuesdays are quite vivid, while they are probably all but gone from the other. What's the difference? The emotional impact associated with the events of 9/11.

There is a technique called *neural linking* that uses that same kind of emotional association to deepen the impact of any belief or affirmation you choose. You accomplish this by linking that new belief with powerful feelings that already exist in association with some other memory.

Neural linking happens to us all the time. How often have you come across a certain smell—the first cut grass in springtime, the burning leaves in autumn, a wool sweater pulled out of a closet, a certain dish on the stove that you haven't eaten in ages—and suddenly a full-fledged memory from the distant past came flooding back to you? This happens because memory is strongly associative by nature. Many of our strongest childhood memories, for example, are forever linked in our brains with a certain smell (your father's pipe tobacco), sound (the next-door neighbor's dog barking), or tactile feeling (the drying saltwater, sand, and sun on your skin at the shore in summertime).

You can put that associative trait to work for you by designing specific links for yourself. Here's how you do that.

First, search your memory banks for a positive event in your life that was especially empowering, a moment where you felt a thrill of accomplishment, excitement, or triumph. What you are looking for is an existing neural pattern in your brain that has some "stickiness," that is, some strong depth of feeling to which a thought can adhere.

Jot down (either in the space here or in your "My Answers" notebook) a sentence or two that identifies this event, so you can return to it easily and quickly later on.

A POWERFULLY POSITIVE EMOTIONAL EVENT

_____

_____

_____

_____

_____

_____

_____

Now, close your eyes and let yourself reexperience that event for a few moments, and examine what you're seeing, hearing, smelling, feeling, and experiencing.

When you're finished, jot down a few of the impressions you had; these don't need to be full sentences, just words or phrases that will remind you of the feelings this experience evokes:

_____

_____

_____

_____

_____

Now, choose one of your affirmations. Choose a statement that is fairly short and that you strongly want to imprint as a new belief. In my case, I chose "I am a brilliant and savvy businessperson," since this is definitely not a belief I grew up with, and yet it has been critical to my achieving success in my business visions.

Now, close your eyes again and let yourself reexperience that powerful memory, evoking all the sensory impressions, feelings, and emotions involved—and while you are at the height of that feeling, repeat your new affirmation, either out loud or just in your mind.

Here's what happens: When an event (whether "real" or in your mind) evokes strong emotion, protein is released along with neurotransmitters as the neurons fire across the synaptic gap, and that causes the event to bind to that neural pathway much more strongly than if it was simply a neutral thought or memory. When you relive that powerful event and bring back that old feeling, more of that protein is released all over again—and when you attach your new affirmation to that event, you are physically bonding that thought into this existing neural pathway.

I'll share an example that I use for myself.

When I was seventeen, I received a scholarship to play basketball for Oregon State University. During one unforgettable game, I played the position of point guard and had the job of guarding an intimidating player by the name of Dan Brodeur. Dan was 6'8" and I was only 6'3". I had a forty-eight-point game—and throughout that game, I limited him to sixteen points. I vividly remember the exhilarating rush of emotion of being able to hold him in check while scoring myself almost at will. It was one of the most emotional moments of my life, a feeling of being totally in the flow.

This feeling was so powerful, so vivid, that I can go back there and drop into the thrill of that game at a moment's notice. So that's what I do: I go back to that moment and reexperience that feeling of being in complete control on the court, on top of the world—and then I think: "I am a brilliant and savvy businessperson."

I attach that exhilarated feeling to this new belief that I want to instill, using the emotion and the neural pathways that are already in place, thereby associating that thirty-year-old feeling that is still so resonant in my mind with this new belief.

EXAMPLES OF EMOTIONAL ANCHORS

Winning my first one-mile race. I felt proud, excited, elated, and exhilarated. I remember the fresh, rich smell of the spring turf and the feeling of my leg muscles still humming from the race, and I can see and hear the crowd cheering for me.

Finishing my degree. I felt fantastic, capable, brilliant, on top of the world. I remember the look on my parents' faces—they were both beaming with pride.

My first date with the love of my life. I felt indescribably happy, like I had suddenly found my way home for the first time. I can feel the warmth of her hand in mine, and smell the fragrance of her hair.

STEP FOUR:
PREPARE YOUR NEURAL IMPRINTING MATERIAL

Imprinting materials are simply physical expressions of your vision and affirmations that you can feed to your nonconscious brain through your senses. The most common examples of imprinting materials are:

- Written statements, typed and laminated

- Audio recordings, including simple voice recordings and voice-over-music recordings

- Subliminal media

- Pictures and vision boards (also called *dream boards*)

For more examples, go to www.johnassaraf.com.

Written Statements. Print out your current, most complete version of your vision statement. Compile your affirmations onto a single page and print that out as well. You can have these laminated at any quick-print shop. You can also three-hole-punch them and keep them in a binder.

Audio Recordings. Make an audio recording of yourself reading your affirmations. You can burn this to a CD or transfer it to your iPod or MP3 player, and not only use it during your neural reconditioning sessions but also have it available to listen to throughout the day.

You can also use this recording of your voice reading your affirmations as a voice-over, on top of a beautiful, soothing musical background. There are companies that sell software designed for this purpose, but you can also use any decent recording or mixing program, such as Audacity, Amadeus, or GarageBand to do this on your home computer.

Subliminal Media. An even more powerful way to feed selected thoughts to your nonconscious brain is through subliminal media. For example, you can create an audio track of soothing music along with a recording of your voice reading your affirmations at a volume level just *below* the threshold of your conscious hearing. What makes this so powerful is that it bypasses your conscious filters and pours directly into your nonconscious mind.

Subliminal media can include audio recordings, video recordings, and subliminal software, which flashes images of your choosing on your computer screen, so that you can be pouring your own visualization into your nonconscious brain while your conscious brain is busy working away at its tasks. One of the great things about subliminal media is that you can play it to yourself throughout the day, without it distracting you from whatever you have to keep your conscious attention on at the moment.

We have produced a companion CD for *The Answer* (www.John Assaraf.com/cd or www.GetTheAnswer.com/cd), which includes an audio track of soothing music along with my voice reading a series of affirmations, and another track with the same affirmations, only this time recorded at a subliminal volume level. You may find this helpful, but the very best subliminal media for you will be those you create yourself.

Pictures and Vision Boards. Cut out pictures from magazines that represent things you want to acquire, activities you want to enjoy, places you want to live, a lifestyle you want to have — anything that offers a pictorial representation of the life you want to be living. Tack these onto a corkboard to create a panorama of your dream life. I keep my vision boards on the wall right above my desk, so that the pictures and images I've chosen will bombard my senses throughout the day, surrounding me with things I want to acquire, achieve, and accomplish.

I also have a board I call my "achieved" board, where I place pictures of things I've already achieved. For example, on that board I have a picture of that home that I had put on my vision board way back in 1995. Along with pictures of what you *want* to achieve, it's very important to appreciate the things you *have* achieved. The spirit of appreciation and gratitude creates a much stronger connection to the quantum field of infinite possibilities.

THE POWER OF VISION BOARDS

Vision boards, or "dream boards," are an especially powerful tool for imprinting your aspirations on your nonconscious brain, because fully one-quarter of your entire brain's processing power is devoted to the sensory stream that comes in through your eyes. I know that some of us are more visually oriented, while others of us are more auditory or more kinesthetic, but those are minor distinctions compared with the fact that human beings are visual creatures. This is why one picture is worth a thousand words, and why visual images are such a powerful tool for influencing your nonconscious brain.

This is a great place to really exercise your creativity and ingenuity. Have fun! You're designing your future. Go find the car of your dreams, and bring along a friend who can take a picture of you sitting in the car. Even better, take it for a spin, and have your friend make a video of you driving the car. Go find a home you love, clothes you like, anything you can find that you can represent visually.

One of our clients had checks made up for his checking account that featured a picture of a house just like the one he aspired to have. Every time he wrote a check, he was reminding his reticular activating system of the house it needed to be on the lookout for.

One of our clients made an entire video documentary about his amazingly successful business. Working with a few friends, he assembled footage of himself walking into his office and greeting his secretary, who gave him a brief report on the millions of dollars pouring in from his various deals—and of course all of this was made up, fictional, using a borrowed space and a friend in the secretary role. But it looked fantastic. The documentary lasts a good five minutes, and leaves you breathless: It's like a film clip on a day in the life of Warren Buffett or Sir Richard Branson. Brilliant!

And if you start to feel inauthentic or silly, stop and remind yourself that every physical reality starts out as an idea. Every billionaire begins as a child with a dream. Every successful business starts out as a movie in someone's mind.

STEP FIVE: YOUR NEURAL RECONDITIONING ROUTINE

The whole process of designing your vision and affirmations, of sitting down and writing them out, editing them until they're perfect, then typing a clean copy, getting it laminated . . . all that preparation uses your conscious brain's abilities. Now that you have your tools, this is where the real work starts: Now you get to use these tools to imprint these images onto your nonconscious.

You can accomplish this routine in as little as thirty minutes a day. The more time you give to it, the more quickly your new vision and supporting beliefs will become ingrained at the nonconscious level, and the more quickly your goals will take shape in the physical world of events and circumstances. Again, the most important thing is not how long you do it, but that you *do* it.

It's best to do this at roughly the same time every day, because your body is sensitive to its own circadian rhythms. This is a key to successful conditioning that every professional athlete, musician, dancer, and writer knows: A routine practiced five days in a row *at the same time every day* has a far greater impact on your developing abilities than a routine practiced five days in a row at widely different times.

The ideal time for this practice is when you are a little tired and not too focused. That half-awake/half-asleep state when you don't have your conscious filters fully in place is the moment when your nonconscious is most accessible. Ideal times are first thing upon rising in the morning, and last thing before going to sleep at night. We also recommend adding a third time during the day. This might be during your lunch break, or whenever you can break off from the action of the day to find a few minutes of quiet seclusion. If you're someone who steals a few minutes midday to catnap, then that's the perfect time to add in your midday neural reconditioning.

It's also a good idea to practice this routine in the same place every day, if you can. Find a quiet, solitary place where you can be undisturbed for at least ten minutes; turn off your phones, pagers, email alerts, or anything else that might interrupt you.

MEDITATION

Meditation is the foundation of the neural reconditioning process, the ground upon which you will build the structures of new beliefs, goals, and aspirations in your nonconscious brain. People often associate meditation with "relaxation" or "stress reduction," and in fact, most of the early studies focused on the health benefits of meditation, and especially relaxation and stress reduction. But the principal impact of meditation is not that it relaxes you, but that it trains your brain to focus. Meditation is such an effective stress reducer precisely because it allows you to focus on relaxing (which is otherwise surprisingly difficult to do).

Larry Ellison, the CEO of Oracle, requests of his top managers that they practice meditation consistently, three times a day. Phil Jackson, the legendary L.A. Lakers coach, has for years trained his players in how to meditate. A 2003 story in *Time* magazine reported that ten million Americans said they were meditating regularly, double the number from a decade earlier.[7]

In the last twenty to thirty years, a huge amount of research has been conducted on the mechanics and benefits of meditation. More than 1,000 scientific studies on the effects of meditation have been conducted at more than 250 independent universities and research institutions in 33 countries. These studies, many of which have been published in leading scientific journals, have shown that meditation:

- increases focus and concentration;

- increases powers of observation;

---

7. Joel Stein, "Just Say Om," *Time* (August 4, 2003).

- increases energy levels;

- increases creativity and intelligence;

- improves memory and learning ability;

- reduces stress and increases inner calm;

- increases happiness and self-esteem;

- reduces anxiety and depression;

- improves overall state of health;

- deepens awareness of the quantum field.

Normally, we are so caught up in our day-to-day life, so involved in doing, doing, doing, that our brain's hectic activity often drowns out finer signals and precludes any hope of our picking up on the information that is most crucial to helping us achieve our goals. Meditation develops the "muscle" of focus, just as free weights can be used to develop the pectorals, abdominals, and other body muscles.

Meditation conditions the brain, allowing us to tap into the source of all our ideas, the quantum soup of infinite consciousness. Meditation is what gives you control of your brain waves. Meditation trains your brain so that you are better able to focus on and broadcast the message of your new goals and vision, and also better attuned to receive the answers, the tools, and the resources you need to fulfill that vision.

It accomplishes all this by developing your capacity to modulate and regulate the different frequencies of brain waves you are emitting.

BRAIN WAVES

Beta (14–100Hz): These are the fastest and shortest of the common brain waves and are not conducive to deep learning or imprinting. This is our normal, everyday waking state. Some scientists include gamma waves (24–70169Hz) in this category. Gamma waves, according to some researchers, are emitted when we are making new neural connections. Research on Tibetan meditators found they emitted a flood of gamma waves.

Alpha (8–14Hz): These brain waves are associated with relaxation, deep learning, relaxed focus, light trances, increased serotonin production, presleep or prewaking drowsiness, higher intuitive factors, meditation, and the beginning of access to the nonconscious mind. Access to the quantum field begins with alpha brain waves.

Theta (4–7Hz): These brain waves are associated with dreaming (REM) sleep. They are also associated with the production of catecholamines (vital for learning and memory), increased creativity and ability to tap into universal intelligence, integrative emotional experiences, potential changes in behavior, and increased retention of learned material. High levels of access to the quantum field are available through theta brain waves.

Delta (0.1–4Hz): These are slow, very long brain waves associated with dreamless sleep and the release of human growth hormone (HGH). Trained monks can access this level of the quantum field in an awakened state.

The four common levels of brain waves can be compared to the four gears of an automobile, with beta being first gear, alpha second, theta third, and delta fourth. Most of us function in the beta range all day long. Can you imagine driving that sports car in first gear for hours at a time, with your pedal to the metal? Of course not. Yet that is essentially what most of us are doing to ourselves. We're burning out our systems. No wonder so many of us are falling prey to stress-related illnesses. And no wonder the regular practice of meditation has such a significant beneficial impact on those same illnesses.

It isn't that beta is "bad"; there's a lot of power in first gear. That's the gear you use when you first start out; it has the power to move the car from standing to motion. And first gear is great for treacherous conditions, like slick ice. But driving around that way all day? You'll fry your gears.

Likewise, there's a lot of power in the beta range of brain waves. It's great for absorbing new information, for focusing on certain tasks you've never done before. It's what you're using to read these words. But like first gear, beta won't take you very far. Once you've gotten the car rolling, once you've got the initial information figured out, you want to drop back into second gear.

As you start to do this, a fascinating thing happens. When you shift your car into second gear the wheels start turning faster and your car travels faster, yet your engine slows down. How is that possible? It's in a different gear. The same is even more true in third gear, and fourth. Less effort from the engine. Less fuel, less wear and tear. Less stress. Less heart disease, less stroke, less irritability, less frustration and anger, less depression and anxiety—and you're getting more accomplished!

That's also a description of your life when you regularly recondition your brain with meditation.

SHIFTING THE GEARS IN YOUR BRAIN

Meditation will help you stop spinning your wheels and start achieving those things that matter to you. Most of us are working way too hard. Being wildly successful in business takes hard work, and plenty of it. But hitting your head against the wall doesn't help. Nor does spending so much time and effort struggling to build your business that you never have the chance to enjoy your life along the way. If you're working at building a business the way most entrepreneurs do, you're working way too hard—and chances are good that your business is headed toward failure at the same time.

Working harder is not the answer. Nothing in nature "works hard," yet everything in nature works. "Consider the lilies of the field," says the famous biblical passage, "how they grow: they neither toil nor spin; and yet I say to you that even Solomon in all his glory was not arrayed like one of these."[8] Lilies don't stress over how they're going to grow, nor does anything in nature. Why not? Because they don't need to "work hard." They just live their natural life and fulfill the blueprint around which their physical self is wrapped. The lilies of the field are guided by the clarity of vision tucked within the energetic "idea" of the lily that lies at the heart of the plant.

Your business is no different.

---

8. Matthew 6:28–29 (NKJV).

HOW TO MEDITATE

Find a quiet space somewhere in your home where you can be undisturbed for a few minutes. You'll want to start off with just six or seven minutes; that's plenty at first. Your mind is like mental muscle, and you want to start out working this mental muscle just as you would a bicep or quadricep.

Simply sit quietly and comfortably, in a chair or on the floor, hold your hands any way you like. The most important thing about meditation is that you find a position that is comfortable for you. It doesn't have to be some specific posture or anything that is unusual or uncomfortable for you. Just sit in such a way that you are relaxed, then close your eyes, and focus on your breath going in and out.

Take a slow, deep breath in through your nose, and let it out through your mouth. Take another two or three breaths like that, breathing in through your nose and out through your mouth. Then, just let your breath move freely in and out through your nose, focusing your attention on the base of your nostrils.

Continue doing this for six or seven minutes.

You'll find that your mind starts to wander off and becomes engaged in this thought or that thought. When you notice this, don't judge it or criticize yourself, just let yourself notice what is happening and gently bring your attention back to a focus on the passage of your breath, slowly in and out, and to a focus on the base of your nostrils.

Continue sitting in that relaxed posture and just watch your breath.

The first few times you do this, you may feel as if you spend your entire time chasing after your mind, bringing it back to focus on your breath, only to find it dashing off again. It can feel like you're babysitting a child who keeps running off every chance he gets, forcing you to run after him. Don't worry, that's okay. Don't let yourself think you're failing at this. You're not. You're doing just fine.

You may find it continues for days like this. That's okay, too. Remember that what you're doing is applying the magnifying glass of your frontal lobe to the "sun's rays" of your conscious mind. You are beginning to exercise your muscle of conscious focus, just like exercising a pectoral or hamstring. It doesn't matter how "well" you focus on your breath; what matters is that you do the exercise. In time, you'll find that your focus comes more and more easily.

In the quantum universe, observation and focus are critical. There is no force in the universe more powerful than intent. By exercising your frontal lobe and by practicing the observation of your breath, you are strengthening your ability to quiet your mind and exercise the power of intent and focus.

Practice this every day.

After about two weeks, extend your meditation time to fifteen minutes. After another two weeks, if you can, extend it further to thirty minutes. However, the most important thing here is that you keep the consistency of practicing this regularly, every day. If you miss a day, just treat it the same way you treat your wandering focus: Okay, you missed a day. Don't castigate yourself or chalk this up as a "failure." Just bring your focus back to what you're doing, and resume your practice the following day.

As you continue this practice regularly, you'll start to notice that your entire day changes. Everything seems to slow down, and you seem to have time for everything. You start to feel a profound sense of connection with the universe around you. And most important, you start seeing the elements of your dreams, goals, and aspirations come into focus and take shape in your life.

Meditation has all sorts of fringe benefits for your health and your life, but it especially shines as a powerful ground for neural reconditioning. Developing your ability to access the different types of brain waves will make it vastly easier for you to achieve your goals.

Remember how often the average human being loses focus? Every six to ten seconds. Through meditation, you develop the ability to stay locked onto your goals like a laser—and when you do, you open the possibility for the quantum field to respond, resonate, and supply all those elements you need for the fulfillment of those goals. In other words, you exercise the Law of Attraction.

Now, to this base of general brain conditioning let's add the steps of neural reconditioning.

THE NEURAL RECONDITIONING PROCESS

Immediately after you finish your few minutes of meditation, follow this with a few minutes of visualizing your business vision, just playing it through your head as a mental movie. Just like meditation, visualization begins by sitting in a relaxed position and closing your eyes, but this time you create a mental picture of the scenario you are visualizing.

I see myself visiting my banker. She greets me warmly by name and comments on how well my business is doing. I'm wearing the clothes I want, driving the car I want, eating the food I want, having the health I want, being in the relationship I want—I'm living the life I want, and I see that playing as a movie in my head. I'm already living it, over and over again.

Or, I see myself during a performance review. I'm selected for a promotion, based on the impact I've made by successfully managing my team.

At first, this may seem awkward and unproductive. That's all right. The more you practice this, the easier it will be, and the clearer the images will become.

This is where clarity pays off: Always seek to picture precisely the same images, day after day. When you do your homework and make your material crystal clear, you pave the way for faithful daily repetition. Soon you'll find that you can quickly and easily evoke these pictures and put them up on the screen of your mind, viewing them as you would a movie in a darkened theater, with yourself in the lead role. It's the film adaptation of the thrilling book called *My Stunning Success*.

And by the way, even though we're using the term *visualization* here, don't forget to create a compelling sound track. Your visualization can also include vivid tastes and smells, tactile sensations, and gut feelings. In fact, the gut feeling is really the bottom line. The best film directors know that they are using the tools of shape, color, movement, sound, and every other tool they can for one purpose: to evoke a visceral response. It is feeling that you are going after, the vivid experience of being in your successful dream business, and whether you arrive at that feeling through sights, sounds, smells, or sensations of your skin matters not at all. They all lead to the same destination, which is *how it feels* to be there.

After your visualization, take a few minutes to go through a declaration of all your affirmations. You might read these out loud from your laminated sheets, or if you have created an audio recording, you might read along as you listen. As you go through them, let yourself feel the truth of them. See a picture in your mind, or feel within yourself what it feels like to have achieved or to have exemplified each one of these statements.

It's that simple: a few minutes of meditation, a few minutes of visualization, and a few minutes of affirmation.

STEP SIX: USING NEUROTECHNOLOGY

Technology has given us all sorts of wonderful tools we can use to continue bombarding our nonconscious brain throughout the day with our visions and declarations of the world we want to create. Here are some of the most common forms:

Audio. You can have your affirmations playing while you're jogging or working out, cleaning house—anytime you would ordinarily listen to music.

Subliminal Audio and Video. Likewise, you can play subliminal audio and video recordings to yourself throughout the day. One great advantage of subliminal audio recordings is that they play their messages directly to your nonconscious, and don't distract your conscious focus from whatever you're engaged in at the time, so you can play these even when you're busy at other tasks.

Subliminal Software. There is software available that will play your affirmations to you by flashing them "invisibly" on your computer screen. Your conscious mind will not be aware of these messages, but like audio subliminals, they will play directly to your nonconscious brain, so you can have them broadcasting to you while you're busy at work on your computer focusing on other tasks.

Audio Support for Meditation. There are also quite a few wonderful CD programs available to help put your brain into a meditative state.

IN SUMMARY: THE NEURAL RECONDITIONING PROCESS

A. First thing in the morning, midday, and last thing at night:

- Meditation

- Visualization

- Affirmations

B. Throughout the day, as practical and available:

- Various forms of neurotechnology (software, subliminal audio, etc.)

FEEL THE DOUBT AND DO IT ANYWAY

As you first start going through this daily process, you may feel a nagging sense of discomfort, anxiety, or doubt. When you say, "I am now earning five hundred thousand dollars a year," you may hear another voice in your head that says, "No, you're not! Why are you lying?"

Don't let this throw you. This is completely normal. What you're feeling is your psycho-cybernetic system doing what it's designed to do: alerting you to the fact that you're making a change in course. It's simply the lookout in your brain, watching where you're headed and sending you an alert message: "Captain—new goals, dead ahead! We're having five-hundred-thousand-dollar thoughts! We've changed course—what should we do?"

The key is to feel it, sense it, and appreciate the fact that your psycho-cybernetic system is doing its job, doing what it does to keep you safe—but don't interpret that with a "Retreat!" response. Interpret it as the thrill of moving into new territory. Reply to your own message: "I know, it's okay, that's exactly where we want to be headed. Full speed ahead!" Let that sense of anxiety or discomfort translate into the thrill of adventure, and tell yourself exactly what I told my son in those two weeks before kindergarten: "You're gonna have a blast!"

And know this: There is a point where everything flips. You'll find that you get to a place where you start to see opportunities that line up with that $500,000 goal, and when that happens, you'll also start to see your behavior change and your choices change. New opportunities will show up in your life, new resources and new situations. You'll start to see your business change—in fact, you'll see your *life* start to change. And all that happens because of one and only one thing: because first *you* changed.

8

NEURAL RECONDITIONING FAQs

The following are questions that real-life clients have asked us, in tele-conferences, workshops, and correspondence, after going through training in the neural reconditioning process. If questions have come up for you, hopefully they will be addressed by some of our answers here.

Q: Does the order in which I do the different parts of this process matter?

It makes sense to meditate first, spending a few minutes putting your brain into a good, clear condition before moving into the rest of the routine. But in terms of your vision, affirmations, audio tools or visual tools, mental movies and neural linking with past memories, or any other part of the process—there's truly no right way or "best" way to do this. We've shared what works for us; feel free to tinker with this order to better suit your specific needs.

As with physical exercise, where you want to work out all your muscles and not just one or two, it's good to have a variety of tools, materials, and approaches. But the key here is to find what works for you. This is not a recipe that you have to follow exactly or it won't come out right. This is like taking a handful of basic, delicious ingredients and making a great-tasting sandwich. Are there rules for making a sandwich? Well, it's probably a good idea to have the bread on the outside, but that's about it. And it's *your* sandwich. Make it the way it tastes best to you.

Q: *Thirty minutes? I don't know if I can carve out a full half hour every day—that's a lot of time!*

Okay, if you can't do thirty minutes, how much *can* you do? Or let's put it this way: How much time do you think transforming your life and achieving all of your goals is worth? Fifteen minutes? Seven minutes? We know you're busy. We're all stretched, and that's fine. We are less concerned with *how much time* you invest in doing this than we are that you do *something*, and do it *every day*.

Thirty minutes a day is ideal, but even if you invest just seven minutes you will see phenomenal results within thirty days—*if* you genuinely devote those seven minutes a day to this process, day after day, consistently and fully. Move that to fifteen minutes or more, and you will see results that are nothing short of spectacular. And don't forget, once you start meditating you'll find that your whole day feels less stressful. Somehow you seem to be moving briskly through a world that has slowed down a little bit, so you feel like you have *more* time.

Q: *I feel awkward when I read my affirmations out loud.*

That's okay: Feel the discomfort and do it anyway. Creating your vision involves taking a risk, the kind of thrill you experience when you go skydiving or bungee jumping for the first time. Your body may literally tingle with the sensation of the chemical warning signals: *Danger! Danger! You are now proceeding outside of normal safety zone!* For you, this signal may take the form of: *This feels phoney and unnatural!*

Creating and imprinting your new vision takes courage, because by definition you are stretching beyond the limits of your current beliefs. Most people seek to achieve only what they already believe is possible—but you can do far more than that. Robert Browning wrote, "Ah, but a man's reach should exceed his grasp. Or what's a heaven for?" We say your reach should dramatically exceed your grasp—or what is *living* for?

If you want to achieve your goals, you have to take yourself through this process of designing the beliefs you want *before* you believe them.

You can't wait for all those new beliefs to feel genuine; they won't feel genuine until you believe them, and you won't really believe them until you've done what it takes to turn them into mental habits. You must create the vision first, then create the beliefs you'll need to match and support that vision, and then give your nonconscious brain the task of absorbing those new beliefs. At that point your conscious brain will feel comfortable.

Q: I've attended a lot of seminars and spent thousands of dollars on self-improvement training and materials, but I'm still sort of frozen in my current life. I understand what you've described here, but I can't seem to take action to make it happen for me. Do you have any suggestions?

First and foremost, look at the words you're using and the beliefs you're holding. When you say something like "I'm frozen in my current life," you're perpetuating the very state of affairs you say you want to change. Be careful what you say to yourself in the back of your mind—because someone really important is listening!

So let's get rid of "I'm frozen." No, you're not, not at all. You are what you say you are. You can tell yourself, right now, "I'm freeing myself up to take this new approach." Remember, don't focus on what you're *not* doing; don't tell yourself you're *not* in action. Focus on what you *want* to be doing; see yourself doing that.

And don't worry about the money and time you've invested in seminars and materials. That's not wasted money. Everything you've learned is inside you, stored in the unconscious brain, just waiting for you to put it into action. But the answer is not in the information—it's in the *application* of the information. And that's where you're going to begin. Starting now.

Q: My biggest challenge at the moment is moving past procrastination. What would you suggest?

You could start by changing your belief from "I am a procrastinator" to "I'm someone who takes action and gets things done." Get that belief anchored in your nonconscious brain, and it will become the truth so quickly it will amaze you.

Q: I'm in my seventies—I wish I'd known about this earlier in my life! Now I feel like it's too late to really make much of a change.

You're never too old to start right now. And the effects can be so profound, it's worth doing, no matter what your age or what your circumstances. Over the past ten years that we've been sharing this approach, we've received tens of thousands of letters and emails from people all over the world telling us how it has led to more money, more health, more fulfillment, more satisfying relationships, and stronger spiritual connections than they had ever thought possible.

Something else about older people: The latest research suggests that by doing this work, you will actually reduce or slow down the potential for Alzheimer's. As you build all these new neural connections (remember plasticity!), you are keeping your brain alive and vital.

Q: How do I spot my limiting belief system? I have a company making a half million dollars a month, but I want to double that: I want to be making a million a month. So I'm doing well, but not as well as I'd like—and I don't know what belief is holding me back. How do I know what I need to focus on every day?

If you want to know what the current software in your brain is doing, just take a look at your current business results. That's what we call your current *mental financial capacity.*

Right now, what we know is that your current mental financial capacity is running at about $6 million a year for your company. If you want to increase that to $10 million or $15 million a year, we need to go into the brain to change the software, to change your belief about what is possible for you and your company to achieve. By staying with your regular meditation and the practices of the neural reconditioning process (don't forget, consistency is the key!) you'll recalibrate your psycho-cybernetic mechanism and redirect those parts of your nonconscious brain that feel like they're holding you back.

Here's the final part of it: When we talk about your conscious and nonconscious mind as related to achieving success, what we want to do is allow your reticular activating system to see all the opportunities for you and your company out there that are at the $10 million or $15 million frequency, as opposed to what you're seeing right now, which is limited to those opportunities that resonate at about $500,000 a month.

To do this, continue every day to reset your mental financial capacity by staying with the neural reconditioning process. And don't forget the astronauts: This process may take as long as a month.

Q: *How do I know when my nonconscious is getting in the way of what I want to be producing?*

You'll start doubting, having anxiety and fear about what you're about to do. Anytime there is a disconnect between what your nonconscious is programmed to achieve and what your conscious mind wants you to achieve, you'll start to feel doubt, fear, and anxiety.

The first thing is to simply notice that disconnect and realize that your nonconscious brain is sending you a signal based on your old conditioning—*not* based on what you're capable of achieving. Remember that it takes a good thirty days to really take root. What you want to do is stay with the neural reconditioning process, and you'll find that every single day you do it, the anxiety and doubt from your old beliefs will become less and less evident.

The key is to be aware of it, stay on it, and move right through it.

Q: *I've been doing all this bombardment of my nonconscious brain, and I notice all sorts of things are starting to change in my life. I'm even starting to see life differently. Sometimes I want to put the brakes on!*

When you retrain your brain, it starts looking for images out there that match up with this new internal image, so new things just start showing up in your life. You've started seeing things you weren't seeing before, and tapping into frequencies that you never tapped into before, because *you* have changed. You don't need to put on the brakes; instead, just keep reflecting on the vision and declarations you've articulated, and make sure they accurately describe the life you want to create.

For example, if you're worried that your business will become so successful that you won't have any time for your family or for quiet time for yourself, for reading or studying or whatever you like to do to deepen and develop yourself personally, then add those elements that are obviously important to you into your vision.

Remember, this is *your* vision. You get to design it the way you want.

Q: Your neural reconditioning program inspired me; it worked and I have enjoyed great success. But I'm afraid I may fall back into my old patterns and slide back to where I was before. How do I stay focused?

The first way is to make sure you're committed to doing the work, day in and day out. Make yourself reminder notes to review where you stand with the entire process, perhaps at the beginning of every week. Second, you might consider working with a coach. Last, add a statement to your reprogramming routine that will address your concern in a positive way, something along these lines: "I am building on a solid new unconscious foundation to take my success even further."

Q: When I first went through this process, I wrote out my core abilities, my one-year goals, my business vision, affirmations, everything. How important is it to revisit that, and how often?

The game never ends; you've got to keep recommitting to the process. Every time you set your goals higher, every time you push the goalposts out further, or set your foot on the path to some new goal or aspiration, you have to recommit to the process of articulating that goal and then imprinting it onto your nonconscious brain. We've been doing this for over twenty years, going from goal to larger goal to larger goal. Every time we set the financial bar higher for our company, we recommit to the process—and our whole team recommits to the process. That's what it takes.

Q: Is it okay to bombard my nonconscious by listening to my affirmations while I look at my vision board, or should I do one thing at a time?

Remember that you are dealing with a supercomputer of absolutely mind-boggling power. It has far more capacity than we give it credit for. Don't worry about giving it more than it can handle—you'll never use your full capacity in this lifetime.

Q: I'm using the phrase debt-free *in my vision, but I'm concerned that my nonconscious will register the word* debt *and focus on that, with the result that I'll keep manifesting exactly what I don't want.*

Great question! It's important to phrase your goals and vision in positive terms. However, it is okay to use the terms *debt-free, alcohol-free,* or *drug-free.* The associations we have in our minds are already clear on what *debt-free* means; we subconsciously emphasize the *free,* so it doesn't seem to cause us to go in the opposite direction (i.e., toward debt, alcohol, or drugs). We've used these phrases with people for years, and never once have we seen any negative impact from them. We all clearly know what the term *debt-free* means. On the other hand, saying something like, "I am no longer letting abusive men control and ruin my life," seems to us to be clearly creating a word picture of exactly what the person *doesn't* want. Far better to say something like, "I attract into my life only people who love me, respect me, and act in my best interests."

Q: I've been applying the neural reconditioning techniques every day for about a week now, and I've noticed that I have been quite irritable. I am wondering if this is some sort of detox or by-product of the neural reconditioning.

You're absolutely right. Whenever you introduce a new idea or new direction, you're setting up a different vibration in the brain, and that creates a cognitive dissonance or conflict with your existing beliefs that reverberates throughout your body. You are creating new neural pathways that correspond to your new beliefs, while at the same time you're letting your old pathways atrophy. But those old pathways, which correspond to the nonsupporting beliefs you're letting go of, have had their firing thresholds lowered from years of repetition, and they are trying to fire off their habitual impulses. So you're setting up conflicting signals in your body, and it's normal to register that as a sensation of anxiety or stress. That's what the psycho-cybernetic mechanism is all about.

So yes, you very well may feel a detox type of reaction to this process. You're forcing the brain to move into a higher order of functioning, which shows up as you actually release chemicals that reflect that. But remember, at the border of chaos is where we find the most growth. Get excited by the sense of turmoil; it means you're on your way!

Q: I can really see how all this would work. I have started to work on writing out my vision and affirmations, but I just haven't been able to get myself to finish them. I can't seem to get myself to actually sit down and go through the whole neural reconditioning process. Can you give me any insight into how to deal with this?

If you find you haven't done this work, here's the question you could pose to yourself: "What stories am I telling myself as to why I haven't done this work?" The way you do anything is the way you do everything. If you're dragging your feet, ask yourself, why? What reason are you giving yourself that you can't do this? Your habits are forcing you to behave in the same old way you always have.

Here are some other questions you might ask yourself: "How well is my inactivity working for me in my business and my life? Wouldn't it be nice to make a change?" You've got nothing to lose but your old habits, and everything to gain.

Q: What motivational audios do you recommend I listen to? Is there any particular author you recommend?

There are quite a few excellent speakers who are master motivators, who have done their homework, achieved great things in their own lives, and are talking from experience. But again, the key here is not the information; it's the application of the information. It's the Law of Action. If you're like most of us, you already have much more information than you will ever be able to fully use.

We all tend to think there's a magic pill just around the corner—the next teacher, the next audio program, the next workshop, or the next book. It's ironic that we're saying this—after all, what you're holding in your hands is yet another book! But the truth is, no matter how good the information may be, it will do you absolutely no good as long as it stays only in your conscious mind. You have to apply it, put it into action, and put it into action *in such a way that it gets into your nonconscious brain.* That is the only way any information can consistently serve you and support you in changing the path of your life.

Q: I've actually manifested a few incredible things in my life, including some unexpected income and a new job. At the same time, I don't feel I really know what it is that I want.

If you're thinking you don't know what you want, guess what instruction you are giving your nonconscious mind? That's right: "I don't know what I want." So shift that instruction; give your reticular formation a different search string. Instead, you might say, "I would like my nonconscious to bring me some options for what it is I would like to achieve," and then let your nonconscious get to work.

Ask yourself this: "If I *did* know what I want, what would that look like? What would that feel like?" The questions you pose to yourself are very, very powerful. Remember, we are dealing with infinite resources. We have to let go of our present results and our present conditioned mind and move to a higher order of thinking that is fully supported by the universe.

One more thing: As you're doing this process, make sure to pay attention to what *is* changing and what *is* working.

Q: What do I do if I do all this, and it still appears to not be working?

Go back to look at the natural laws we discussed. Natural laws always work; even when to us they may not appear to be working, they absolutely are working. The only question is *how* are they working. Are you clear about your vision? Are you being consistent in your neural reprogramming?

Remember the Law of Gestation. If you want to lose ten pounds, there are two ways to do it: You can have it surgically removed, and it will take a matter of minutes. Or you can begin to exercise a little every day, watch how you're eating, and steadily move toward your ideal weight. That will take weeks or months, but you're a lot more likely to keep it off that way. In other words, it will really work.

Finances work the same way. You can hope to win a lottery or go rob a bank, both of them quick ways to get the money you want. The problem is, the first is unlikely and the second is illegal. Or you can plant the vision and beliefs you need to support those financial goals. That way will take more time, but it's legal and inevitable. You have to wait for the seed to grow, and you have water it and weed it every day, but if you do, it *will* come to fruition.

Q: I've heard people recommend very short, one-sentence affirmations, while others recommend long, descriptive paragraphs. Which do you prefer, and why?

The only real question here is, what works for you? We like to use various types of expression. But there's no right or wrong way here. Shorter statements are easy to remember and can be quite forceful. Full paragraphs allow more room for description, for evoking your various senses and making things vivid in different ways. It all works. Which one feels right to you? Do you want to try both?

Q: What kinds of vision boards do you have?

As we mentioned in chapter 7, John has several boards. One is his "achieved" board, which he uses to continually remind himself of the things he has accomplished. Another is his "health" board, where he displays photos of the physique he wants to maintain, pictures that illustrate the kind of lifestyle he wants to have, and agreements he has made with himself concerning his health. On another, he puts photographs of things he wants to acquire, like watches and cars, and things he's going to do, like flying a jet aircraft.

Q: How do I tell the difference between uncomfortable growth, which I want, versus the discomfort of heading in the wrong direction, which I don't want.

Great question! Try asking yourself this: "Am I moving toward what I want? Am I heading in the direction I want to be heading? Am I headed toward something that is genuinely fulfilling?" Ask yourself, "Is this goal worthy of my life?"

Naturally, we often find ourselves heading in the wrong direction, and we have to adjust and change course. Discovering that we need to shift direction is not the same thing as falling down. Anytime we stretch ourselves, we're uncomfortable. Yes, there is a deeper part of us that loves growth and seeks fuller expression. That's our creative side. But our smaller self loves comfort and opts for the status quo.

The thing we need to remember is that change is the very essence of *everything.* There is actually no such thing as the status quo; it's an illusion. We're always changing in one direction or another, so in that sense we're always leaving our comfort zones. The question is, in what direction are we heading? Is it one we've chosen, or are we just moving by default along whatever track we happen to find ourselves?

Q: Can you say a little more about the neural linking thing? I want to make sure I'm doing that right.

Think of this as hitching a ride. When you hitch a ride, you're using someone else's vehicle to get from point A to point B. In the neural linking process, you're using a neural pathway that already exists to hitch a ride for a new idea. You bring up that neural pattern by thinking about that memory and evoking the emotion in it, which releases a flood of positive chemicals—and then you bring in the new idea to hitch a ride on that feeling.

Q: Should we be saying these affirmations out loud?

You can say them out loud or in your head, whatever feels right to you. If you're not used to doing this, get in front of a mirror and look at yourself as you read your affirmations and declarations. Here's what's going to happen: You are going to feel very uncomfortable watching yourself doing this! In fact, you might feel like an absolute idiot. And here's the wonderful thing about this: As soon as you start to feel comfortable with it, you'll know that the neural rewiring is under way.

Q: I believe in the value of setting financial goals beyond my comfort zone: "I earn ten thousand dollars a month easily and effortlessly." But what happens if that does not come true after several months? Doesn't this start creating a cognitive dissonance in my own conscious mind?

That can happen, but ask yourself this: What are you doing above and beyond your neural reconditioning to pursue that goal? If a salesperson sets a goal of earning $10,000 a month but never picks up the phone to make sales calls, it's just not going to happen. An affirmation alone will not cause results to happen in your life, unless you have the right plan to back up that affirmation and are taking daily action in accordance with that plan.

This is why the Law of Action is such an important complement to the Law of Attraction, and it's also the reason for the last of the "Five Musts" (see page 101): "You must take daily action."

The quantum universe is not a bell captain, it doesn't just hop to it when you snap your fingers. This is an intelligent universe. When you place your order by creating a clear picture of what you want and cast it out into the quantum sea by conveying it to your nonconscious brain, the universe responds to that order in the most economical, effective, and intelligent ways. The specifics of that response may show up very differently from anything you could have conceived. But those results will never show up for you if you are not in action.

Do you have the right plan to back up your affirmation? If you do, and you are taking action, then when the time is right, new opportunities will line up to make that happen.

Q: While I'm visualizing, I get this little critical voice in my head that says, "That's not possible!" How do I turn that voice down?

First, remember that this mind chatter is completely normal, and in fact, it's not a negative. It's your psycho-cybernetic mechanism doing exactly what it's designed to do. You might hear it as, "You're not smart enough, you're not savvy enough, you don't know enough about business, you're not tough enough . . . ," but all it's really saying is, "Whoa! Course change! Danger, Will Robinson—course change!"

You know what I do when I sense that voice chattering away in the back of my mind? I laugh. I say, "Oh, my gosh, look at that, isn't it amazing how that kicks in? That's my psycho-cybernetic mechanism! What a miraculous thing the human brain is!" and then I go right on with my visualization.

Q: What do I do with all the negative thoughts that seem to creep through my mind on their own, even when I don't mean to have them?

This is a great question. Dr. Daniel G. Amen, medical director of the Amen Clinics and author of *Change Your Brain, Change Your Life,* coined this wonderful term, *automatic negative thoughts,* or ANTs. And that's exactly what it feels like sometimes: like you have ants crawling around in your brain.

The ANTs go marching one by one,
Hurrah, hurrah
The ANTs go marching one by one,
Hurrah, hurrah
The ANTs go marching one by one,
The little one stops to suck his thumb,
And they all go marching down to the ground
To get out of the rain—
Boom, boom, boom—
The ANTs go marching one by one,
Hurrah, hurrah . . .

It's a brilliant way of describing that near-obsessive neural crawl that most of us have felt at one time or another. It can really feel like those negative thoughts have a life of their own, a little colony of creeping things taking dominion over our brains.

But as much as it might *feel* like that, it's *not* like that. They are in fact *your* thoughts, not an alien force, and they do fall under your control and command. Those thoughts are coming from your brain, because if there is one thing your brain loves to do, it's communicate. The brain is designed to send out signals—constantly. That little voice in your head is simply the neurons between your ears firing off electrical and chemical impulses across synaptic gaps.

So if you're wondering how to make that chatter go away, you can stop wondering right now. Outside of meditation it's *never* going to go away. What you can do is determine its content and spin: positive or negative. First, ask your brain to make you aware whenever this is happening. Often the parade of ANTs has been going on for so long that we have learned to ignore it consciously. The first step is to bring this chatter back under the scrutiny of your magnifying glass, so that you are consciously aware of it. Place this order with your neural kitchen: "Whenever that little stream of negative thoughts comes marching over my picnic, bring it to my conscious awareness."

Then, every time you become aware of the negative chatter, consciously redirect the impulse by thinking the polar opposite. When you notice yourself thinking, "This sounds interesting, but it'll never work for me," let yourself have the thought, "This sounds amazing—and I can see that it will absolutely work perfectly for me!" When you find yourself thinking, "This is too hard," reply to yourself, "This is incredibly easy. This comes to me with no struggle or effort at all." When your ANTs go, "I'm not sharp enough, I don't deserve success," turn the thought to, "I am so ready for this, the timing is perfect and nobody deserves it more than I do!"

TRANSFORMING ANTS

ANT (Automatic Negative Thought)	New Empowering Belief
I could never accomplish those business goals, because I don't have the skills it would take to pull them off.	I can easily acquire all the skills I need OR find all the perfect people I need with those skills to help me.
I'm afraid to try this. What if I mess up and fail miserably?	Being afraid is a normal feeling in the face of something new. I feel the doubt and do it anyway—and I triumph, every time.
I'm not sharp or savvy enough for this.	I am a successful and savvy businessperson.
I'm not really sure exactly what to do.	I always have crystal clarity of purpose and focus.
Things never go right for me.	Things have an amazing way of always working out for me.
I could never do that.	I can achieve whatever I set my mind to.
I'll never be able to learn this.	Learning new things comes to me easily.
I'm not bright enough.	I am smart and capable.
I always have problems.	I see solutions in every situation.

Although we're saying this is simple—and it is—that doesn't mean it's easy. You may need to sit down, take some time, and go through this with pen and paper in hand. It may take days of observing your own thoughts to unravel just what it is those ANTs are saying. If your negative thoughts have been running freely around the picnics in your brain for decades, don't feel discouraged if it takes a few days or weeks to find them. It's worth the effort: Track them down and work out what those negative messages are, then take the time to work out just the wording you want for their polar opposite. Write those new statements out, and add them to your list of affirmations.

If this seems tedious or unnecessarily thorough, think again. Remember, even though it may seem like your conscious mind is in charge of things, it actually exerts control over only a very tiny fraction of your thinking. It is a big fish in an extremely small pond—and your nonconscious brain is the whale in the ocean that is actually in charge.

The reason it's worth it to take the time and care to sit down and work out this list of positive thoughts is that *this is where your conscious mind shines.* Use the strength of your logical frontal lobe to design those thoughts you *want* to have running around your brain—and then once you've designed them, feed them to your nonconscious brain and let it exercise *its* strength.

How do you "feed it to your nonconscious brain"? Repetition. It's the same way you learned to drive a car, the same way a concert violinist takes excruciatingly awkward finger movements and turns them into unconscious routines that seem fluid and effortless.

Changing the language means accepting that you're in control. Now those particular neural pathways that triggered negative thoughts will gradually stop firing, and as they do, their firing threshold will rise so that they become less and less prone to fire again. At the same time, as you repeat your new positive thoughts, their corresponding neural pathways will grow stronger. Neurons that fire together wire together. With repeated firing, you'll *lower* the firing threshold of these new pathways, making it easier and easier for those thoughts to repeat themselves: a self-reinforcing cycle.

How long does this take? Actually, it happens instantaneously. The moment you have a negative thought, you release a chemical message into the bloodstream that perfectly matches that thought. And if you catch that impulse right at its inception and replace it with your new positive thought, you'll instantly switch the content of the electrical impulse your brain is firing. That, in turn, will instantly convert the nature of the chemical message being sent, and flood your bloodstream with the new positive thought—and as a result, your brain will register the feeling, "Hey, I'm feeling pretty good right now!"

While this process happens instantaneously, that doesn't mean the *habit* changes instantly. If you have been letting this little army of negative thoughts march around your brain for decades, it's unreasonable to expect that you can transform all those ANTs overnight or by next week. Be patient with yourself. They won't go away all at once—but they will go away. What you're doing is the equivalent of mowing down an old lawn and giving new seeds time and space to sprout. It takes a little time. Remember the Law of Gestation.

Remember, too, that this is not a vague idea cooked up by pop psychology: Everything we're describing here is based on hard science, revealed over the last decade by new technologies that have allowed us to look directly into the brain and observe the real-time brain function of patients experiencing depression, anxiety, and other chronic manifestations of doubt, worry, and fear.

So, yes, it takes some time, but once you begin the process, you will probably be surprised by just how quickly it happens. At first, it feels like a lot of effort without much result, but soon the momentum of the process begins to take over. It's like pushing a stalled car downhill to get it started: It takes the most effort to get it rolling those first few inches. After a foot or two you can feel the weight of the car itself working for you. Before you know it, the car accelerates through sheer momentum—and now the engine sparks into life. Hop in, and you are off and running. The muscular effort that it takes to start the process is the focused power of your frontal lobe; the car's engine is the power of your nonconscious brain.

Within you is all the brilliance, all the intelligence, and all the resourcefulness you need in order to build your dream business and create your ideal life. Within you is a genius yearning to express itself. All you need is to learn how to use your conscious faculties to tap into the phenomenal power of that nonconscious brain of yours.

9

THE IMPORTANT THINGS:
MURRAY'S STORY

When I was young, my family was told that I had a learning disability and that I would never amount to much. After repeating a year in school and continuing to fail, I was pulled out of the Toronto public school system and sent to a school that was "equipped to handle my special needs"—in other words, a school for kids who couldn't make it in the regular system. The expectation was that after finishing school, I would go to work in a factory, and that would be that. Sure enough, my first job was with a company that put me to work cleaning sewers a hundred feet below the city streets. I figured that was a pretty accurate reflection of my net worth.

But I didn't want to live a below-average life; I didn't even want to live an average life. I saw clearly that I wanted to create financial freedom for myself, and that this was never going to happen as long as I had a menial job. I saw something else, too: The two guys who were running that waste disposal company were no smarter than I was.

I eventually left the sewers and went to work at a factory where I operated a metal press making aluminum kettles. I worked at a number of other jobs, none of them very exciting, until a moment came when something inside me shifted, and I took a radically different course.

I was working for Bell Canada at the time, a $50 billion company, which at the time was the largest telephone company in the world. I was a technician, a cable puller, one of the guys who went out and installed phone systems for customers. During my years at Bell, I'd heard a lot of customers complain about the exorbitant rates that came with a monopoly. *If only there were some competitive companies*, they would grumble. After hearing that for a while, I started asking them, "If I started my own phone company, would you do business with me?" The answer always came back affirmative.

When deregulation came to the Canadian telecom industry in 1979, I saw my opportunity. I didn't know anything about how to run a large business, let alone how to start one. However, I had something most of my coworkers didn't: a genuine passion for what I was doing. I knew that better phone service improved the quality of people's lives, so I greeted that opportunity with a commitment to provide outstanding work. And I knew the telephone industry. The market was hungry for a competitive service. I could keep working as an employee, earning low wages, or I could provide that competitive service as the owner of a telecom business. So, at the age of twenty-four, I left Bell and started my own phone company.

All the messages I'd been given for twenty years had fostered a firm belief that I would never amount to much. But I had a passion for more, and that compelling desire was too strong to be contained. I knew in my bones that it was time to build a new belief. The process I put myself through was what we now describe in our work as *neural reconditioning*, but at the time, I didn't know that's what I was doing. I just did it.

The string of experiences that took me from sewer to boardroom taught me something that would change the course of my life: Building a successful business is not rocket science. I saw plenty of academically accomplished people in business who were brilliant, who knew more *stuff*, intellectually, than I would ever know. But they weren't the ones who were running these companies, and often they were not the ones living their dreams, either.

I knew that success in business was my ticket to the better life I envisioned, and I knew that the path to that success did not lie in academic brilliance: It lay in figuring out the critical components of running a business—any business—and learning how to make those components work correctly. And I was pretty sure that I could do that.

It occurred to me that what people had called my "disability" was just a different way of looking at things. John operates very well from intuition; for me, it's practically the opposite. My brain processes information in a very compartmentalized, sequential way. I don't read a lot, or spend a lot of time in theoretical or abstract thought. I'm at my best when I'm working methodically and analytically, with a concrete, tangible process right in front of me. I've always had a very no-nonsense, bottom-line view of life, and I found that I could hone this sense into a strong ability to look at a business and quickly diagnose its problems, and see how to fix them.

THE SCHOOL OF HARD KNOCKS

My new phone company, Alternative Communications, Inc. (trade name: All-Tel), became Bell Canada's first competitor, and I stayed in that business for a few years, long enough to taste success.

It was not an easy time. In addition to the fact that we were going up against the largest phone company in the world, a slew of telecom giants from the United States, Europe, and Asia also showed up to do battle on this newly competitive turf. In my company we were more determined than we were prepared. We took plenty of hard knocks. Several years later, my marriage had fallen apart, but I'd learned quite a bit about business. Now a single dad with a seventeen-month-old daughter, I walked away from the business and spent the next few years as an employee, once again.

I went to work as one of the charter employees of a new company, Telecommunications Terminal Systems (TTS), which wanted to build the first national telecom in Canada that spanned all provinces (until that time, each province had been regulated independently). I helped the company accomplish this by creating a national dealer division, and building it to revenues of about $60 million. Then I stopped and looked at what was happening. Here I was again, helping someone *else* make money. So I decided to go into business for myself, a second time.

I created a company called New Opportunities Corporation

(NewCo), which looked for promising new technologies to develop. One of the first companies we got involved with was a venture that was revolutionizing the digital storage of audio information. Have you ever stopped in front of a home on sale and noticed a box on the "For Sale" sign that said to tune in to a local FM radio station for more information? If so, you've seen one of our products. We ended up owning two national FM broadcast licenses in Canada and the United States, and we worked out deals with real estate companies, airports, and McDonald's.

NewCo evolved into an incubator company that worked with new ventures in media, technology, engineering, import, energy management, manufacturing, and more. We were like an investment company, but in addition to financial backing, we took an active role in running each company, including its management and marketing.

After running NewCo for five years, I took a corporate executive position with a $350 million media company that owned twenty-six radio stations, thirty or so magazines, and fifty-five newspapers. I worked with them for two years, building a place-based media division, and then I moved on again, forming a partnership with a group that owned a private television network. You've probably had the experience of waiting to board a plane and watching the airport's television network on monitors at your gate; we were the first company in America to provide that kind of private television network.

By this time I had clearly established a pattern: I never stayed at any of these business ventures for longer than a few years. I wasn't really interested in carving out a career in any one industry, or in running any of these companies long term. What did interest me was figuring out how to run them, taking them from wherever they were, setting them on a track to success, and then moving on to learn more.

After working in everything from telecom and technology to network marketing and personal development, I had applied and honed my approach in a wide range of fields. It was time to put it to the test. Now I wanted to take on the challenge of building something huge from the ground up.

INDIAN MOTORCYCLE

I have always been a passionate motorcycle enthusiast. In 1994, I had bought an Indian Motorcycle T-shirt and thought, "Too bad . . . This used to be a great brand." In its day, Indian Motorcycle was bigger than Harley-Davidson, but it had closed its doors in 1953. Yet the brand had been so compelling that even now, after languishing in bankruptcy for nearly half a century, it still had the power to evoke a compelling sense of quality and identity.

That thought I had about Indian when I bought that T-shirt in 1994 was stored away in my unconscious brain, along with countless millions of others. When I was ready, the Law of Attraction brought the thought to my conscious attention. In 1997, three years after buying that T-shirt, I got a call from a friend, Rick Genovese, telling me he had an opportunity to buy into a company that owned the rights to the clothing company for Indian. I described to Rick the strategy that would be required to pull this venture off successfully; he listened, thought about it, and decided he wasn't interested in doing it himself. But I knew this was a project I could pour myself into. I put together a consortium and made a bid on the Indian Motorcycle name.

At the time, there were a dozen other bidders for the trademark, including groups with far more clout and power than we had. Rick Block, the court-appointed receiver, was looking for a very specific formula (e.g., bid offer) that he believed was required so that the creditors were confident that they would get their money back. Rick was originally my greatest advisor and one of the smartest business people I had ever met. Nobody believed that this little group from Canada had even a ghost of a chance. But we had a different belief—and our belief prevailed over the odds. Our bid of $23 million—for just the name—was accepted. We now owned the Indian Motorcycle brand. Along that journey, Rick and I became close friends.

Before we opened our doors, we spent a full six months doing nothing but evaluating and planning, going through the exact same processes we're taking you through in this book. We figured out precisely who our ideal customer was, which business models were optimal for us, and what strategies and tactics best fit our business model. I had five presidents reporting to me, and we had to make sure that everything we did satisfied all our objectives and our larger vision, as well as our personal goals and values.

Most of all, we had to make sure we had identified the critical components that would ensure that it all *worked*. We had to make sure we didn't get lost in complexity—that we operated at all times with a clear view of the big picture, that we translated that larger vision into clear focus, and that our focus always translated into the critical actions that would catapult Indian Motorcycle into stratospheric success.

When we finally opened our doors, we came out with our brand blazing. We opened up the first Indian Motorcycle Café and Lounge, a 30,000-square-foot complex that included a five-star restaurant and a retail clothing store. Then we opened up two more Indian Motorcycle Lounges, put our clothing line into 800 retail outlets, and produced a line of 450 licensed Indian Motorcycle products.

And of course, we built motorcycles. Boy, did we build motorcycles. We had a partner, Ray Sotelo, who owned a manufacturing company called California Motorcycle. Rather than starting a new manufacturing arm from scratch, we paid our partner $20 million, took California Motorcycle, and changed its name. We built a half-million-square-foot, fully robotic manufacturing plant in Gilroy, California, the garlic capital of the world. We put our motorcycles into 250 motorcycle dealerships and opened a parts-and-services division. In addition to our regular Indian-branded line, we also built a few thousand custom motorcycles and established a private-branded division that built a thousand private-labeled machines.

In our first year, we generated $75 million and had a company valued at $300 million; we were the largest employer in Gilroy and we went on to become the second-largest U.S.-based motorcycle company in the world. The Indian Motorcycle success story drew significant media attention, and was featured on CBS, NBC, and CNN, in *Forbes* magazine, in hundreds of newspapers, radio stations, and magazines globally, and on two thousand websites in seven countries.[9]

---

9. Later, in 2000, I left Indian Motorcycle for other adventures; unfortunately, the company didn't fare that well in the years that followed, and it went bankrupt in 2004. As of this writing, it has been bought out of receivership and is being resurrected once again.

SOLVING RUBIK'S CUBE

I've taken you through the Indian Motorcycle story not to brag but to make a point. Since starting All-Tel in 1979, I've been involved with thirteen successful businesses, helped engineer corporate turnarounds, and launched start-ups in such diverse industries as hospitality, retail, media, consumer products, technology, training, energy, e-commerce, software, and entertainment. I've helped thousands of other business owners increase their revenues, profits, and value. Working with all these businesses has shown me that running a successful business is not that complicated—as long as you understand how to look at it.

Imagine that we've blindfolded you, sat you down in a chair, and put a Rubik's Cube in your hands. If you started moving the pieces randomly, twisting each section this way and that, eventually you would get all the colors to line up perfectly. However, we would need to give you some bathroom breaks, because it would take time. How much time? Scientists have estimated that it could take you up to *six billion years*.

That's a long time.

Now let's modify that experiment slightly. This time, we'll blindfold you again, sit you in the chair, and hand you the cube, only now we'll also bring into the room with us someone who knows the Rubik's Cube inside and out. He won't tell you what to do. He'll just comment "Yes" or "No" every time you make a move.

Will this shorten the time it takes you? Absolutely. This time, it won't take six billion years; it won't even take one billion. How long will it take to match up all the colors?

Less than two minutes.

Your business is a lot more like that Rubik's Cube than you might imagine. It's not that your business is all that complicated. (A Rubik's Cube, after all, has only six colors and six sides.) It's just that at every turn, you're faced with choices. How do you know whether to twist the block this way or that way? Whether to put your marketing dollars into this direct-mail piece, or that website, or this radio ad? Exactly what to say when people ask, "So, what does your business do?" Or what to say in your ad? When an ad campaign doesn't seem to be getting the results you hoped for, how do you know which feature of the ad to change? Making all these decisions could take you six billion years— or it could take two minutes.

For example, in 2002, a couple of years after I left Indian Motorcy-cle, I took over the operation of Dave & Buster's Canada, a famous food and entertainment complex. The company's revenues were fall-ing drastically (30 percent on sales of $16 million), their business value had plummeted from $9 million to $1 million, and they couldn't pay their bills. After I took this operation through the process you're learn-ing in this book, revenues stopped falling, and then started rising again.

As with the Rubik's Cube, if we hadn't known exactly which way to turn at every juncture, it could have taken years to find our way, and Dave & Buster's Canada didn't have years. But we did know which way to turn, and after just eight months, we sold the company for $8 mil-lion, an eightfold increase in value.

Whether you are a small-business owner or a Fortune 500 execu-tive, a plumber or a dentist, the manager of a fitness center or the owner of a daycare center, the principles of Business Mastery™ are the same. Growing your dream business—*any* dream business—is a systematic process that boils down to this: You need to know, out of all the possible things you *could* be doing, which are the critically important few ac-tions that you *must* take. And you need to be doing those few things every single day.

10

VISION, FOCUS, ACTION

"Lights, camera, action!" So goes the famous cry of preparation that heralds the shooting of a film scene. And there's some interesting wisdom buried in that three-word announcement.

Lights comes first for a reason. On the movie set, the director first makes sure the scene is set and lit properly. Setting up the lighting is not only one of the most expensive aspects of preparing the movie set, it is also the one that takes the longest time. A film crew might spend many hours setting up a scene and getting it lit properly for only minutes of actual shooting time.

Business works the same way. After buying the Indian Motorcycle name, Murray's team spent six months setting the stage, making sure they had their "set" properly constructed and perfectly illuminated by clear planning. They didn't transact a nickel's worth of business for those six months; in film terms, the camera wasn't running. Before they could shoot a foot of film, they had to make sure they had just the right *vision* perfectly in place.

Next comes *focus*. Once the stage is set and properly lit, the director makes sure the camera is in position, with just the right angle and lens. There might be a hundred things going on in that scene, but the director knows exactly where he wants to point the camera to get the results he's looking for. In business, there may be a hundred things going on at once. It may look complicated, but it's not—if you know where to focus. Before you take any action, you *must* know where to point the lens.

Finally, it's time to roll film. The actors have all learned their lines and they're ready to walk onto the set and do their part. But before a line is uttered or any gesture is made, the director has already seen it in his head, so the moment something is off, he knows it. It's the same in business. You have to know what actions are critical for the scene to work.

Vision, focus, action. This is the business version of "Lights, camera, action!" It's a mantra that will help you build your dream business, or position you for success in any company or corporation.

Vision means keeping the big picture in mind at all times. People unnecessarily complicate things. There are details, sometimes hundreds of details, in any business, and they're important—but they're only details. There are only a handful of key moving parts to this machine. The Rubik's Cube has only six colors. That's why *focus* is so crucial. You need to have the right lens so you can focus on the big picture and see which handful of actions are critical to your success.

We recommend that you use three kinds of "lenses" to keep the big picture always in focus: a *gap analysis*, a *revenue plan*, and a *sales process map*.

GAP ANALYSIS

In chapter 6, you set specific financial goals. A gap analysis is simply a more detailed way of defining those targets—and the ground you need to cover to get there. You create a gap analysis simply by charting where you are today compared to where you want to be in the future.

For example, suppose your business currently has annual revenues of $100,000, and you want to increase that to $250,000 within the next year. That means your gross revenue gap is $150,000. Now you know what your revenue plan and sales process map need to accomplish (we discuss these in the next few pages). This also gives you a practical way to track your progress and compare your current results with your projected results, to make sure you're on target.

A gap analysis need not be solely about money; it can deal with other goals as well. *Financial goals* might include such items as revenues, profits, cash flow, assets, available cash, expenses, payables, receivables, debt, credit, and revenue sources. But any business also has measurable *nonfinancial goals*, such as the number of satisfied customers, the number of salable products and services you offer, and the inventory you keep on hand. And you also have *personal goals*: the number of hours you work per week, the number of days you work per week, your level of stress, how much vacation time you take, how many personal days you take, and so on.

To create your own gap analysis, simply choose numbers that represent the goals that are most important to you and your career or business, list where you are with each of those measurables today, and write down a number for each category that represents *where you want to be* at a specific time in the future. Typically that would be a year from now, or at the close of your next fiscal year. The distance between the two sets of numbers is the gap.

REVENUE PLAN

A revenue plan is a description of the formula that takes a business from one side of that gap to the other. A revenue plan is easy to develop. Simply list all the products and services your business provides; then multiply each by the prices you charge; then multiply that by how many units of each you expect to sell for the specific period you've chosen.

If the results from your revenue plan match the objectives on your gap analysis, terrific. If they don't, then you need to make adjustments until they do. For example, if you own or run your business you might raise your prices, or adjust the number of units you expect to sell, or both. Once you have your revenue plan where you want it, you now have a simple road map for reaching your targets—a road map to which you'll want to return regularly.

That, by the way, is the real strength of your revenue plan, and its most important aspect: that you return to it again and again, and compare it to the actual results you're getting. It does little good if you file it away in a drawer and forget about it. Like a general's battle plan, a revenue plan is only as valuable as you make it; use it often, and make adjustments according to what you find.

SALES PROCESS MAP

Once you have your revenue plan in place, your sales process is the key tool you're going to use in order to make in happen. Your sales process includes choosing the most appropriate channels for getting your message directly to your ideal customers, and choosing the right marketing strategies and tactics for delivering that message effectively (which we will look at in some detail in chapter 14).

We sketch all this out with a sales process map. A sales process map can run to several pages, or it might fit on a cocktail napkin, depending on the business's level of complexity and scope, and how much detail you go into. But it is simply a picture of a sequence of specific, sales-related activities that, when performed properly, will result in a predictable and measurable sales outcome. The typical components of this sequence include steps to: 1) identify your ideal customer, 2) generate leads, 3) qualify prospects, 4) present to and interact with these prospects, 5) convert prospects into customers, 6) service customers and follow up with them, and 7) upsell.

Most businesses don't track this complete process, and never take the time to map it out in explicit detail. They should. Charting this process causes you to think it through carefully. Like the revenue plan, the sales process acts as a blueprint that you can refer back to constantly, adjusting as you learn, and as your business grows.

THE STRATEGIC CORE OF YOUR BUSINESS

These three types of planning are all simple methods for applying *vision, focus, action* to your business. Each focuses on the big picture to create practical actions by asking and answering a specific question. The gap analysis answers the question "Where are we going?" The revenue plan answers the question "What will it take to get there?" And the sales process map answers the question "How will we accomplish that?"

> Gap Analysis = Where you need to go.
> Revenue Plan = What will get you there.
> Sales Process Map = How you'll accomplish that.

We developed these three steps in our work with large corporations, but we've used them with businesses of every size and scale. Your business can benefit immensely by going through this three-step process on a regular basis, say, once per quarter, to chart your course and make sure it's taking you where you want to go.

At the core of all your planning lies another simple question: "How do we generate revenue?" This question is such a powerful way of applying *vision, focus, action,* and it is so central to building your business, that we think of it as the *strategic core* of the business. In fact, we are going to devote most of the rest of this book to growing revenue; but before we do, we need to explore one more universal law.

THE LAW OF COMPENSATION

In earlier chapters, we looked at a few of the great universal laws that govern our lives: the Law of Attraction, the Law of Gestation, and the Law of Action. There's one more law we need to describe here, because it holds the secret of choosing the right strategies and tactics for building your dream business: the Law of Compensation.

The Law of Compensation is an expression of how cause and effect operates in the marketplace. Monetary compensation doesn't happen by chance or by accident; it occurs as the natural and inevitable result (the *effect*) of a specific set of circumstances (the *cause*). If you can create precisely the right circumstances, you will automatically generate the result. The Law of Compensation describes those specific circumstances:

Compensation occurs when enough people want what you offer.

Sounds simple, doesn't it? It *is* simple. And like all universal laws, it is also incredibly powerful. The more you explore this law, the more you come to see the keys to success that it holds within its elegant simplicity.

What you offer (your product or service) is the result of an idea you've had. That idea is the seed of the eventual compensation. When you have a clear, focused, vivid idea that translates into a commercial offering that matches up with something enough people want—and want badly enough to pay for it—then you've created compensation. In the simplest terms, your idea is the cause, and compensation is the effect. Like everything else in the universe, the success of your business starts with an idea. But simply having that idea, no matter how strong, clear, vivid, or valid it may be, is not enough. *People have to want it.* And for that to happen, they have to *know* about it.

You plus your business idea does not yet equal a viable business. In fact, you plus your idea plus the full development of that idea—capital investment, research and design, a facility, plant, staff, inventory—still does not yet add up to a business. The magic point where all these ingredients actually cross the threshold from idea to reality, where they go from being an acorn to becoming the beginnings of an oak, is the point where *customers* come into the equation.

You plus customers who want what you're offering—*that's* a business.

Compensation occurs when enough people want what you offer.

It doesn't matter whether you're a baker, a doctor, a corporate CEO, a manager, a café owner, an athlete, a writer, a computer engineer . . . No matter what you do, if you are out to earn an income at it, this law applies to you.

INSIDE THE LAW OF COMPENSATION

We can break the Law of Compensation into three questions. First, is there a strong desire in the marketplace for the product or service you offer? Next, is your offering outstanding? And finally, are you or your team sufficiently skilled at marketing this offering to induce people to pay for it?

THREE CONDITIONS OF THE LAW OF COMPENSATION

Your business will be compensated to the degree that it satisfies three requirements:

1. There must be a strong need and/or desire in the marketplace for your product or service.

2. Your offering must be outstanding.

3. You or your team must have the ability to market and sell your offering.

That last factor is especially worth noting. It's not enough to have an exceptional product offering. There is a popular myth in business that goes something like this: "If you have the right product at the right time, the public will beat a path to your door." Sorry, but that's not how it works. They won't beat a path to your door—they *can't*—if they don't know about you. And reaching them with the right message is not easy in these intensely competitive times. The buying public is so saturated with media and marketing messages that it takes a highly focused and determined effort to slice through the clutter and reach your target market with enough impact to gain their attention. If you don't accomplish that, *your business won't grow.* It's that simple.

You have to have a great idea. Then you have to turn that idea into an outstanding product or service. And you also have to be very, *very* good at marketing and sales.

MARKETING AND SALES: THE KEY TO BUILDING REVENUE

We did a study many years ago to see who the most successful real estate agents in our company were. We found one thing in common among all those individuals who were earning $500,000 a year or more: They were all spending *at least 80 percent* of their time in front of potential customers. We also found one thing in common in the low-end group, those who were earning anywhere from $25,000 to $40,000 per year: Every one of them was spending *no more than 20 percent* of their time in front of customers.

No matter what your business is, sales and marketing is its most important function, its lifeblood. Marketing and sales is the engine that drives every business. Whatever else you're doing, you've got to be able to get in front of people so that they can make an informed buying decision about your offering.

Now, "getting in front of people" can mean many different things. It might involve face-to-face contact, or it might take place over the phone or through the Internet. It might include reaching out to people through the vehicle of television, radio, postcards, kiosks, or any one of dozens of other vehicles. But whatever the method, if you or your sales and marketing team are not in front of qualified prospective buyers more than 50 percent of your time, you are wasting your most precious resource, which is *you*.

You may be asking, "But what if that's not my strength? What if I'm not especially good at marketing or sales?" That's a great question. If marketing and sales is not your strength, then don't waste a moment trying to make yourself better at it. Instead, get someone on your team who *is* better at it. Whether you do this by hiring or outsourcing, networking or bartering, masterminding or taking on partners, make this your first priority.

THREE CRUCIAL QUESTIONS

In any business we have ever been involved in, there are three questions we ask ourselves every single day: "How can we achieve more profits per sale?" "How can we achieve more sales per customer?" And finally, "How can we get more customers?"

Each of these questions corresponds to one of three basic ways to optimize the revenue-building capacity of your business. The first question looks for ways to optimize each sale; the second looks for ways to optimize each customer; and the last one looks for ways to optimize your entire business.

1. Optimize sale: *How do I get more profit per sale?*

2. Optimize customer: *How do I get more sales per customer?*

3. Optimize business: *How do I get more customers?*

There are numerous ways you might answer the first question. You might find ways to raise your prices, or decrease your costs, or do both at the same time. You might be able to bundle separate components together and thereby create a new composite offering that can command a higher price; or, you might be able to do the reverse, creating greater profits by unbundling components and making them separate offerings.

There are also many ways you might answer the second question. It took considerable cost and effort to acquire the customers you already have; why not try to sell them more? This might mean expanding your product line or range of services, or it could mean doing more to make your existing customers aware of other offerings you have that they might not know about. There might be a back-end sale or "upselling" component that you can add into your process.

In the chapters that follow, we're going to focus on question number three, and explore that most fundamental way of growing your business: *attracting more customers*. In fact, we are going to take that question to a whole new level, giving you the keys to skyrocketing growth and genuine financial freedom, by adding one critical word to that question:

"How do I get more *ideal* customers?"

That's where we'll go next.

11

YOUR IDEAL CUSTOMER

A hundred years ago, a shaggy-bearded economics professor at Switzerland's University of Lausanne made an intriguing observation. Vilfredo Pareto, keenly interested in the political and social implications of economics, observed that the majority of Italy's real estate was concentrated in the hands of a minority. Specifically, 80 percent of the real estate was owned by 20 percent of the population. Over the years, reflections of Professor Pareto's observation began showing up in many different disciplines and applications, and it eventually came to be known as Pareto's Law, or the 80/20 rule.

You can see the 80/20 rule operating in virtually any and every realm of human activity. Look through your emails from last week. You'll probably find that 80 percent of them went to 20 percent of the people in your address book. Look in your closet or your kitchen cupboards. You'll find that you wear about the same 20 percent of your wardrobe and cook with about the same 20 percent of your cookware, about 80 percent of the time.

While the numbers are not always exact, the general rule applies everywhere you look. Studies in leading North American banks consistently show that 15 to 20 percent of bank customers generate up to 95 percent of bank profits. Some 5 percent of all Internet sites generate about 85 percent of all Internet traffic. And on and on it goes.

THE POWER OF SIXTEEN

Applying Pareto's Law to your business tells us that the majority of your revenue (roughly 80 percent) is generated by a comparatively small percentage of your customers (roughly 20 percent). If we could identify exactly who those 20 percent are, we could use that law to leverage your efforts in some amazing ways. For example, what if you focused more of your time on the 20 percent and less time on the other 80 percent? What would happen? Let's take a look at the numbers.

The 20-percenters currently generate 80 percent of your business. That means they're generating four times as much business as the 80-percenters. But hang on, it gets better: Not only are they generating four times as much revenue as a whole, but there are also four times *fewer* of them. That means that each of your 20-percenters is generating *sixteen times* as much revenue as an individual 80-percenter.

Now, what if *all* your customers were like those 20-percenters? What if you could replace your current 80-percenters with a whole new crop of 20-percenter-type customers? You'd have something like *sixteen times* your current revenues.

We can take this one step further, too, because even though your current 20-percenters are the best customers you have right now, they may not be your *ideal* customers. Can you imagine how powerful it would be if you identified exactly who your ideal customer was, and then found simple, practical ways to fill your business with exactly that kind of customer?

That's exactly what we're going to do over the next few chapters.

THE AMAZING POWER OF THE IDEAL CUSTOMER

You're no doubt familiar with the amazing power of compounding interest, which has often been called "the Eighth Wonder of the World." There is a similar force in business, just as powerful and in many ways more important: the power of the *compounding customer*. Customers who love what you do for them will tell others, who will then tell still more people. There is no marketing force more powerful than positive word of mouth from a satisfied customer. This is not news to you; everyone knows this. The question is, how do you create that positive word of mouth? Most businesspeople strive for it by looking for ways to improve what they do, and that's certainly a good thing to do. But there's another critical place to look: *Make sure you are attracting the right customer in the first place.*

Your ideal customer is the one who not only buys your product or service, but who buys it and uses it with passion. Your ideal customer is the one who *really wants* what you have to offer. The ideal customer doesn't just use your product, she *loves* your product. She doesn't just purchase your service; she feels that she couldn't live without it.

The more ideal your customers are, the fewer returns and complaints you'll have, so you'll generate that much more customer satisfaction. Once you start getting the right message to the right customers, they'll not only buy from you, they'll keep buying from you forever. They'll spend more money with you than the average customer ever would. They'll tell their family and friends to buy from you, too. Identify your ideal customer and you'll soon find you are working less and earning more—a *lot* more.

Why don't more businesses take advantage of this amazing opportunity for leverage? Because they have no idea who their ideal customer is.

WHO IS YOUR IDEAL CUSTOMER?

The only way you will attract your ideal customers to your business is if you first create a crystal clear picture of who they are. Your ideal customers may be walking past your business unnoticed, right now, but if you haven't created that clear picture in your brain, your reticular activating system is filtering them out. Remember how the brain works: *You only see what you're looking for.* So let's find out exactly what customers you want to look for.

Your ideal customer profile is vital to every facet of your business. It has an impact on product development (you want to develop product features that your ideal customers value), customer service (you want to meet the servicing criteria your ideal customers deem the most important), and marketing and sales (you want to take your ideal customers' highest values and concerns into consideration in crafting any marketing materials and sales script). Your ideal customer profile is so central to your business that every employee in your business should be thoroughly familiar with it. In fact, lack of employee knowledge and understanding of the customer profile is a common reason for business failure.

Let's start with the simple question, "Who is my ideal customer?" Take a moment to write out your thoughts about what he or she looks like. These can be as short and simple as one or two sentences. As we go through the rest of the chapter, we'll refine and develop this picture further. By the time we're finished, it may have changed quite a bit. For now, just briefly describe your ideal customer in your "My Answers" notebook.

MY IDEAL CUSTOMER

_____

_____

_____

_____

_____

As examples, here's what you might put down if you owned a day-care center, a dining and entertainment complex, or a small architectural firm. And by the way, we're not saying these are the most _accurate_ profiles; these are just starting thoughts, representative of the kinds of descriptions people tend to come up with when we have them first start looking into this question. Later on in this chapter, we'll have the chance to revisit and look at each of these examples in more depth.

MY IDEAL CUSTOMER IS . . .

For a daycare center:

My ideal customer is a busy mom, probably employed and with a household income of, say, $70,000 or more, with one or two preschool-age children.

For a dining and entertainment complex:

My ideal customer is a man, age in the twenty-five to forty-five range, with enough disposable income to want to take a group of his friends out for a good time at a moderate price.

For an architect:

My ideal customer is a couple, under thirty-five and in an income bracket of $100,000 or more, with a growing family and looking to build a new home.

DESCRIBING YOUR CURRENT CUSTOMER

Now let's describe your *current* customer. Think about all the customers you've dealt with over the past few months and start to note some basic demographic information about them, such as age, gender, and income level.

- Are your current customers mostly men? Mostly women? A fifty-fifty mix, or some other combination?

- Is there a certain age group or range that tends to buy from you, such as thirty-five- to fifty-five-year-olds, teenagers, or baby boomers (customers in their fifties and sixties)?

- Are most of your typical customers single or married?

- Do you know your current customers' approximate income level? If not, do you know what zip code they live in? Zip codes tend to correlate with income ranges.

This information will be enormously helpful later on, when we look at how to reach your ideal customer and what to say when you do. Demographic information can play a huge role in crafting the right marketing message; reaching a twenty-five-year-old woman requires an entirely different message than you'd need to reach a fifty-five-year-old man, and you would sell to a single person quite differently than you would to someone who is married. This information is so valuable that we've created a form you can use for conducting your own current customer surveys. We've included a copy of this form in appendix 1, and we've also made it available for free download at www.GetThe Answer.com/forms.

We suggest you select a few of your current customers to interview— at least three, and a dozen would be better. The more customers you survey, the more complete your information will be. And by the way, this is something you *don't* want to delegate to employees or others in your business. The customer survey is such a crucial piece of the strategic plan that you'll want to do this yourself.

You'll note that there are two versions of this form: business to consumer (B2C) and business to business (B2B). This is because the questions you want to ask will differ slightly depending on whether your business sells primarily to individual customers or to other businesses. For example, gender, age, and marital status are relevant questions for individual customers, but not necessarily for organizational customers. For businesses, you'll want to record such demographics as the number of employees, headquarters location, and organizational structure, details that would be irrelevant for individuals. A business's location and its number of employees can serve as good indicators of the type of company culture you'll be dealing with and the number of subordinates you may have to speak with in order to get your sales message to the decision maker. There's a big difference between a New York–based business and a California-based business, and you would deal with clients at Google very differently than you would deal with clients at IBM.

CASE STUDY: AN AUTO INSURANCE COMPANY

Jack Rued, one of our colleagues, had a vivid experience with the value of client demographics. In the mid-1980s he was brought in to work with one of the nation's largest auto insurers. Sitting in a conference room with one of their VPs of marketing, Jack asked who their ideal client was. The VP told him it was a man of a certain age group and income bracket.

"It so happened that there was a printout of their customer file sitting on a shelf in that conference room," Jack recalls. "I picked it up, handed it to him, and urged him to take a close look at it. He did—and a simple review of their own data revealed that the overwhelming majority of their clients were *women*."

The VP hadn't known the answer to Jack's question; when he described the company's ideal client, he was simply guessing. The company hadn't bothered to take a look at their own marketing demographics. Now that they had, they were in a position to take immediate action, as Jack describes:

"We created a direct-mail piece written by a woman copywriter, addressed to women, and illustrated with images of women. We did a gender selection of the prospect mailing list we were using, carving the men and the women into two separate lists, and we sent this new piece to the list of women. By identifying, understanding, and targeting our actual client demographic, the company's sales jumped that year by about $20 million."

CASE STUDY: HIGHLIGHTS FOR CHILDREN

Jack relates a similar experience more recently with the magazine *Highlights for Children* that involved a more detailed and sophisticated demographic analysis. *Highlights for Children* communicates principally to grandparents, who like to buy magazine subscriptions for their grandchildren.

"In 2001," says Jack, "I took the *Highlights for Children* customer database to a third-party company to help us analyze what we had in some detail. Most people think of grandparents as one category, but looking closely at our list, this company was able to track all sorts of demographic differences: There were couples, widowed grandmothers, grandparents living with family versus on their own, grandparents of various levels of disposable income . . . The variables were amazing, and we ended up identifying eight distinct subgroups.

"Once we had that information, we began communicating distinctly to each group. We launched an email campaign that sold the exact same product lines to everyone, but we used different language and text composed specifically to connect and communicate with each distinct demographic group."

That one email campaign returned a conversion rate 30 percent higher than normal.

WHY DEMOGRAPHICS IS NOT ENOUGH

Demographics is valuable information, but it's limited. It tells you who your business serves, in a broad sense, and where you might find that customer. That is, it identifies your universe of potential prospects. But this is not nearly enough information to define your ideal customer, because it doesn't really describe what these customers are looking for.

Let's say you own a daycare center, and the demographic information you've gathered tells you that your current customer is female, married, employed, twenty-one to forty-five years old, has one to three children, and has a combined household income of $70,000 or above. Now, when you go looking for additional customers, you have a precise fix on the demographic profile of people you're looking for, and this information can also help you determine *where* you might find them (as we'll see in chapter 14).

DAYCARE CUSTOMER DEMOGRAPHICS

1. Gender: *Female*

2. Age: *twenty-one to forty-five*

3. Income Level: *$70,000 or above (household income)*

4. Marital Status: *Married*

5. Number of Children: *One to three*

6. Education Level: *N/A*

7. Job Title: *Employed*

8. Geographic Market: *Local*

But here's the problem: This demographic information tells you only what these women *need*. It doesn't tell you what they *want*. And that difference can make or break your business, because not all customers are alike. The ideal customer will be included among those people who want the service or product you provide.

Out of this universe of working women who need daycare, some want inexpensive daycare that will essentially babysit their children while they're at work. Others want daycare that will offer educational classes to their kids, with certified teachers providing that instruction. To this second group, price is not an issue, but it's likely to be crucial with the first group. A third group may be more interested in daycare that provides a loving, nurturing environment with a very low staff-to-child ratio to ensure that each child receives personal attention.

That's three distinctly different groups—and this presents you with a decision. You cannot serve them all. No business can be all things to all customers, nor should it try to be. If you want this daycare center to become your dream business, it is imperative that you decide exactly what kind of daycare center you want to run and which group of women you want to attract and serve as your customers. Once you make that critical decision, you can then throw all your resources behind that decision and create a daycare service that nobody else in your area can even hope to match.

Demographic information alone will not tell you which of these three groups you're dealing with. That's why it's imperative that you also gather *psychographic* information—information about what your customers *want*. This is the ultimate purpose of your survey interviews.

PSYCHOGRAPHICS

Along with our basic demographic data, we're going to give our customer profiles some dimension by adding psychographic information. Demographics give you characteristics that identify the abilities, needs, and interests of the customers who are purchasing your product or service. Psychographics help to identify the motivation or reasons they are making this purchase. Demographics describe *who* is buying your product or service; psychographics describe *why*.

Your prospects buy what you sell because they have specific wants. Your job is to know, understand, and deliver the solutions for those wants, and since they will vary widely depending on the specific business, it's critical that you know *exactly* what they are.

When you call your customers to set up these survey interviews, tell them you are working on a project to improve your business because you want to be the best at what you do, and ask if they would be willing to help. Offer to give them a small gift, such as a discount or bonus, if they'll give you a few minutes of their time. If they have time right now, great; if not, make an appointment when it's convenient for them.

Once you are on the phone with them, ask them a few simple questions about their experience as a customer of your business. You will probably already have much of the demographic information. The real purpose of the call is to gain insight into the psychographics—the customer's wants and subjective experience—that lie behind the objective data of name, address, and age bracket. You can learn this information by asking some simple questions, such as:

- Why did you become our customer in the first place? Why do you do business with us?
- What do you like most about our business?
- Are there any other products or services you would like to see us offer?
- If you could have anything you wanted from a (insert your business here), what would it be?
- What do you like *least* about our business?

When you ask this last question, people will often tell you, "Oh, everything is fine," but don't give up that easily! You're placing a burden on them by asking them to solve your problem, so make it a little easier by making it specific: "What is the most frustrating or inconvenient thing about doing business with my company—or for that matter, with any other company in this business?" Find out what single thing, no matter how small or trivial, bothers them the most about doing business with a business like yours.

Make sure you ask open-ended questions, that is, questions that cannot be answered with a simple yes or no. Yes and no don't tell you much. You want usable information.

Then take it one step further: Ask them about other types of businesses. Ask them what frustrates them most about grocery stores, dry cleaners, restaurants, movie rental stores, doctors' offices, clothing stores, and so forth. You'll often uncover an important unmet want by looking at another industry. Once you've discovered a hidden frustration, you can look for ways to make sure you've eliminated it from *your* business.

"Is all this really necessary?" you may be wondering. "Calling my customers and walking them through an interview . . . Don't I already know my customers well enough? I mean, I deal with them all the time!"

Yes, this *is* all necessary. This is part of the process that will set you above and apart from the competition, that will make you the extraordinary option, the top choice, the cream of the crop in your field. Why? Because while you may *think* you know what your customers want, you probably don't know them as well as you think.

One of our clients, a portrait photographer, had always believed his customers valued fast turnaround, low prices, and technical expertise. When he completed this interview process with a small group of customers, he was startled to find that they hardly mentioned *any* of those benefits. As it turned out, the number one thing his customers valued was his *creativity.* Not only was he good at using soft lighting to bring out the best features of his subjects and unique camera angles, but he found clever ways to get their children to smile for the camera. That single bit of market-research insight inspired him to come up with even more ways to serve his customers' wants and distinguish himself from the competition.

Trust the process and invest the time in the research. And by the way, this is something few if any of your competitors are doing.

DEFINE THE GAP BETWEEN YOUR CURRENT CUSTOMER AND YOUR IDEAL CUSTOMER

The psychographics section of the interview form provides a list of traits that reveal information about what aspects of doing business with you are most important to that customer. As you interview your customers and complete their demographic information, turn to that section and check off those traits that seem to apply to each customer. (It's best to do this in pencil, because you may change your mind as you think back on your interview.) After finishing your interview, review this list. Once you are satisfied you've represented this customer as well as you can, list the five traits that seem to matter most to that customer, ranking them from one to five in order of that customer's preference.

When you've completed all your interviews, lay out all your filled-in survey forms side by side and look over the information you have, highlighting or circling items you find in common among the various samples. You're looking for patterns that reveal the typical customer that your business is presently attracting. Again, this is not necessarily the ideal customer that you *want* to attract; we need to start with a clear grasp of where things are right now.

Then take a blank survey form and write at the top, "Summary Customer Profile," and enter information that represents a composite picture or average of all the customers you've surveyed. Now take another blank form and write at the top, "Ideal Customer." This time select the top five psychographic characteristics that *you want and expect* from an ideal customer—and compare the two lists. Do they match? If not, then you've just discovered that your current customer is *not* your ideal customer. And now that you have a clearer picture of exactly who you're looking for, you are in a much better position to target your marketing message to attract that ideal customer.

EXAMPLE: DAYCARE PSYCHOGRAPHICS

Returning to the example of the daycare center, let's say you've recently taken over this business and inherited an existing clientele. From your work in chapter 6, you've identified your core strengths and unique abilities, and you know your passion is to provide young children with an excellent education that will give them a head start in school. However, after conducting a half dozen surveys with your current clients, it's clear that your daycare is currently serving women with limited income who wouldn't be able to afford any higher-end services.

What you have is a daycare service that *competes on price alone*, which is what most daycare centers do. The top five traits you recorded from your customers might look like this:

✓ Provides payment in full

✓ Doesn't question invoice accuracy

✓ Prefers annual service contracts

✓ Is easy to work with

✓ Is cooperative, not overly demanding

If you wanted to build a daycare empire, a chain of centers that competed mainly on price, then this would be a pretty good description of your ideal customer. But that's not what you want. What you want is a daycare center that provides young kids a first-rate educational experience. When you listed the five characteristics that you want and expect from your ideal customer, it might have looked more like this:

✓ Selective about who she does business with

✓ Wants to be kept informed as to problems/progress

✓ Wants the latest innovations

✓ Appreciates a job well done

✓ Speaks highly of us—sends us referrals

These two lists are completely different: Not a single trait from the first list appears on the second. If this was your daycare center, chances are pretty good that you would be experiencing a fair amount of frustration with your business. You might not know why. Is it a marketing problem? A staffing problem? A location problem? The answer is none of the above. The real problem is that *your clientele and your business vision don't match.*

You're not serving your ideal customer. And once you see this clearly, it can make all the difference in the world.

CASE STUDY: FUNDAMENTAL FITNESS

When Suzanne Thomas bought a neighborhood gym facility in August 2006, she soon realized she had her hands more than full. The previous owner had let the place fall into serious disrepair and it needed a complete face-lift; its record-keeping and other business systems were antiquated; and years of neglect had earned the place a very poor reputation in the neighborhood. Although she had corporate management experience, this was Suzanne's first solo enterprise, and she knew she needed to master her learning curve rapidly. The initial refurbishing had saddled her with cost overruns, and the financial picture was far from rosy.

When Suzanne came to us in early 2007, one of the first things we asked her to do was identify her ideal customer.

"I hadn't thought at all about what kind of customer I wanted," says Suzanne. "I had just been trying to serve whoever showed up. Murray told me, 'If you try to be everything to everybody, you end up being nothing to anybody.' So I began asking myself what I really *wanted* in a clientele."

A lot of gyms sell as many memberships as they can, knowing that quite a few of these people will never actually come in and use the equipment. Suzanne decided that she wanted people to come use the equipment.

"I wanted to target our business to a specific type of customer: a person who has a genuine commitment to fitness, who is going to spend some time and money pursuing it, and not just run through a quick routine first thing in the morning."

Once Suzanne had identified who she was looking for, she spelled it out right on the center's website:

WHO WE WORK WITH

- "Motivated" people who want to improve their quality of life
- People with a high degree of personal accountability and drive
- People who understand the value of knowledgeable professionals
- People who need/want to improve their functional abilities
- People who want to improve their health and/or feel better
- People who want to reduce their health costs
- People willing to invest in their health for the long term
- People willing to build relationships based on mutual trust and respect
- People with a high follow-through on advice
- People not shopping for the lowest-cost provider
- People who expect a friendly, knowledgeable staff
- People who want a place to feel comfortable in, whatever their current fitness level

Within six months of working with us and immersing herself in our educational and coaching environment, Suzanne's business had more than doubled membership, and had boosted revenues by 240 percent. Even better, she is doing what she loves and loving what she does, gaining tremendous satisfaction from providing her customers with health and fitness results they can sustain for a lifetime.

The needs and desires of Suzanne's customer now match her own passion to a T, and that has made Fundamental Fitness her dream business. We'll revisit Fundamental Fitness again in the next chapter and see how the process of identifying her ideal client also showed Suzanne some powerful ways to innovate in her business.

CASE STUDY: MOUNTAIN SUN ARCHITECTURE

David Clarke started his Alto, New Mexico–based architecture company, Mountain Sun, in 2000. When he began working with us in August 2007, we asked him to define his ideal client. Answering this question led to a revelation for David.

"In a good firm," says David, "about 70 percent of the business is repeat business. When I looked through my own client list from the past seven-plus years, I found I had less than 10 percent repeat business."

Most of David's existing clients were residential customers. Once they had built their home, they typically no longer needed his services. This meant he was constantly having to chase down new clients.

"John and Murray got me to ask myself what clients I wanted to attract. Who could provide significant repeat business?"

The answer, in a word, was developers. They regularly initiated new projects, whether they were commercial or residential, subdivisions or shopping centers. David focused on creating new relationships with a handful of developer clients who were interested in an environmentally friendly approach, and it revolutionized his business.

An even more interesting revelation came when David asked himself this question: Why had it taken him more than seven years to come to what now seemed a fairly obvious realization? The answer was *belief.*

"I'd never focused on my ideal client because I was always feeling financially overwhelmed. I was carrying some debt, and believed that getting out from under that debt would be a long, difficult struggle. Driven by the feeling of having to chase money, I was too wrapped up in finding *any* client to think about looking for my *ideal* client."

So David began creating a new set of beliefs about his talents, which included crafting a set of affirmations around his being a highly skilled and capable businessman, fully in control of a thriving business.

"This picture was completely foreign to me," says David, "but I steeped myself in it." David put up vision boards all over his house, and he soon found himself bidding on exciting projects on an entirely new scale.

But before we finish David's story, there is one more element to our survey we need to look at: identifying the decision makers.

IDENTIFY THE DECISION MAKERS

As you conduct your customer interviews, it's also important to learn exactly who plays what role in the decision-making process that leads to the purchase of your services. In most business transactions, you'll find there are three distinct roles involved: a decision maker, an influencer, and the actual user of the product or service. Most businesses never take the time to think this through, and they can miss the boat as a result.

For example, let's say you've determined that your ideal customer is female, married, and has two kids. In most households fitting that demographic profile, the wife is generally the *decision maker* for household expenditures; she's the one who decides to have the carpet cleaned, the house painted, the car serviced, the fence built in the backyard, and so on. Her husband is typically the *influencer*; he doesn't want to do any of the work, but he wants to okay the cost of the purchase. In the end, they're both *users* of the product or service.

Suppose you own a chain of pizza shops and your typical customer is a family of a certain income range. How do you market to this family? Before you even consider that question, let's gain a little more clarity: Who are the decision makers, the influencers, and the users here?

It's easy to identify the users: Everyone in the family is a user. However, it's typically the parents who place the order, so the parents are the decision makers. But what about the kids? They may not make the decision, but they sure do influence it. In fact, the kids are not only influencers, they are often very influential influencers. If you want to sell more pizza, throw in a free dessert for the kids when you make your delivery, and the kids will continue influencing their parents to order pizza only from *you*.

In order to market and sell effectively, you need to know who it is that you need to reach. This may include, but not be limited to, your customer, because the end user of your product or service is not always the only person involved in the buying process. For example, you may have an insurance policy targeted to men, but as you delve more deeply into your customer profile, you discover that it's the wife or girlfriend who evaluates the policy and makes the buying decision. Once you've learned this, you'll create and direct your marketing message toward the woman, even though you know she is not your end user.

This situation is especially common in B2B transactions. In fact, here you often find that you're dealing with influencers or even decision makers who are not even users of your product or service at all. You'll commonly find yourself dealing with subordinates who require their bosses' approval before they can make the purchase.

Let's say you are marketing a service to a large corporation, but the person you actually sell to is a middle manager. What does he want first and foremost? To keep his job, which may very well be on the line. Knowing this ahead of time will prepare you to market to him and even train him on how to go sell your product or service to his boss, the decision maker, which you probably won't have the opportunity to do yourself. Now not only will the middle manager be well prepared to sell your product, he'll look good to his boss, which is what he wants most of all.

CASE STUDY: DAVE & BUSTER'S CANADA

When Murray went into Dave & Buster's Canada, the company was in trouble. Sales had been decreasing since it first opened. One of the main reasons was that they had targeted the wrong client profile. Their marketing was aimed primarily at a twenty-five-to-forty-five-year-old male, whom they believed to be their ideal customer. But when Murray's team took a close look at the decision-making process that actually brought that ideal customer into the food and entertainment complex, they found something fascinating: That customer was not the predominant decision maker. Who decides where the date is going, where the family's going out for dinner and fun, or where to hold a special event, like a birthday party or corporate event? The person typically making those decisions is a woman.

Murray's team decided that it would be smarter to communicate to women. They started aiming their marketing at women of a certain demographic, and that shift in marketing strategy played a significant role in taking Dave & Buster's from having a value of $1 million to $8 million in just eight months.

CASE STUDY: MOUNTAIN SUN ARCHITECTURE

After deciding to target developers as his ideal client, Mountain Sun Architecture's David Clarke learned the critical importance of identifying the decision maker when he bid on a fairly large project building town houses. "That project was backed by a team of investors, but I was dealing with just one guy," David says. "I threw out a pretty high price, and they jumped on it. Then my contact came back and said his partners wanted to pull out a few elements of the plan and alter the fee structure a bit. I agreed and put together a contract." Weeks went by before David finally heard back: The cost was still too high, and they'd decided to go a different direction.

"Part of the problem, I realized, was that I never dealt with all the decision makers involved, just that one guy," says David. "I was determined not to make the same mistake on my next project."

His opportunity came when he had a chance to bid on a project for a developer who was building seventeen homes in a small subdivision. This time, David went out of his way to make sure he spoke with every single one of the project's investors, and got a sense of each person's interests and concerns.

"I soon learned that there was one gentleman in particular who was really pulling the strings in this group—and I made sure that I thoroughly and completely addressed every one of his issues," David says.

This time, Mountain Sun got the job.

PUTTING IT ALL TOGETHER: YOUR IDEAL CUSTOMER PROFILE

Most businesses put significant time, money, and effort into attracting more customers. But simply serving *more* customers is not nearly as critical to your success as serving *the right* customers. When you match your business with the right customers, they will not only buy your product, they will serve as your advocates and ambassadors, sing your praises, tell the world about you—and *bring you new customers*. This is why it's well worth it to do the market research and define your ideal customer with as much clarity and precision as you can.

Now, let's put all this together and create your Ideal Customer Profile. Reread the description you wrote of your ideal customer at the beginning of this chapter. Go back over your summary results from your customer surveys, and revisit the prioritized list you created of the psychographic traits you want and expect in your ideal customer. With all this information freshly in mind, now take a few moments to create a revised picture of your ideal customer, making it as accurate, detailed, and complete as you can.

MY IDEAL CUSTOMER

_____

_____

_____

_____

_____

_____

Do you see what you're really doing here? You're creating *another vision board*, but this time, instead of building a picture of your dream business, you're building a picture of the *dream customer* that this business attracts. Once again you're creating a crystal clear image, using the magnifying glass of your prefrontal cortex and its amazing powers of focus, imagination, and analysis—and as you define this image and impress it upon your nonconscious brain, the Law of Attraction will bring it into your life, and into your business. Just as with any vision, once the picture is in sharp focus, you will nonconsciously marshal all the resources within you and without you to manifest that picture.

Now we're going to turn this same high-clarity lens onto your business offering, to make sure you match your business's performance with your ideal customer's highest expectations.

12

INNOVATING YOUR BUSINESS

So far we've painted a general picture of what your ideal customer wants; now it's time to get more specific. To know how to find your ideal customers and then create the right marketing messages and materials to reach them and attract them to your business, you need more targeted, pinpointed psychographic information. You need to identify and thoroughly explore what your customers need and what those customers want.

Need and *want* may sound similar, but they're different as day and night. For example, let's say I need a new car to get to work every day, but I really don't have the money for it in my budget. I don't *want* a new car, because I feel I can't afford it. On the other hand, if I *want* a new car, I will probably find a way to get it—regardless of whether or not I truly *need* it.

Which are stronger, needs or wants? If you have kids, you know the answer without having to think about it. Your child *needs* new clothes for school; he *wants* the latest video game. And even if we are better at masking our feelings, when it comes to our wants, we adults are no different from kids. Nobody really *needed* an iPod when it was introduced to market, yet look at how many people *wanted* one (and bought one!). Young or old, no matter our demographics, our wants tend to be a much more powerful driving market force than our needs—and *that's* where you want to focus your marketing message.

We got a good start on identifying our customers' needs and wants with the basic psychographic information we gathered in chapter 11; now we're going to take a closer look by identifying our current customers' most urgent *hot buttons*.

YOUR CUSTOMERS' HOT BUTTONS

Hot buttons are the problems, frustrations, and concerns that matter most to people as they consider the possibility of doing business with you. Your customers' hot buttons are the most pressing reasons they have for becoming your customers. Because we are all individuals, you might expect that people's hot buttons would vary widely from customer to customer. It turns out that when it comes to reasons to buy a given product or service, we all tend to share the same few hot buttons for any given type of business.

When you call a moving company, an airline reservation desk, or a roofing contractor, what expectations do you have? What results do you want to see above all? You want your possessions packed and moved fairly quickly without being broken. You want the reservation booked accurately and you don't want to wait a long time while you do it. You want your roof repaired right the first time, so it doesn't leak, and you want the bill to come in close to the estimate. And that's what all the other customers want, too.

Sounds simple, right? It actually is, yet an amazingly large number of businesses never take the time to identify precisely what their customers' hot buttons are, what that means in terms of their specific business, and what the very best ways are to address those expectations—let alone how they can communicate all that to their ideal customers and prospects.

Once again, we're dealing with clarity and focus. Your job is to identify and define the three to five hot buttons that top the list for your business; in other words, the top needs and wants that lead customers to turn to your business. While this list varies from business to business, it tends to be quite consistent *within the particular industry* to which the business belongs, so before we go any further, let's determine what that industry is for you.

For this purpose we use a classification of five distinct kinds of industries: *service, professional, retail, wholesale,* and *opportunity/entrepreneurial.* Here is a short list of examples of various businesses that represent each industry (a more comprehensive list appears in appendix 2, at the back of the book). If you don't see your specific business listed there, then make an educated guess as to which industry best describes your business. (By the way, roughly 70 percent of U.S. businesses fall into the service sector, which is why we list it first.)

INDUSTRY CLASSIFICATIONS

Service: automotive services, banking, education, real estate, food service, daycare, etc.

Professional: advertising, attorney, accountant, physician, dentist, architect, etc.

Retail: automotive dealer, clothing store, restaurant, bakery, florist, office equipment supplier, etc.

Opportunity/Entrepreneurial: consultant, home-based businessperson, broker, direct marketer, online-service developer, etc.

Wholesale: computer hardware, paper products, food products, packaging and containers, etc.

In appendix 2 we've also provided a list of those hot buttons that are most common for clients in each industry, listed in order of importance for that specific industry. You can use this list to help you determine which are the three to five absolute top-priority hot buttons for your specific business. Keep in mind that these are listed in order of priority; in other words, for any business in the service industry, "Fix it right" (the first one on the "Service Industry: Common Hot Buttons" list in appendix 2) will tend to be the number-one hot button. We sometimes see situations where other hot buttons may be more appropriate than those listed, but not very often. Still, if you genuinely believe the hot buttons that apply most to your business are different from those listed, then go with your gut; nobody knows your business better than you.

You also may find the information you've gathered from the last chapter has already identified some of your business's top hot buttons for you. In the daycare example, if you decided to accommodate those customers looking for the lowest-priced daycare in the area, then obviously *price* would be one of your top hot buttons. If you decided to service the group that wants educational instruction by certified teachers, then *expected results* would probably remain the number-one hot button. If you decided to cater to the group wanting the low teacher-to-child ratio, then *customer service* might be number one.

Now, look through the list of hot buttons for your industry, and select what you think are the top three hot buttons for your specific business.

MY BUSINESS'S TOP THREE HOT BUTTONS

1. _____

2. _____

3. _____

"WHAT ABOUT PRICE?"

When we go through this exercise with clients or with our seminar audiences, there's one question that people often raise right off the bat: "What about price? Why doesn't price rank very high on any of these lists?" Businesspeople often expect that price would be their customers' number-one hot button, or at least one of the top three. In reality, it's often one of their last considerations. Most customers are willing to pay more—*if* you offer enough value to warrant the higher price.

This brings us to a key insight: What matters is not so much price as *value*. Value determines price, not the other way around. So what is value? That turns out to be the million-dollar question, because value is a relative term. Relative to what? To what your customer thinks, feels, and says it is. Value, in a word, is what your customer *wants* and *needs*. And that is such a critical discovery for your business that it's worth any effort to identify and define exactly what that is.

When your marketing and advertising looks just like everyone else's marketing and advertising, then your customers can't easily determine the true value you provide. Without any real distinction, your product or service becomes just another commodity. And in the absence of information about value, potential customers will default to the lowest price as a differentiator. You absolutely *must not let that happen*—because if it does, it's over. If you don't find a powerful way to differentiate yourself, then the only way left to compete is price. And if your business has gotten to a place where it can compete only on price, it's time for you to get out of that business. It has become a no-win situation for you, because there will always be someone willing to undercut your price.

Fortunately, we have *never* encountered a business where that situation actually applied. In fact, if you provide more value than your competition and you communicate that value to your prospective customers, you may even be able to *increase* the price you charge for your product or service. Again, most customers will pay a higher price—*if* they understand the superior value that your product or service offers them (think BMW!).

A TALE OF TWO ATTORNEYS

Mary is looking for an attorney to handle her divorce. She speaks to two attorneys and asks them both what they would charge for their services. The reason she asks this question is simply that she doesn't know what else to ask. She has never been through a divorce; this is all new to her. She doesn't know what issues are involved or how attorneys might differ, so the only thing she can think to ask about is their rates. (Remember that this is the norm, in any industry and for any business. In the absence of information about value, prospects will always default to price shopping.)

The first attorney replies by telling her that he charges $250 an hour, and he would be happy to handle her case. "When would you like to book our first meeting?" he adds, as he opens his appointment book. Mary declines to book a date just yet; she wants to check the second attorney's rates first.

When she reaches the second attorney, she asks the same question—but she receives a very different response. This time, the attorney replies by first asking Mary a few questions about her situation. After he has listened to her for a few minutes, he begins to tell her about his service.

"Well, Mary, our practice is a little different from most family practices in the area, especially concerning divorce proceedings. Our goal is always to reach the most amicable and fair settlement possible for both parties—not only for our client, but for *both* clients involved.

"In approaching it this way," he continues, "we have found that over seventy percent of our clients have been able to achieve a cordial ongoing relationship with their ex-spouses, and they generally move past the divorce and on with their lives more quickly." And this is not just hype; he tells Mary that he'll have his secretary send her a packet of testimonials and survey data his firm has compiled that backs up what he's telling her. This law firm presents that same information on their website, in their brochures and other promotional materials, and in any public-speaking engagements they do. Why are they so consistent in making this information available and reinforcing its message? Because it speaks directly to their ideal clients' hot buttons, and illustrates the law firm's unique value.

"This positive approach," he continues, "has made it easier on both our clients and their ex-spouses—but especially so for any children involved, whom we regard as in many ways the most important parties to consider in the whole process." The attorney goes on to explain that his firm has developed several new approaches to help achieve this goal. And in doing this, he tells her, they have found that they typically are able to finalize a divorce 25 percent faster than the norm.

Finally, he tells her that his rates are $300 per hour.

Which one do you think Mary will choose? Chances are good that she'll go with the second attorney, because he took the time to tell Mary about the special features his firm provides, and how she will benefit from them. He informed her as to his firm's *value*. The fact that his firm's rates are 20 percent higher than the other firm's may be offset by shorter billing times, and even more so by the improved quality of life Mary will enjoy by pursuing this more positive approach to her case.

If the second attorney had not taken the time to educate Mary but had simply told her, "My rates are $300 an hour," he would have lost this client to the first attorney.

MATCHING WANTS WITH SOLUTIONS

No matter what the business is, every customer comes to it with certain problems, concerns, and frustrations. If you can identify what those are, if you can discover what it is that your ideal customer truly wants and then provide a solution that satisfies that desire, they'll buy from you each and every time.

In order to discover your ideal customers' genuine desires, we are going to crawl into their heads, using the information we've gathered so far, and analyze their hot buttons. Specifically, what does each hot button actually *mean* to them? Once we've done that, we'll compare that information with the product or service your business offers, to see whether or not your business solves those problems and fulfills those wants in a way that meets your customers' expectations. To do this, we're going to methodically examine each hot button and ask:

1. What does that hot button really mean to your ideal customer?

2. Does your business presently match that want with an ideal solution?

If you can answer that second question with an enthusiastic and unequivocal "Yes—absolutely!" then you deserve congratulations. But check yourself for honesty. For most of us, running our business through this exercise will reveal, if not outright flaws and deficiencies, at least areas where we could stand to improve. Remember, we're asking you if your business matches what your customer wants, not just with a solution, but with an *ideal* solution.

These two steps alone are not enough, because simply *meeting* your customers' expectations will not make your business extraordinary. What you really want is to meet *and exceed* your customers' expectations. And to do that, we need to ask a third question:

3. What could you do that would create an extraordinary solution to that want?

This third question gives you the opportunity to brainstorm, and to truly *transform* your business. What you're looking for are creative and imaginative ways to innovate, to improve your business offering so that it will be so exceptional, so extraordinary, that it will provide not just *good* solutions but *outstanding and amazing* solutions—solutions that will put your business in a class by itself.

For example, let's say you own a plumbing business, and your ideal customer has a leaky pipe in her basement. Plumbing falls under the "service industry" category. Checking the list of hot buttons for the service industry in appendix 2 tells us that the hot button that tops the list for this group's ideal customer is "Fix it right."

That's pretty generic; what does that really mean? Once you've identified a particular hot button, it's important to spell out exactly *what that hot button means to your customers,* in terms that are specific to your business. In other words, you are using that hot button as a way to define the specific expectations your customers have for your business. We like to express this as an "I want . . ." statement, so that we stay focused on the *customer's want.* In this case, we can come up with three statements:

CUSTOMER WANTS ("I WANT . . .")

1. I want my broken water pipe fixed so it stops leaking.

2. I want the plumber to use quality materials so that it doesn't leak again.

3. I want the plumber to have the proper training and expertise so that it doesn't leak again.

The next step is to describe the solution your business presently offers that fulfills these wants. Since we're shifting from the customer's point of view to your business's point of view, we do this step as a "We . . ." statement.

OUR SOLUTIONS ("WE . . .")

1. We repair broken pipes by replacing the entire pipe, not just the fitting.

2. We use the highest grade of copper piping available on the market today.

3. We require our plumbing staff to be certified master plumbers with a minimum of five years experience.

So far, you've identified what your customer is looking for and how you meet that expectation—but simply *meeting* expectations is not going to build your dream business, attract your dream customers, and make them customers for life. Doing all that requires taking the next step.

EXTRAORDINARY IS MANDATORY

This is where the real power of defining hot buttons kicks in. Remember what we saw in chapter 6: *Extraordinary is mandatory.* This is where we're going to apply a methodical focus to make your business extraordinary by solving your ideal customers' most urgent wants and fulfilling *their* idea of value in an exceptional way.

Returning to our plumbing example, the first solution was, "We repair broken pipes by replacing the entire pipe, not just the fitting." That's a good solution, but it's not extraordinary. In fact, that's probably what most plumbers do. What could you possibly do to innovate and add extraordinary value to this type of repair? What additional steps could you take that no one else in your industry is taking?

Well, after you replace the entire pipe, you could do a physical inspection of all remaining plumbing features and check for corrosion. Instead of simply replacing the customer's broken pipe, taking her money, and leaving, you could painstakingly go through her entire home and check for any other corroding pipes that might create other problems in the near future.

The benefit of this approach is that it may save your ideal customer future water damage, along with the cost of a future service call. If one pipe is bad, chances are good that several others are in the same state of disrepair. Your customers will appreciate such attention to detail—especially since most plumbers don't take the additional time to do such an extensive inspection.

This single innovation begins to separate your plumbing business from all your competitors. It also provides you with a huge marketing advantage, because now you can market this additional service as a standard part of what you provide for *all* your customers. This one innovation increases the value of the service you provide. In fact, it would probably even allow you to charge more than your competition.

A little additional brainstorming on the second and third "I want . . ." problems and their current "We . . ." solutions yields additional innovations. For the "quality materials" customers want, you could install polypropylene piping that carries an additional ten-year guarantee that copper piping doesn't offer. And for the customer's expectation of "proper training and expertise," you could require that all your master plumbers earn six CEU credits in additional training annually.

INNOVATIVE THINKING ("WE COULD . . .")

1. We could do a physical inspection of all remaining plumbing features and check for corrosion after replacing the entire pipe assembly.

2. We could install polypropylene piping that carries an additional ten-year guarantee that copper piping doesn't offer.

3. We could require that all our master plumbers earn six CEU credits in additional training annually.

Finally, we complete the process by summarizing the benefit that all of this will ultimately bring to the customer:

We save you from future water damage plus the costs of future service calls.

Are you beginning to see why this exercise, if performed carefully and thoroughly, can absolutely revolutionize your business?

A DAYCARE CENTER'S HOT BUTTONS

Let's run through this process once again, this time using the daycare example.

Daycare falls into the *service* industry classification. One hot button in this industry is "Expected results." When someone does business with a service, they expect specific results from that service. But we need to define exactly what those specific results *are*, because that means different things for different professions. If I have LASIK surgery performed, I expect my vision to be corrected to 20/20. If I visit a chiropractor, I expect my back to stop hurting.

This is why we need that first step, the "I want . . ." questions. The daycare owner *must* define exactly what that hot button means to the customers she deals with every day. The best way to do this is to imagine that you are the customer, and ask yourself, "What would I want?"

Asking ourselves this question, here's what we come up with:

1. I want my child to receive actual instruction by real teachers, instead of just being watched by babysitters.

2. I want to know for sure that my child is being well cared for by competent staff members.

3. I want staff members who don't get irritated or frustrated when dealing with kids all day long.

These seem like reasonable expectations that most parents would have as they consider whether or not to place their child in your daycare center. Now, here are the solutions we find within that daycare business that match up with those customers' wants:

1. We hire staff members with instructional experience.

2. We provide all parents with written monthly incident reports concerning their children.

3. We rotate our staff members throughout the day to keep them fresh.

Those are good solutions—but not *great* solutions. What could we do to raise the bar so high, to create such unique value and extraordinary service, that we would clearly stand out from all the other daycare facilities in our area? We want to step outside the box and come up with new, different, better, and more innovative ways to improve on what we're already doing.

Brainstorming the first line, the one about staff members' experience, we come up with this idea:

1. We could require all staff members to be accredited teachers who specialize in accelerated learning for preschool children. Their credentials would be made public, both online and in the facility itself.

That sounds much more impressive and reassuring to parents considering daycare than simply telling them, "We hire staff members with instructional experience." And here is the benefit from that innovation:

The child will be better prepared when starting grade school.

Brainstorming the second "we" solution, how we report to our customers on their children, we come up with a really amazing idea that goes way, way beyond the scope of written monthly progress reports:

2. We could install WebWatch, a 24-hour webcam system that allows parents to log on to a website and observe their child at any time during the day.

Just think of the benefits this would offer the customer:

Parents will feel they're in control. This greatly increases their peace of mind, and removes all concerns and worries regarding staff competence and safety.

If you were a parent, wouldn't you gladly pay additional fees to be able to log on to a password-protected website and see exactly what your children were doing and how they were being treated, anytime you wanted to?

THE CREATIVE POWER OF BRAINSTORMING

As you work through this process, always remember this cardinal principle of brainstorming: *There are no stupid ideas.* Give your creativity full rein. Jot down whatever ideas come to mind, no matter how crazy they might seem at first. In fact, the most powerful innovations often come from ideas that seem outlandish or impossible when they first pop up.

In this example our client was a pediatric dentist who specialized in treating school-age kids, nine through eighteen. What would the hot buttons be for this dentist's ideal patients? For one thing, their kids are in school during the week, and in most American households today, both parents work outside the home. In order to get children to their dental appointments, one of the parents has to take off work, drive across town to pick up the child at school, drive her to the dentist, wait an hour or two in the waiting room while the dentist fixes the child's teeth, drive the child back to school, and then finally return to work.

Obviously, this is quite a hassle for the parent, not to mention loss of time at work, loss of wages if he or she doesn't have comp time as a benefit, and the cost of gas. Virtually every one of our dentist's clients faced this problem. He started brainstorming to see if he could come up with a way to innovate in this area and solve this problem for his clients.

First he thought about buying a van and hiring a driver to pick up the kids at their schools and drive them back and forth to their appointments. When he looked into this, he found that the premiums for the insurance he would need to cover himself in case of an accident were prohibitively high.

What about hiring a taxi service? They have their own insurance, and what's more, he wouldn't have to invest in the vehicle. As he researched this idea, he ran into another problem, not around cost but around the issue of trust. When he ran the taxi idea by some of his clients, he found that they had very strong reservations about having their children picked up and driven across town by unknown cabdrivers. Many parents said flat out that never under any circumstances would they allow their children to be picked up and driven to their appointments by taxicab.

Finally, the dentist had an idea that was so wild that at first he dismissed it as preposterous: What about a limousine service? After some investigation he discovered that limo drivers are carefully screened for alcohol and drug use, and they have to pass a rigorous background check. That should certainly handle the parents' concern about safety. And can you imagine how the kids would feel about walking out to their very own limo, with the driver holding the door for them, in front of their peers? The kids would go nuts! Hiring a limo service would also solve the insurance problem, because limo services are required by law to carry ample insurance.

But wouldn't this be tremendously expensive? That's what the dentist thought. In fact, the idea seemed so crazy that he almost didn't even bother to check it out. But it didn't seem crazy to us. The dentist does business during the day, which is a slow time for most limo companies, who do the bulk of their work in the evenings. It turned out that they would welcome the opportunity to provide their services to the dentist, to bring in some additional income during their slow time. In fact, they agreed to reduce their normal rate from $60 per hour to $25 per hour— a discount of more than 50 percent! This meant it would cost the dentist an average of $200 per day, or $1,000 per week.

So far so good, but now we were looking at adding $50,000 a year to the dentist's costs. Would it be worth it?

We looked at some numbers together and he decided to take the plunge. Business doubled almost overnight. His revenues increased by about $350,000 annually, all for an additional cost of $50,000 per year—which, by the way, was a tax-deductible business expense. What's more, to offset that additional cost, he raised his rates, and no one even blinked at the increase. The perceived value to the parents was worth the increase many times over. And how many parents would ever leave a dentist who was thoughtful and caring enough to provide such a service? The long-term value of this dentist's business shot through the roof.

In this example, who was the decision maker? Probably Mom: She wants only the best for her child, and the limo idea would bring her tremendous peace of mind. The influencer was probably Dad: He would feel tremendous pride that he was providing for his child in such style. This would also appeal to his ego. The user (and additional influencer) is obviously the child, who would love the status and excitement of being picked up at school in a limo. He'd come home from school on appointment days excited and thrilled with the experience. In fact, in another few months, he'd probably start asking, "Hey, Mom, how soon is my next dentist appointment?"

CASE STUDY: SCHLITZ BEER

In the early years of the twentieth century, Schlitz beer, then the fifth-bestselling beer in the United States, hired a man named Claude Hopkins to help them increase their market share. At that time, the rage in beers was purity. All the big brewers were blasting the word *pure* in their advertising, spending fortunes on two-page spreads so they could write the word in larger type than their competition.

In order to get to know his product, Hopkins took a tour of the Schlitz brewery. What an eye-opener! He learned that the air in the cooling rooms was carefully filtered so that the beer would remain completely pure as it cooled. He was told that the beer filters contained white wood pulp, which was used despite its extremely high cost because it provided by far the best filtering of any material available.

He saw men carefully cleaning each pump and pipe twice daily to eliminate any chance of contamination. He saw how every single beer bottle was cleaned and sterilized, not just once or even twice, but *four separate times* using custom steam-cleaning machinery before being filled with beer. And although the Schlitz brewery was situated on the shore of Lake Michigan, which back then was not even slightly polluted and would have provided an easy and inexpensive source of more clean water than they would ever need, Schlitz had dug a four-thousand-foot artesian well to provide the purest, cleanest water possible.

Hopkins was stunned at the lengths to which the brewery went to maintain their product's purity. He asked the people at Schlitz why they weren't telling the beer-buying public about all the amazing steps they were taking to actually *ensure* their product's purity, instead of simply screaming "pure" like everyone else.

Because, they told him, they were just doing what every other brewer was doing. That was just the way it was done. Hopkins thought about this. "This may be the way it's done," he concluded, "but *I* certainly didn't know that. And I don't think anyone else knows it, either."

He told Schlitz he wanted to base their entire ad campaign on educating the public—in great detail—about all the elaborate steps they took to guarantee the purity of their great-tasting beer.

The Schlitz people thought he was nuts, but they eventually gave him the go-ahead, and Hopkins created the ads. He told the world about the cooling rooms with their meticulously filtered air, about the zealous cleaning and sterilizing routines, and about the artesian well that went the extra mile. Beer drinkers responded in droves. Within a few months, Schlitz catapulted from fifth place in beer sales to a tie for first.

Hopkins educated customers about what was extraordinary about the beer business—and he did it first. Any brewer *could* have told that same story; it's just that none of them had bothered. And now it was too late: If any other brewers tried to copy Hopkins's ads, they would have looked like they were playing follow the leader. (If anything, it would have just helped bolster Schlitz's popularity!)

The moral is this: If you're not unique in your industry, then innovate so that you are. And if you think you can't afford to innovate, take a look at what you're already doing. Even if all your competitors are doing it, too, if nobody else has drawn attention to it, maybe you can be the first.

CASE STUDY: FUNDAMENTAL FITNESS

While doing the work to identify her ideal client, Fundamental Fitness founder Suzanne Thomas carefully researched her potential client demographic and noticed that the older population in her area was largely being ignored by her industry.

"These people are not as strong as they used to be," says Suzanne, "and they're susceptible to all sorts of health problems. They badly need a fitness program that speaks to their unique needs, yet nobody was offering any programs designed for them."

Once she had identified this specific demographic, it was easy to create an innovation to serve them: Fundamental Fitness started offering programs tailored specifically for seniors during the middle of the day. "This is normally our downtime," explains Suzanne. "The moms have already taken their classes and gone home again, and most of our other clients are at work. So we offered seniors a discount to come in between eleven o'clock and three o'clock, and we had staff here ready to show them around, work with them, and take some of the intimidation out of being in a gym facility."

Suzanne continues to look for new ways to innovate and provide her clients with unique benefits.

"We started offering yoga. We offered Zumba, a Latin American dance-exercise routine, and it took off like a rocket. We offer nutritional counseling, group fitness coaching, and mentoring. We have daycare for moms so they can come in and get a little relief, and work out in the mornings and in the evenings. Starting this week, we're offering ballroom dancing."

CASE STUDY: MOUNTAIN SUN ARCHITECTURE

When David Clarke put in his bid on a project to build seventeen town houses, he took the time to find out his potential clients' major hot buttons. "I was proposing a fairly good-sized fee," says David, "and their biggest concern was value: What were they getting for that fee?"

David had done some careful research and found that in traditional construction practices, there was a "normal" waste factor of about 30 percent built into the job. By using specific design methods, collaborative processes, and some advanced new software—and hiring a few people who knew that particular software application inside and out—David devised a way to cut that waste by nearly one third, which represented a huge financial savings to the contractor.

David described this approach in his proposal, and the key investor in the project (the one he had identified as the key decision maker, as we saw in chapter 11), was so impressed that he called David personally to talk to him about his cost-saving approach. Having done his homework so he could offer that one innovation, says David, was instrumental in securing this lucrative contract.

CASE STUDY: CANADIAN ACADEMY OF SENIOR ADVISORS

Rhonda Latreille, B.A., M.B.A., C.S.A., is the cofounder and president of the Canadian Academy of Senior Advisors (CASA), which she started initially with John Ostaf and Dr. John Crawford in the summer of 2003. Rhonda and her husband, Herb Latreille, are now the sole owners of CASA, and maintain the exclusive licensing rights to offer the Certified Senior Advisor (C.S.A.)® designation in Canada, a credential first introduced in the United States in 1997 as part of a plan to teach professionals about the health, social, and financial aspects of aging so that they could offer more age appropriate, relevant, and ethical services and products to a maturing population. "It's basically Gerontology 101 for professionals," says Rhonda. "The bottom line is that we teach professionals how to make their business more boomer- and senior-friendly."

Rhonda started with the business model she had inherited from the States: offering a course of twenty-four different modules, presented over a three-and-a-half-day event. "We were flying in experts from all across North America. With the flights, hotels, and other costs, it was a very expensive proposition with a brutally high break-even point."

Rhonda and Herb had poured their own resources into launching the company, and after two years, CASA had hit a wall. "We had good revenue coming in, but our profit margin was nonexistent," Rhonda says. "It was a struggle on every level—financial, logistic, and emotional. Just keeping up was exhausting. We knew we couldn't keep going the way we were—it was just not sustainable."

When Rhonda started working with us in the fall of 2005, we suggested she look for some way to offer the program on a smaller scale and in less time.

"At first I simply could not see how John and Murray's suggestion could possibly work," says Rhonda. "We also had a correspondence-course version of the program, but people liked the excitement of the live event. And with twenty-four modules of nearly an hour each, that made three solid eight-hour days. How could it possibly be compressed any further while maintaining the scope and standards of our renowned faculty? There was no way—because my reticular activating system was eliminating any other possibilities from view."

After a few months of coaching and neural reconditioning, John and Murray again advised that a new delivery model simply had to be considered, and this time Rhonda suddenly had an epiphany: "I now saw that we could create a combination of live classes *and* correspondence—and that by doing that, we could actually provide our clients with the best of both worlds: the experience of the live class *without* the financial drain of being away from their clients for a half a week."

Which is exactly what Rhonda did. CASA set up a one-day program to launch the material, flying in *one* faculty member (instead of eight or ten) to give participants that personal touch and live-event experience, and completed the course by leading the group through the rest of the material via a correspondence-style self-study.

Their clients loved it. The break-even point for a class immediately went down by 300 percent—and because attendance at the event no longer meant that their clients had to lose four days of work, CASA was able to attract more clients. Suddenly they were generating a profit.

One year after signing on with us, CASA's revenues had increased by 41 percent. After twenty months, revenues had nearly tripled in less than two years.

YOUR BUSINESS'S HOT BUTTONS

Now it's your turn. Go back to the list you made earlier in this chapter of the top three hot buttons for your business, and work through this process yourself. For each hot button, look for at least one or two "I want . . ." statements that describe exactly what your customers want from your business, and the "We . . ." solutions you presently offer.

If you honestly cannot think of what your ideal customers want, just ask them. Conduct a quick, simple survey by calling several of your best customers and asking them what problems or needs they most count on your business to solve or address for them. If you're just starting your business, choose two or three potential customers and ask them what their expectations are when they're in the market to buy what your business offers. Ask your family members, friends, or neighbors. Remember, there are no right or wrong answers here. You're simply analyzing what each hot button means from your ideal customer's point of view.

What if you can't come up with any "We . . ." solutions to match a particular customer want? Then you've just identified a significant deficiency in your business—you're not even *meeting* your customer's expectations, let alone *exceeding* them! If for any reason your business doesn't offer a solution to any of the "I want . . ." statements you came up with, then we urge you to make this aspect of your business your first priority!

AND NOW, INNOVATE!

It's no exaggeration to say that this last step of the process may be the most important single bit of business brainstorming you ever engage in. The ideas and innovations you generate at this point could positively revolutionize your business.

Review the work you've done so far, and then start to think up brand-new ways you might improve on each current solution you've identified. Take your time. Be open to any and all new ideas and possibilities. Keep a little notebook and pen handy at all times, and jot down every idea that pops into your head, no matter how wild or impractical it might sound at first. Many of these ideas may turn out not to be feasible or cost-effective—but you won't know for sure until you write them all down and then research each and every one of them. Remember the pediatric dentist: It only takes one idea—if it's the right idea—to put your business in a class by itself. And this is exactly what *must* happen if you want your business to become irresistibly attractive to your ideal customers.

For each innovative solution you come up with and decide to pursue, identify the greatest single benefit that this innovation will give your customers. This is where the care you took in identifying your top three hot buttons pays off, because now you can walk through this whole process for each one of the remaining hot buttons on your list.

It takes time to go through this entire process thoroughly for every hot button—but we can't even begin to describe how valuable it is. Don't skimp on this; this is where you'll create that edge of excellence that makes all the difference, and will lead to huge increases in revenue and profits. As you do, ask yourself this: How many of your competitors do you think are going through this exercise? *None of them.* This will give you a huge competitive advantage over your competition. Completing this process will move you and your business into the big leagues.

IDENTIFY THE BENEFITS THAT MAKE A DIFFERENCE

We breezed over that last step, the one about the "greatest single benefit," without going into it in any detail. Let's pause here for a moment to take a closer look.

The whole process of examining hot buttons and innovating your business isn't complete until you have filled in that last section by identifying the greatest single benefit your customer gets from the process. Why not? Because that benefit is the whole point of the exercise. It's the holy grail of business development: a compelling reason why your customer will always choose to buy from you, and not from your competitor.

In order to do this effectively, it's critical that you know how to distinguish among three things: features, advantages, and benefits.

- *Features* are the tangible components of your product or service.

- *Advantages* are the results produced by that product or service.

- *Benefits* are the emotional experiences produced by those features and advantages.

People don't buy cars; they don't buy homes. They don't buy a meal at a restaurant, a piece of jewelry from a jeweler, or a membership at a fitness center. They buy how that car, home, meal, pendant, or workout routine *will make them feel*. People don't buy features or advantages. They buy *benefits*.

For example, let's say you buy a car with a 400-horsepower engine. The engine is a feature, a physical component. The car accelerates from 0 to 60 mph in 5.5 seconds; that acceleration is an advantage produced by the engine. But when you go that fast that quickly, you also get an adrenaline rush, a sense of power and control that can't be put into words. *That's* the benefit—and *that's* what the customer wants.

Think for a moment about the book you are now holding in your hands. A *feature* of this book is that it brings together decades of research from such widely divergent areas as neuroscience, quantum physics, business coaching, and practical, hands-on business development. That feature gives the book the *advantage* of having a uniquely comprehensive, whole-person approach to business growth. The *benefit* of this approach is that it gives you *the answers you need* to make your business wildly successful.

How excited would you have been about this book if we had called it A *Multidisciplinary Look at Neuroscience, Quantum Physics, Business Coaching, and Hands-On Business Development?* Not so excited? How about this: A *Uniquely Comprehensive Guide to Business Growth?* Chances are, you still wouldn't be convinced this was a book you wanted or needed. So we titled it *The Answer*. Any one of these three titles would have been just as truthful and just as accurate. But we went with *The Answer* because you're our ideal customer, and *the answer is what you want*.

Know exactly what your ideal customer wants and exactly how you fulfill and exceed that expectation, and you've got a business that's destined for greatness.

13

FINDING YOUR BUSINESS'S DNA

If you've ever seen a karate demonstration, you've probably seen a person break a wooden board or even a brick with his foot or bare hand. Impressive, but with the right training, you could probably do that, too, right? Yes, but now picture this: In the aftermath of tornadoes in the American Midwest, steel plates have been found that had been run through *by pieces of straw*. What force could possibly cause something as flimsy as a piece of straw to penetrate a sheet of steel?

That's the power of focus. It's the same force we brought to bear on creating your vision for your business and the supporting beliefs you needed to support that vision. It's the same force we used to craft your picture of your ideal customer. And it's the force we're going to use now as we clarify the very essence of your business. We'll do this by creating a message that speaks specifically to your ideal customers—a message so targeted and powerful that every ideal customer who hears it will immediately ask, "How do you do *that*?"

How can one simple message possibly be so powerful? Because, of all the advantages and features your business offers, it focuses on the benefits your customers want. By highlighting these benefits, this message will make your ideal customers realize that you are not just the best business that meets their individual needs and wants—you are the *only* one that does.

This message is known as a *Unique Selling Proposition*, or USP, and it is the DNA of your business.

USP: YOUR DNA

Your USP is the most important single benefit that you offer to your buyers, the one that differentiates you completely and unequivocally from your competition. It focuses on the unique characteristic of your product or service, both in terms of what is especially important to your customer and in terms of what it is that you offer that your competition does not. It is the reason your customers will insist on buying from you and nobody else.

People often see a USP as simply a clever marketing message, but it's much, much more than that. A strong USP forms the foundation for how you innovate your brand, determine your pricing, train your employees, and make thousands of decisions about any and every aspect of how your business operates. Wal-Mart has created the largest retailer in the world and produced some of the wealthiest individuals on the planet by faithfully and constantly using their USP to define every aspect of their business:

"Wal-Mart: Save money. Live Better."

A well-crafted USP gives you the ability to communicate what you do in a single sentence so that everyone gets it. Most companies can't do that. They might have a mission statement somewhere, filed away or tacked up on a wall, but 99 percent of the employees wouldn't be able to tell you what it is.

If you walked into the boardroom of Ford Motor Company or General Motors and asked each person in the room to describe the company's mission in thirty seconds or less, you'd probably hear something different from each person. How do we know this? Because you can see it in their results. GM has lost track of their ideal customer; they are trying to be all things to all people, which is a recipe for disaster.

However, ask that same question in the boardroom at Lexus, and we'll bet that anyone in the room would be able to nail it in a sentence without blinking an eye—and it would be *the same sentence*, no matter which person you asked: "Lexus: The Pursuit of Perfection."

Why? Because they know their USP. They know who their ideal customer is and they know who *they* are.

Notice that the USPs of Wal-Mart and Lexus could not be more different. Wal-Mart's is based on the lowest possible price, while Lexus's is based on the ultimate in quality and is therefore aimed at the high end of the price scale. But that's not the point. The point is, they each do what they do very well—in large part because they know their own DNA.

While many businesses create taglines and mottoes to capture attention and create a memorable impression, your USP does far more than that. It is the heart and soul of your business. Your USP conveys what it is your business stands for, and it communicates this both to the outside world and to everyone in your business. Your USP helps you engage all who come into contact with your business, from prospects and customers to employees, suppliers, and investors.

In this chapter, we're going to show you a few examples of outstanding USPs and walk you through the process of creating one yourself.

A POWERFUL BENEFIT STATEMENT—NOT FEATURE STATEMENT

Creating a genuinely effective marketing program starts with developing a clear, concise message that explains exactly what your business does and how that benefits your ideal customer. That is the purpose of a Unique Selling Proposition. Crafting a compelling, powerful USP is a vital step toward differentiating yourself in a competitive market. Your USP will become one of the major causes of your future success, not only with regard to your marketing, but in everything you do, from product development to customer retention.

It's not enough to create a USP; you must also *use* it. Once you've invested the time and care it will take to design the perfect message, you then need to integrate it into every step and every touch point of your business: your business cards, stationery, website and marketing collateral, your marketing scripts, and the language your employees use when interacting with prospective customers.

Developing a powerful USP can make the difference between becoming a huge success or an also-ran. If you want your business to be incredibly successful, if you want your company to be recognized as the preeminent leader in your market or industry, if you want your business to grow exponentially, then you *must* have a remarkable USP.

The majority of business owners today are making the mistake of emphasizing the features of their product or service instead of the benefits they provide to customers. Computers are advertised for their processor speed, memory, and hard drive. Televisions are listed by their features—screen size and type, plasma or LCD, HDTV or HDTV-ready, projection or direct view. Cars and trucks are touted for their horsepower ratings, gas mileage, and options lists. Digital cameras by the number of megapixels they offer. Soft drinks by the number of calories they contain. Who cares? It's all a waste of words, dollars, and—most precious of all—the attention of potential customers.

Features can certainly distinguish one product or service from another, but they are not likely to sway a prospective customer enough to make the decision to purchase, especially if the features are not clearly and readily translated into benefits. Your prospective customer will always ask himself or herself three questions:

What does this mean to me?

Why should I buy this product or service over all the others being offered?

Why should I buy it from *you*?

Your USP will answer all three questions before they're even asked. Your USP must accomplish two tasks: It must tell your customer what, why, and how your product or service fulfills their wants and needs, and it must differentiate your business from your competition.

THE ELEVATOR PITCH

Imagine this scenario: You step into an elevator and the person standing there gives you a friendly nod. You exchange greetings. You ask him what he does, and he tells you. Then he asks, "So, what do *you* do?"

You've got about thirty seconds to respond. What do you say?

This scenario is the classic setup for what is commonly called the *elevator pitch*—a clear, powerful, well-thought-out statement of your business's most compelling value, that you can deliver anytime, anywhere, on the spot, in thirty seconds. In fact, an elevator pitch is really just a statement of your business's USP, delivered in a natural, conversational way.

There is a formula for this that works brilliantly, and it comes in two parts: problem and solution. The problem half starts with the words "You know how . . . ?" and then goes into a description of the problem your customers experience *before* they buy your product or service. The solution part comes next, starting with the phrase "What we do is . . . ," and going on to explain how your product or service happily resolves your customer's problem.

A POWERFUL ELEVATOR PITCH

"You know how . . . (description of customer's problem)?"

"Well, what we do is . . . (description of your business's solution)."

If that sounds like a lot to do in thirty seconds, it's not. Actually, it couldn't be easier. Here's an example:

"You know how when you call plumbers to fix a leak, they make you sit around waiting all day for them to show up?"

Your new friend will be nodding at this point. Of course he knows about this problem. We all do. And even if he's never actually had that experience, he can easily imagine it. *You know how* are magic words: They instantly put the two of you on the same side of the situation, two comrades sharing a universal experience. And most important, you've painted a vivid picture of a problem that you are now about to magically solve.

"What we do is, we treat our customers with courtesy and respect for their time by guaranteeing that we'll arrive within fifteen minutes of our appointment time, and we'll fix the problem properly and quickly so you can do the more important things in your life."

In Hollywood, there's a saying about how to write a good screenplay: "In act one, you get your hero stuck up in a tree; in act two, you throw rocks at him while he's up there; in act three, you get him down again." A good elevator pitch is like a thirty-second movie: You get your hero up a tree, and then you miraculously get him safely down again. You've created a word picture of a problem—and of how you solve it.

As they sometimes say in the advertising business, "Wound 'em, then heal 'em." In order to capture someone's attention, you have to tap into their emotions—in this case, the pain our potential customers feel when they're suffering with leaky plumbing and don't have a plumbing service as trustworthy, reliable, and attentive as ours. We tap into that pain, and then we lead them out of it, healing their suffering.

ENGAGE WITH EMOTION, JUSTIFY WITH LOGIC

All good selling engages the customer with emotion, but emotion is not all there is to it. Logic comes into play as well. It works like this:

People buy based on emotions, and they justify their purchases with logic.

That's why you want to mention your product or service's specific features, too, and not only the benefits it provides. While benefits are what customers really want, the features will satisfy their need to justify their emotional buying decisions with logic.

That first phrase, "You know how . . . ," must always connect to your customer's most compelling emotions. Think about the things that anger or frustrate them when they find themselves in the situation you are describing. What frustrates you when you go to the doctor? More than likely, it's the long wait. If you're a health professional in private practice, that's probably a great place to innovate. What would happen if you offered a ten-minute no-wait guarantee? This would also be a great place to focus on how to create emotion for your USP.

What frustrates you when you go to a restaurant? It may be the long wait for a table, or the noisy kids at the next table, or the slow service, or the inconsistent quality of the food. There's plenty of room there to innovate and create a memorable USP.

Tap into a strong emotion, and prospective customers will pay attention to your USP.

CREATING A CONCISE USP

There are times when you'll engage someone in conversation and use that elevator-pitch version of your USP, but to capture the very essence of your competitive advantage, you need to reduce that explanation to a single, short, catchy phrase or slogan. The best way to do this is simply to start jotting down phrases and parts of sentences. Don't evaluate or even think about what you're writing; just let your mind wander over the various benefits your business offers, and get your random thoughts down on paper.

Many professional copywriters use a simple yet fascinating tool in situations like this. It's called a *Mind Map*, and here's how it works: Take out a sheet of paper, and in the center of the page write down what your business does. In the example we're working with, we would write the word *plumbing*. Then begin listing all the benefits your business provides your customers as those benefits randomly occur to you (see the example below).

FIXED FAST   FRIENDLY   FIXED RIGHT

ON TIME — PLUMBING REPAIRS — NO WAIT

GUARANTEE OR FREE   CONTACT IF RUNNING LATE   15 MINUTE ARRIVAL TIME

The powerful thing about a Mind Map is that it allows your creativity to operate unhindered, without imposing any kind of rational or analytical structure on it. This is actually the way the human mind works: in random sequences. Your brain doesn't really have structured thoughts; it has thoughts triggered by millions of stimuli at once—and *after* we've had the thoughts, our analytical process begins poking through them and looking for ways to sequence and rearrange them.

With Mind Mapping, one thought can immediately trigger another thought that goes in an entirely different direction—and that thought, or the next, or the one after that, may be the thought that really captures what you're looking for.

PRIORITIZE THE BENEFITS

Once you've completed brainstorming your Mind Map, go through the benefits you've recorded and pick out those that seem like they would be the most powerful from your customers' point of view. Put yourself in their place and ask, "If I needed a plumber, which of these would mean the most to me?"

From our Mind-Mapped brainstorm diagram we've picked out the phrases *on time*, *no wait*, and *guarantee or free* as offering the strongest benefits, since we absolutely hate to wait around for someone to finally show up. What about *fixed fast*, *friendly*, and *fixed right*? They're not bad, but if we're hiring a plumber, we pretty much assume those benefits. What's more, every other plumber makes those same claims. *Contact if running late* is really more of a negative than a positive. And *fifteen-minute arrival time* means basically the same thing as *no wait*, but it doesn't sound quite as compelling.

After sorting through them all, we end up with these three benefits: *on time*, *no wait*, and *guarantee or free*. Putting all these together to build a powerful and compelling USP in a single phrase, we come up with:

"On-time plumbing repairs with a no-wait guarantee—or it's free."

If we heard a plumber say this, we would want to ask them, "How do you do *that*?" And that's exactly what a USP is supposed to do: get your prospects to engage you in learning more about your product or service. Everyone who hears your USP—in either its elevator-pitch or its slogan form—should instantly ask you, "How do you do that?" If they don't, you have some additional work to do.

CASE STUDY: RE/MAX

In the 1970s, most real estate offices paid their agents through a fixed split-commission system that offered little incentive for top performers, and the industry experienced a very high turnover rate, creating lots of relatively inexperienced and unprofessional Realtors. Dave and Gail Liniger wanted to change that, and they vowed to rid the industry of its amateur image by creating a national real estate sales force that would establish themselves as professionals of a higher standard.

In creating their company, RE/MAX, the Linigers created a USP that they emblazoned on the sides of their trademark red, white, and blue hot-air balloons. This USP trumpeted the essence of their mission and their unique value from the skies, until virtually everyone in the country had seen it: "Above the Crowd!®" In time, RE/MAX added another slogan, "Outstanding Agents, Outstanding Results.®"

RE/MAX has grown every single month for more than thirty years. They've been able to achieve this remarkable result because they've remained true to their terrific USPs.

CASE STUDY: INDIAN MOTORCYCLE

When Murray took over the Indian Motorcycle name in 1999, he knew the company needed to identify and communicate the brand's value, which required it to develop a USP. In order to do that, the new company first needed to identify its ideal customer.

The new Indian Motorcycle knew it didn't want to compete with Harley-Davidson and sell to bikers. It wanted to cater to a clientele that had more disposable income, to the professionals—doctors, lawyers, and others—who placed a value on higher quality and had the money to pay for it. The company decided not to build a $13,000 motorcycle to compete with Harley-Davidson; we decided to build a $40,000 motorcycle that would be in a class of its own. Instead of producing a $195 leather jacket that competed with everyone else's brand, Indian Motorcycle produced a $1,200 jacket that made a statement.

The new Indian Motorcycle wanted to attract customers who would value those products enough to pay higher prices. And it wanted to honor the values of Murray's team as well: They wanted to do something of great quality. Once they went through this careful process of identifying what it was they were really up to, they had their USP: "When quality is worth more than price."

The new Indian Motorcycle company used its USP as a lighthouse to guide all its decision making—and that image evoked the Law of Attraction. Once it opened its doors, it started attracting customers like crazy.

When you create your USP, you're creating a thread that, when you tug on it, unravels the entire structure of the company and lays everything out clearly for all to see.

CASE STUDY: OUR OWN BUSINESS

We went through this process ourselves when we began laying the foundation for how we were going to serve business owners. We poured dozens of hours into the process of identifying our ideal client, and dozens more into defining and refining different versions of our business vision and Unique Selling Proposition.

Our purpose is to help people build their dream businesses—not just "large businesses," but their *dream* businesses. We are not focused purely on money or financial success. We're interested in great achievements, the realization of people's biggest dreams. In our view, building a successful business is not an end unto itself; it's a vehicle for creating and expressing a dream life. Genuine success is something you achieve on many levels—not only financially, but also in your health, your family and personal life, your spiritual life, and more. Success isn't a singular thing; instead it's the full expression of a successful life, in all its dimensions.

So how do we express all that in a single phrase? When we went through this process, here is the USP we ended up creating:

More business, more money, more life.™

CASE STUDY: FUNDAMENTAL FITNESS

Let's take another look at Suzanne Thomas's innovative approach to the fitness business she renovated. Along with identifying her ideal client base and finding innovative ways to serve that clientele, Suzanne dedicated some time to carefully defining the heart and soul of Fundamental Fitness and distilling that essence into a short USP. The first thing she looked at was the distinction of price versus value.

"In the gym industry," says Suzanne, "everyone else competes on price. I decided not to do that. Instead, I wanted to offer a quality product."

Suzanne had defined her ideal clientele as people with a serious commitment to improving their fitness. She also realized that her clients were especially busy people who *wanted* to devote the time to their fitness, but for whom discretionary time was at an absolute premium. To her ideal client, time held far more value than money. Once she had carefully identified her ideal client's top-of-list needs and wants, it didn't take her long to define Fundamental Fitness's Unique Selling Proposition:

"We get you in the best shape of your life in half the time."

When people ask, "How do you do that?" Suzanne says she and her staff are ready with the answer: "When you come into our center, we spend time with you showing you exactly what to do, how to do it, and when to change it. We spend the time up front to make sure you are genuinely well educated in what you need, and then we're there to support you in accomplishing that."

Here are some more examples of great USPs we've heard:

USP EXAMPLES

- When what you drive says who you are.

- We help people stay at four-star hotels for Motel 6 prices.

- We turn your financial liabilities into assets that work for you.

- Fresh, hot pizza delivered in thirty minutes or less—guaranteed!

- Guaranteed for as long as you own your car.

- Fifteen minutes could save you 15 percent on car insurance.

CREATE AN ELEVATOR PITCH FOR YOUR BUSINESS

Now it's your turn. Review the work you've done in identifying your ideal customer's hot buttons and the innovations your company provides that make you stand apart from the competition. Consider the most pressing, most compelling, most painful or frustrating problems your customers face that cause them to look to you and your business.

Complete the "You know how . . ." and "What we do is . . ." statements as concisely as possible. Fewer words will have more impact.

MY ELEVATOR PITCH

You know how . . . _____

_____?

What we do is . . . _____

_____.

YOUR CONCISE USP

Now take a stab at boiling your elevator pitch down to a single, catchy, memorable slogan. Again, give yourself time to play around with as many different phrases as you can think of. Use Mind Mapping; go back to your hot button exercises and think through your customers' top problems and benefits again. Put yourself in your customers' shoes and ask yourself, What is the biggest frustration, challenge, or pain that a business like this one might solve or address for me—that is, if that business were truly amazing, genuinely in a class by itself? And what would it feel like?

Take some time to work up a short USP. Don't worry if it's not perfect, and don't worry if it takes a while to come up with just the right sentence or phrase. Remember, you want your USP to compel your prospects to inquire about your product or service. Keep writing and rewriting it until it does. It could take days or weeks or even months to get it right. How do you know when you've gotten it right? When people respond by saying, "How do you do that?!"

MY USP

_____

_____

_____

CASE STUDY: WORLD VENTURES TRAVEL

Is it worth all that effort? Just ask Dave and Yvette Ulloa. Dave is a former police officer with the LAPD; Yvette worked in economic development for the city of Burbank. Together they joined a network marketing business in the travel industry, with big dreams of financial freedom. However, by the time they came to us, their business had stopped growing and had even begun to decline. They had reached about the same income level they'd had in their former jobs, but they hadn't been able to break through that ceiling and take it to the next level. Part of the work they did with us involved resetting their "neural thermostat" and creating some new beliefs through neural reconditioning. Another big piece of their work had to do with defining their ideal client and arriving at a clear USP.

Dave and Yvette offer their clients the opportunity to set up an in-home travel agency that books trips and vacations for families. Their very first USP sounded like this:

> **We help people diversify their income portfolio options while taking trips.**

It's long, it's wordy, and worst of all, it's not compelling. In fact, most people who hear the phrase *diversify their income portfolio options* start to frown as their brains go to work trying to figure out exactly what was just said.

This kind of wordy, jargon-laden slogan is amazingly common. For some reason, businesspeople often think they have to use complex terms to impress prospective customers. In fact, the exact opposite is true. Prospects don't want to be impressed. They just want to know how your product or service is going to *benefit them*.

Dave and Yvette worked with us for a full three months on their new USP, and they finally got there:

We help people make money while taking dream vacations.

Now *that's* a USP. It's short, it's compelling, it grabs your attention, and it makes you instantly want to ask, "How do you do that?"

That benefit-rich slogan is only ten words long. The time it took them to come up with it averages out to more than a week per word! Was it worth it? Consider this: In the few months after implementing this new USP, their revenue increased by more than 400 percent!

That's the power of a compelling USP. That's why it's worth taking the time and effort to create one, and why you then want to integrate it into everything you do.

LET YOUR USP BECOME YOUR MANTRA

Once you've created a powerful, compelling USP, the next step is to integrate it into everything you do and repeat it until it becomes part of the very DNA of your business.

Dave and Yvette use their phrase at every networking event they attend, and they walk out with prospects galore. They use it at chamber of commerce events, at seminars, and whenever they introduce themselves to strangers. They use it on their website. They use it anywhere and everywhere, and whenever they do, *everyone* who hears it has the same response: "Really! How do you do *that?*"

A good USP is like a beacon. It attracts customers by the droves. It drives your profits through the roof. It gets your staff on the same page. It reduces disputes and mismanagement of projects within your business by providing a specific focus. It brings huge success to areas that used to be difficult, such as marketing. It is the most powerful tool your business will ever own.

A lot of people have fun with this part of the process. But remember, it *is* a process, and it's important to take the right steps in the right sequence. It might be tempting to plunge in and start brainstorming on your USP; that's the fun part, the sexy part, the "me" part. But you *must* do the other steps first. There's no point in working on how to best position yourself to attract your ideal customer until you've determined who your ideal customer is, and what he or she wants.

Once you do have your ideal customer profile, then devote as much time as you need to develop the right USP. And once you have it, return to it periodically and take a fresh look—tweak, refine, reexamine. There will always be a new and better way to get your message out to your ideal customer, and you continually need to be on the lookout for that new and better way for as long as you are in business.

14

REACHING YOUR IDEAL CUSTOMER

Now that you know who your ideal customers are and what they want, and you've expressed the way your business satisfies those desires in a single, powerful phrase, let's explore how to reach those ideal customers by creating the ideal marketing for your business.

Marketing is all about improving the odds of communication: crafting just the right message and finding the right channel and form of communication to convey that message to the right people. There are several ways to go about this. You can get expert opinions on what you should do. You could start with an intuitive sense of how you've acquired your customers. Or you might reason it out. However you arrive at your initial strategies and tactics, your next step is the phase that marketing is famous for: test, research, tweak, and test some more.

LOOK FOR YOUR CUSTOMERS WHERE THEY ARE

You may have heard the joke about the guy outside the bar who is scuffling around on the ground under a corner streetlight. A policeman comes along and asks him what he's doing. "I lost my keys," the man replies. The policeman helps him look, but after ten minutes they find nothing. Exasperated, the policeman asks the man, "Are you sure you dropped them here?"

"No, I dropped them way over there, by my car," the man replies, pointing at a parked car twenty yards away, "but the light's better over here."

No matter how hard he looks, that guy is never going to find his keys—and the same thing applies to your business. No matter how much money or effort you put into a marketing campaign, you're not going to attract your ideal customers unless you go looking for them where they actually *are*, and not just where the light happens to be.

We worked with a client who was a chiropractor seeking to expand his business. He talked with other chiropractors in his area to see what they were doing to attract more clients, and learned that they were sending out flyers in the mail. One colleague he talked with had rented a mailing list, printed up flyers, and sent out mailings to five thousand names.

"How did it work?" our friend asked.

"Not that great," said the colleague, "I got two leads."

The total cost of his campaign was $600. Those were two expensive leads—and neither one of them ended up actually becoming a client!

Before doing anything, our client asked himself, "Where is my ideal client?" Most of his best clients came to him suffering from back pain. In many cases, this pain would keep them up late at night. The pain was not so agonizing that it would send them to the hospital, but it was bad enough that they couldn't sleep; nor could they do much else that required focus, like reading. So they would end up watching television on the couch until late at night.

Our client researched the cost of advertising on the local cable TV network, found it to be quite reasonable, and ran a series of inexpensive late-night cable TV ads. He got 125 leads in just four days. Total cost of the campaign: $500. That's four bucks per lead—and *dozens* of them became paying clients.

That's the difference a little planning can make.

CHOOSE THE RIGHT DISTRIBUTION CHANNEL

Our chiropractor client understood that the first step in thinking about how to reach your ideal customer is to decide *where* are you most likely to find him. Another way to put this is to ask, What is the right *distribution channel* for your business?

A distribution channel is the model or vehicle through which your customers will make their transactions with your business. The particular distribution you choose for your business will also determine where your ideal customer is most likely to hear your message. Below is a list of the seven basic distribution channels (a brief description of these seven channels appears in appendix 3).

- Direct sales

- Sales agents

- Phone sales

- Mail order

- Online

- Retail

- Events

Your business may take advantage of one or more of these channels. Each will require a specific and distinct communication strategy.

For example, when Murray went to work for Telecommunications Terminal Systems in the early eighties, they wanted to create a coast-to-coast telecom company that would be the first national organization of its kind; previously, such companies had operated only within individual provinces. Murray knew that they could never achieve this objective through the channel of direct sales (or at least, not on their timetable), so they went with the distribution channel of *sales agents* and set up a national network of dealers. Using these dealerships as local service providers, Murray's team was able to create a national presence that helped the company generate $60 million in revenue within a fairly short time.

Think back to what you learned from creating your ideal customer profile and put yourself in your ideal customers' shoes, just as the chiropractor did. Where are they, and what are they doing when they are most likely to be experiencing that need or want that would bring them to your business? What do their days look like, or their nights? What magazines do they read? What are their media habits? If yours is a B2B business, then what trade publications and other business media are your customers using to inform themselves and stay current?

With your ideal customer's everyday life in mind, walk through that list of seven distribution channels, and see which one is most likely to match up with your customer. In other words, through which channel are you most likely able to reach your prospects with your marketing message?

CASE STUDY: COACHING FRANCHISE

When we were going through the original planning for our new franchise company, we knew from the start that we wanted to have a global impact and touch the lives of millions of businesspeople. We also knew that we wanted to preserve a sense of immediacy, and to maintain that quality experience with our clients no matter how large we grew. At the beginning, we began thinking about the ideal distribution channel to accomplish those goals.

It wasn't a quick or simple choice, because there were many candidates. We could have used the direct sales channel, for example, by creating branch offices run by our central headquarters in San Diego. Or, again going with direct sales, we could have built a massive facility here in Southern California, like a university, and designed educational programs that would bring clients from all over the world to this one location. We could have decided to license to other organizations; and there were several other options we looked at, any one of which would have been feasible.

We spent months looking at all the various channels and models, and finally concluded that there was only one model that perfectly fit the results and the experience that we wanted to create: franchising, a type of *sales agent* channel. To create the kind of passionately committed client experience we were after, we needed representation at the local level: We needed to have people on the ground in each locale, people who understood the unique qualities, character, economic conditions, and other aspects of that region in a way that we could never hope to do from one central location. We could have hired several thousand people around the world, but then we would have a structure with employees working at great distances from the home office, and we didn't think they'd have the same stake in the process as someone who had paid a significant franchise fee to develop opportunity in his or her own area.

We decided to use a two-tiered franchise model, creating a group of roughly one hundred master franchisees (whom we call *regional own-ers*), who would then develop and support a network of fifteen hundred local franchisees (*business partners*) within their region. Franchise op-erations are moving away from such two-tiered models, because they take profit away from the franchisees and put it into the hands of the corporation. But it made perfect sense to us: Relinquishing a piece of profit would support our long-term vision by giving us far greater con-trol of the brand, the integrity of the training model, and the quality of the client experience at the local level.

The franchise model also allowed us to focus on our core competen-cies. Our most highly developed skills and abilities are in the areas of training, sales, marketing, management, and infrastructure. Achieving the same goals with a direct sales model would have required creating a company with some one thousand employees and one hundred man-agers, which would have introduced a colossal distraction from what we do best. Clearly, franchising was the best distribution channel for us: No other model quite fit.

We designed and launched our business mastery program, started growing our executive team, and got some experience under our belts. A year into the project, after more than three thousand businesses served in thirty-three countries, we made the final decision to proceed with franchising, and we spent a year getting the regulatory processes in place, so that by the time our company was two years old and we had fully tested our program, we would be ready to start selling franchise rights, first nationally and then internationally. Right on schedule, we sold our first ten regions, and we've been growing steadily ever since.

CHOOSING THE RIGHT CHANNEL FOR DAYCARE

Let's return to our example of the daycare service and see how we could use what we now know to choose the ideal distribution channel for reaching our ideal customers.

Based on our work in chapter 11, we know that the ideal customer for your daycare service is a woman, from twenty-one to forty-five years of age, married, with one to three children, employed, a homeowner, with a total annual household income of $70,000 or more. Based on our work in chapter 12, we also know what our customer wants: safe, affordable daycare that will provide an educational component within a nurturing, loving environment.

Now, where will we reach her? Let's look through the seven major distribution channels.

Our ideal customer's age range suggests that she is probably Internet-savvy, making the *online* channel a good possibility. Because she is a homeowner with young kids, chances are good that she spends the majority of her nonworking hours in the home, which makes reaching her on the *phone* through a telemarketing service a good possibility. Also, given the nature of the service, most parents would probably want to come visit the daycare center in person before making their decision about using our services, which puts us in the *direct sales* channel.

What about the rest of the list? We can eliminate retail and mail order right off the bat, because daycare service is not something we can move through either of those channels. The last two channels, sales agents and events, don't seem conducive to our business, either. This leaves us with three candidates: *direct sales, phone sales,* and *online sales.*

By the way, this is a typical number of distribution channels to be considering at this stage. Although there are seven possible distribution channels to choose from, you'll almost always find that only a few apply to any given business. And by prioritizing these and examining them more closely, we can often narrow our options down to one.

Which of these channels is most likely to reach your ideal customer? The best way to answer this is to put yourself in your customer's shoes and imagine walking through her typical day. Like virtually all parents of young kids, she's probably swamped early in the morning as she hurries to dress herself and her kids, make breakfast for the family, drop the kids off at daycare, and get to her job on time. She's probably just as busy in the evening, too, not to mention completely exhausted by then. If we're going to reach her by using a call center, the only times we can reach her at home are in those early-morning and eve-ning hours. Given her hectic schedule and state of mind during those hours, how receptive is she likely to be to a telemarketing call? Scratch phone sales.

What about the online channel? This sounds logical—but take an-other look at that day we just walked through. How much time is she spending surfing the Web? Because she has so little free time, chances are good that she just gets online for the essentials, like paying bills, making some quick purchases, and possibly catching up with friends and family via email.

What's more, she is probably not even looking for a new daycare provider, because she already *has* daycare. Your daycare may offer sub-stantial advantages over her present provider, but she doesn't know that yet. We need to reach her with a message that will inform her about the superior benefits your daycare offers, but trying to generate leads on-line by creating a website is probably not going to do the job.

In less than five minutes, we've narrowed the field of distribution channels down to one: direct sales. You are now one of the few daycare owner/operators in your area, perhaps the *only* one, who already knows which distribution channel has the greatest chance of success for pro-moting and selling your service. You know where you will have your greatest chances of increasing customer response rates, which will al-low you to spend your marketing dollars with confidence and certainty as you go about increasing your revenue and your profits.

And imagine what your competition is doing. They are spending a small fortune designing, creating, and implementing an expensive website—a website that their ideal customer isn't looking for and will never find. They are hiring the services of an expensive call center that will only annoy their prospects.

But not you. You know which distribution channel has the greatest chance for success, based on the careful work you've done creating clarity and focus around your business. You're hiring some local moms whose kids have already left the nest to work for you part-time as sales-people, getting out the word about this unique, well-run, learning-oriented daycare center that allows parents to see their kids via webcam anytime they please.

CHOOSING THE RIGHT MARKETING STRATEGY

Now that you know where to reach your ideal customer, it's time to consider what marketing strategies you might use to get your message across. Here is a list of sixteen different strategies to consider. (This list appears, along with a brief description of each, in appendix 3.)

- Advertising (television, radio, print)
- Affiliate and joint venture
- Affinity marketing
- Barter
- Catalog marketing
- Direct marketing
- Event marketing
- Frequent-buyer programs
- Internet
- Outdoor media
- Point of purchase (POP) and point of sale (POS)
- Place-based media
- Promotions and cross-promotions
- Public relations (PR)
- Referrals
- Signage

That's a lot of choices! Fortunately, you won't need all of them. In fact, just as with the seven distribution channels, you'll typically find that just one or two of these methods will prove to be the most effective for your situation, in terms of both cost and response. And with the information you have assembled, that decision will now be far easier to make.

For this daycare operation, the marketing method that makes the most sense to us is direct marketing. This looks promising. We could purchase a highly defined list from a list broker and refine it further using our specific demographic profile information. We could target homeowners who live within a five-mile radius of our daycare center, and narrow that down further to families who have one or more kids and an income range of $70,000 and above. The specificity of this list will yield a small but highly targeted direct-mail list that would be inexpensive to buy, so we might be able to afford a whole series of mailings.

Now that you have your lead-generating strategy in place, you need to develop a tactical plan for the process.

CHOOSING THE RIGHT MARKETING TACTICS

Now that we've decided direct mail is our best option for communicating to our ideal customer, we need to decide on our tactical plan of action for implementing that strategy. Choosing our distribution channel tells us *where* we'll reach our best prospects; choosing the strategy tells us *what* we'll do to reach them; and choosing our specific tactics tells us *how.*

Distribution channel = where

Marketing strategy = what

Marketing tactic = how

In appendix 3 you'll find a fairly lengthy list of possible marketing tactics. This is not a complete list, because new tactics evolve and emerge constantly, but it is certainly extensive enough to give you a wide range of ideas to choose from.

When considering direct mail, we have several options. We could send a sales letter, a brochure, or a postcard. A sales letter might work—if it gets opened; these days, that's a long shot. Most people easily recognize business-related sales letters and will more than likely toss our letter out, unopened.

What about a brochure? A brochure might work if we designed it as a self-mailer—that is, a piece that is mailed by itself rather than being placed into an envelope. Here again, though, we have a problem: A brochure is also easily recognized as promotion and discarded before anyone reads the information.

Also, these different kinds of mailings will differ significantly in cost. Before we make any decision on how much to spend, we need to consider a factor that is all too often ignored.

YOUR CUSTOMER'S LIFETIME VALUE

You're well aware of the fact that before you launch into any marketing campaign, you need to weigh its costs against the estimated benefits. But in order to accurately assess those benefits, you need one critical piece of information: your customer's *lifetime value*.

Lifetime value refers to the amount of revenue and profit you can expect to receive from your ideal customer over the term of your relationship. Knowing your ideal customer's lifetime value gives you a tremendous advantage. This information drives all your lead-generation and marketing decisions, allowing you to focus your marketing dollars with far greater precision, accuracy, and productivity. It allows you to know ahead of time exactly how much money you can afford to spend on efforts to acquire each customer, and results in a far more predictable cash flow.

Not knowing this number leaves many businesses floundering in their marketing efforts, making hasty and ill-informed marketing decisions, some of which can even prove fatal to their businesses. Launching a marketing campaign without knowing this number is like flying a plane without a flight plan.

CASE STUDY: A CATALOG COMPANY'S
CUSTOMER ACQUISITION COST

Our colleague Jack Rued did some work a number of years ago for a catalog company that sold a line of home decorations. This company was basing its customer acquisition costs strictly on the dollar value of the average initial purchase. "They had never really considered the lifetime value of their customer," recalls Jack, "so it had never occurred to them that investing more money in customer acquisition than they got back in initial sales might be a profitable strategy."

At Jack's suggestion, they shifted their acquisition strategy and began investing at a "loss" of $15 for each new customer. "By the end of the first year," says Jack, "we had acquired so many repeat customers that gross revenues had increased by $8 million—simply by looking at the customer's lifetime value and changing our customer acquisition strategy."

Over the course of three years since making the change, the catalog company went on to grow fourfold.

HOW TO CALCULATE YOUR CUSTOMER'S LIFETIME VALUE

Calculating the lifetime value of your customer is simple. First, estimate your customer's *lifetime revenue*, that is, the amount of money he will spend with you throughout his "lifetime" with your business. In the United States, the average consumer moves about once every five years, so we typically use a figure of five years for the lifespan of a loyal customer, assuming that the customer will move out of our business's sphere of influence in five years. Given the particular nature of your business, you may have a typical customer lifetime of ten years, or three months; just give it your best guess.

Let's say you sell a product retailing at $100, and your customer purchases it once every 3 months (4 times per year). Using the default lifetime of 5 years, this gives us a lifetime revenue of $2,000 ($100 **x** 4 purchases per year **x** 5 years). Once you have your lifetime revenue, simply subtract all the expenses involved in generating that revenue, including your total cost of goods sold and the sales and marketing costs involved in acquiring that customer.

Let's say that $100 product you sell costs you $10 to produce and deliver. Because your customer purchases a total of 20 times (4 times per year for 5 years), your total cost of goods sold is $200. Let's also say you spend $90 in sales and marketing expenses to acquire that customer, plus another $500 over the course of the 5 years in communicating with that customer. That's a total cost of $790 ($200 plus $90 plus $500). The *lifetime profit* for this customer would be $1,210 ($2,000 lifetime revenue minus $790 in total costs).

Why is this number so important? Because if you make marketing decisions without knowing the lifetime value of your customer, you're shooting in the dark. And shooting in the dark is never going to create the success you want.

Take the example above: To sell that $100 product, you know it costs you $10 to produce it and another $90 to acquire that customer. When you make that first sale, you will just break even. Is it worth it to spend that much money—or even more—on marketing to that client? Looking at these numbers alone, it doesn't look like it. After all, you're not making any profit, right? You just broke even. You might well be tempted to stop marketing—and if you did, you'd be missing out on a huge opportunity for your business!

Knowing your customer's lifetime value tells you a whole different story. Even though you only broke even on that first sale, knowing your customer's lifetime value tells you that if you continue marketing and selling that product to that customer, you are ultimately going to make a profit of well over a thousand dollars ($1,210, in fact) from that one customer. Lifetime value is the reason cellular phone service companies can afford to give their customers cell phones at ridiculously cheap prices, or even for free: They know they'll more than make it up in revenues from the services the customers use.

What's more, for every dollar of revenue your business produces, you are dramatically increasing your business's *market value*. In some industries the multiple of annual revenues that is used to determine the value of a business can be as high as five, or ten, or even thirty. This means that if you increase your business's annual revenue by $100,000, that could increase the price tag on your business, if you decide to sell it, by as much as $3 million.

CUTTING THROUGH THE CLUTTER

Once you've decided on a marketing strategy, it's time to sharpen the focus of your message to ensure that you reach your prospect with enough impact to cause him or her to pick up the phone, walk into the store, or go to the website and get involved with your business.

Here is the problem any marketer faces: Your prospects are swimming, drowning, suffocating in marketing messages. We all are. In today's media-saturated world, we are exposed to a relentless barrage of advertising messages, from the moment we wake up to the time we go to bed. From television and radio, our morning newspaper and favorite magazines, our email inboxes and the websites we visit, billboards, subway signage, and park benches, messages claw at our eyes and ears for attention around the clock. Now we even find ads on fruit in the supermarket, corporate signage on secluded nature trails, and marketing pamphlets promoting products in dental and medical offices. And that flood of marketing messages is only going to continue to grow.

Because your prospects are inundated with marketing messages, they'll filter most of these messages right out of their conscious thoughts—unless one happens to hit them squarely on their hot button. And because you put the time and effort into investigating exactly who your prospects are, what their most pressing want is, and how your business fulfills it, that's exactly what your marketing message is going to do: make a bull's-eye hit on your ideal customer's hot button with a highly targeted and strategically placed message, compelling the prospect to become involved with your business.

To this end, hiring a professional copywriter is an investment that can be worth its weight in gold, providing you find a good one. (As with any professional, not all copywriters are alike; it's always best to get strong recommendations from the writer's past clients.) But whether you hire a professional or write your marketing materials yourself, you'll want to have a solid grasp of what makes an effective marketing message.

THE CUT-THROUGH-THE-CLUTTER MARKETING FORMULA

Effective marketing copy must:

- *grab* and *engage* the reader's attention;

- give the prospect enough compelling *information* so that he or she can make a cogent decision;

- *offer* a crystal clear, low-risk, easy-to-take next step so that your prospect can take action.

Note that this "next step" action may not necessarily be to plunk down their credit card right then and there to buy your product. It may be to pick up the phone to make an appointment to learn more, to order a free trial, or to visit a retail location. Whatever it is, you want to stimulate a concrete action step that gets your prospect actively involved with your business.

That's the cut-through-the-clutter formula:

grab • engage • inform • offer

Although we'll use the example of a written piece to illustrate this, exactly the same formula can and should be used with any and every marketing communication you create for your business. You can apply it to print ads, radio spots, TV commercials, brochures, flyers, live presentations, websites, e-letters, bag stuffers, coupons . . . *anything*.

Let's take a look at each one of these four steps in detail.

1. Grab

Before it can do anything else, your message first has to gain your prospect's attention, which you'll typically do with an attention-grabbing *headline*.

The headline is by far the most important single part of any ad. If your prospects don't read the headline, then they won't read the rest of the ad, no matter how well it's written. If your headline doesn't do its job, the rest of the project is nothing but a waste of time, effort, and money.

In a print piece, the headline is printed in the largest type; it's where the eye goes first. In a radio ad, the headline is the first thing the listener hears. No matter what the medium, every marketing piece starts with a headline—and that headline must grab the prospect's attention, effectively and immediately.

The right attention-grabbing headline also serves a crucial function that many marketers and business owners don't think about: It immediately *qualifies* your ideal customer and *disqualifies* those prospects who are not ideal. A well-written headline will grab *only* the attention of those prospects who genuinely need or want your product or service—and those are the only ones you want to grab, right?

You have already identified those needs and wants by creating your ideal customer profile in chapter 11, and you further refined and focused those wants through the "hot button" exercises of chapter 12. All this work you've done gives you the raw material you need to draw on for your headlines.

For example, let's say your daycare facility specializes in caring for children ages two to five. Let's say you've discovered that all the other daycare services in your area have a child-to-teacher ratio of about 10:1—that is, there is one teacher for every ten children. You've also learned that one of your ideal customer's hot buttons is making sure their child is getting enough personal, undivided attention and supervision. So you hit on this innovation: You could hire additional staff so that your child-to-teacher ratio would drop to 5:1.

Now we can use that hot button and your innovation to give us the raw material for your attention-grabbing headline:

> *Ever Feel Like Your Daycare Treats Your Child*
> *Like a Number Instead of a Little Person?*

Again, your headline will use the largest type in your entire piece, so that the reader's eye knows exactly which words to read first.

2. Engage

You've grabbed your prospect's attention; that's the good news. The bad news is that you only have it for the next two seconds—and then it'll be gone again. Remember, your customer lives in a world of media overload. Simply grabbing her attention is not going to get your message across, because only a moment after you've grabbed it, you've lost it again . . . *unless* you're carefully following the cut-through-the-clutter marketing formula.

Once you've grabbed your prospect's attention, you must ensure that the very next thing she reads *holds and engages* that attention—and that is the *subheadline's* job. The headline is like tapping on a glass with your spoon at a dinner party to get everyone's attention so you can give a toast. The subheadline is the first line you speak when you actually start *giving* the toast. Imagine your potential ideal customer is saying this to you as she distractedly glances at her watch:

> Okay, you've got my attention for the next ten seconds—what is it you want to tell me? And please, make it quick—I've got other places to be . . .

Your subheadline needs to *engage* your prospect's attention by persuasively promising to provide her with *vital decision-making information* that will resolve a major concern or frustration of hers. In other words, your subheadline builds on the impact of the headline and fleshes it out with enough specifics to make it sufficiently intriguing that the reader will want to read further:

> *Here's How to Ensure Your Child Gets Personal,*
> *Loving, Caring, One-on-One Attention at Daycare.*

Your subheadline will be set in the second-largest type in your piece, and it will be placed directly below (or after) your headline. Again you're leaving no room for ambiguity whatsoever: Your reader's eye knows exactly where to go.

3. Inform

Now that you've cleared some space for your message, you want to give your reader some significant, innovative information about how your business delivers on the promise of the headline and subheadline. This is the task of the lengthiest piece of text in your marketing piece: *the body copy.*

If your marketing piece were a trial lawyer, the headline and subheadline would be your opening statement. It's up to the body copy to detail your case by presenting all the relevant evidence to the jury. Your body copy must convince your prospects that you have the best daycare available. And simply *telling* them that you're the best isn't enough— you have to *prove* it.

In your body copy, make sure you emphasize the *benefits they want*, and not simply the *features you have*. The biggest and most common mistake businesspeople make is to focus on their business's features, and not on its benefits.

It's important to remember that every prospect is looking for the best deal—and this does *not* mean the lowest price: It means the most *value*. Prospects will pay a higher price if they understand the value of your product or service. Therefore, it's imperative that your body copy informs your prospects about your greatest value *with crystal clarity*. Again, this is why all that work you did in the last few chapters is so valuable. Without your ideal customer profile, and your list of hot buttons, and your innovations in place, you won't know the right information to provide in your marketing messages.

For your daycare piece, you'd want to make sure to highlight the fact that your child-to-teacher ratio is *half* that of all other daycare providers in the area. You would want to do this so that you don't come across as maliciously attacking your competition; you're simply informing parents that you have come up with an innovation for your daycare service that has their needs in mind. You might even point out that they're free to inquire at other daycare providers to verify the information you've given them. And, depending on how much room you have in your marketing piece, you might also highlight any other critical innovations you've made in your business.

It's important to make careful choices here. While the body copy is by far the longest portion of the piece, this is still a marketing piece, not an informational pamphlet, brochure, or catalog. Resist the temptation to throw in every bit of juicy information you can conjure up. Yes, you have successfully grabbed and held your prospect's attention—but the rest of the media-saturated world is still plucking at her sleeve, clamoring to be heard. You have a minute or two to inform her—not all day.

4. Offer

You must always end your marketing message with a *compelling offer*. Whether it is a postcard, a direct sales letter, a print ad, a television or radio commercial, a live presentation, or a web page—no matter the form or format, *every* piece needs to close with a compelling offer.

Why? Because if you don't, ninety-nine prospects out of a hundred will simply walk away. Your prospect will not take any action unless you ask her to do so *right now*—and give her a very good reason why.

Your offer has one purpose, and one purpose only: to lead your prospect to take action. This is why the offer step is often referred to as the *call to action*. Your compelling offer needs to be a low-risk or no-risk way to lead your prospect to take the next step in the sales process—to *take action*.

If you sell a low- or moderately priced product or service, the next action step might be to buy. If you sell a more expensive item, the next action step might be to request additional information. One excellent way to encourage your customer to do this is to offer a free informational report.

In our daycare example, the offer might look like this:

Get Our Free Report That
Compares the Child-Teacher Ratio
at All 17 Area Daycares.

When the prospect calls or goes online to request the report, you capture their contact information. If they don't buy from you immediately, you can then continue communicating to them using a series of additional compelling messages (all of which will follow the same cut-the-clutter formula), also known as a *drip campaign*.

Here's how this looks in all four steps:

Grab: *headline*;

Engage: *subheadline*;

Inform: *body copy*;

Offer: *call to action*.

Throughout these last few chapters, we've been using the example of a hypothetical daycare center. Now it's time for us to come clean: There was nothing hypothetical about it. A few years ago we worked with a client who ran a daycare center, and we went through this process with them, developing all the steps we've shown you here. By now you're probably wondering how the daycare campaign went. It went *very* well. In fact, this daycare center went on to absolutely dominate the market in its area.

And whether your business is a local daycare center, a billion-dollar conglomerate, or anything in between, you can do the same.

15

BIG THINKING

You've learned about the Law of Attraction, the Law of Gestation, and the Law of Action. You've learned how to create a crystal clear vision of your dream business and how to imprint that vision and its supporting beliefs onto the powerhouse of your nonconscious brain. You've discovered how to translate that vision into practical strategies and tactics by defining your ideal customer, creating innovations to make your business remarkable, creating a powerful Unique Selling Proposition, and choosing the ideal criteria for creating a powerfully effective marketing campaign. You've got a series of strategic planning tools, including gap analysis, revenue plan, sales process map, and customer lifetime value.

Will all of this guarantee your success? Do you now have The Answer?

Not entirely. Because there is one crucial factor we still need to cover. It is the hardest factor to define concretely, yet it is the essential element that brings together all these other ingredients. That's what this last chapter is for.

If you had a proven, time-tested recipe for the perfect birthday cake, and you gave out copies of that recipe to a dozen different people and set them loose in a dozen identical kitchens, would you end up with a dozen perfect birthday cakes? Of course not. You might have a few perfect cakes, a good number of fairly decent cakes, and perhaps a flop or two. No matter how perfect the recipe, there is always this variable: *the person baking the cake.*

What the individual brings to the recipe is that special ingredient, that element that cannot be measured in tablespoons, minutes, or degrees Fahrenheit. And all truly successful businesspeople have a certain special ingredient in common: *They think a certain way.* And because they think a certain way, they focus a certain way and act a certain way.

What's that special ingredient that makes stunning success possible? *Thinking big.* This chapter is dedicated to looking at what that means.

BIG THINKERS SEE THE BIG PICTURE

The two of us first met in 1980, when we happened to be seated next to each other at a dinner party. We hit it off immediately and ended up talking nonstop for hours. Then we got together the following week to talk some more. We became best friends and stayed in touch over the years. As we compared notes about our experiences in business, we noticed something interesting: Even though our two styles and approaches were very different, we were coming up with surprisingly similar core principles. Even though our brains work very differently, at a fundamental level *we were thinking the same way.*

John had focused his energy on learning how the brain works and how human beings create their reality, both in life and in business. John's explorations had led him to what we described in chapter 3 as the Law of Attraction, the Law of Gestation, and the Law of Action. Murray had focused his efforts on mapping out the components of a successful business and how they interact. His explorations had led him to what we described in chapter 10 as *vision, focus,* and *action.*

Two very different paths, one conclusion: It all starts with vision.

Big thinkers always have the big picture in view, no matter where they are in the process or what they are doing. They look at the whole business as a puzzle, and they see each of the individual pieces as well as the relationship of that piece to the bigger picture. They know at all times exactly where they are *and* where they want to be, and they have a clear picture of what's needed to bridge that gap.

At the same time, big thinkers are flexible, and they understand that goals change as you hit different thresholds. You don't know how things are going to turn out in twenty-five years—you *can't* know. Instead, you create a reachable target to hammer away at, and once you've hit that target you find a new one, and then another new one, and then another.

Big thinkers always know where they're going, even if they don't know exactly how they're going to get there. They know that you cannot achieve what you cannot define, and they go out of their way to define exactly what success means to them.

BIG THINKERS ARE DRIVEN BY PASSIONS, NOT MOODS OR MONEY

Big thinkers are unconditionally passionate about what they do. They know that money isn't success; it's simply one by-product of success. And they know that if they are genuinely passionate about what they do, the money will come. It's very difficult to believe this when you're starting out and may be broke or struggling, but you have to believe it nonetheless. Big thinkers *think big*, even when they are living in a basement apartment and scraping to put together financing for that first venture.

Big thinkers overcome the fear of failure by controlling their attitude, and they control their attitude by staying in control of the pictures they hold in their mind. There are plenty of successful businessmen who have never meditated or heard of the idea of a "vision board," but even though they might not use that vocabulary, every single one of them exercises some form of neural reconditioning.

Big thinkers experience hardship, struggle, defeat, and disappointment as much as everyone else, but because they stay in control of the pictures in their mind, they are not subject to the whims of their moods. Big thinkers know that they'll be successful only if they're willing to risk failure; they know that if they're not willing to take big risks, they won't win big prizes. Big thinkers build businesses with *scope*. The only ventures that interest big thinkers are those that, if successful, have sufficient impact to change their life. To a big thinker, it doesn't make sense to make big sacrifices for small victories. If the win is not big, it's not worth pursuing.

BIG THINKERS STAY FOCUSED

Big thinkers are continuously focused. They simplify their goals so they can succeed in a lot of little steps instead of attempting to make huge leaps. They understand that a long series of little steps will get you where you want to go. Even though they always have the big picture in mind, big thinkers don't get ahead of themselves, and they never discount the value of experience gathered in the process of pursuing a series of smaller benchmarks.

Big thinkers concentrate all their efforts on those areas where they excel, and don't waste time trying to be effective in areas where they do not. Whatever abilities they do not possess themselves, they gather by hiring the very best people they can afford in those areas. Most businesspeople think, "What's the least I can spend to get help?" Big thinkers take the opposite approach. They ask, "What's the *most* we can afford to get the very best help possible?" Big thinkers know that if you surround yourself with the best people possible, your success is already under way.

Big thinkers focus on what their customers want, not on what they want to sell. They put themselves in their customers' shoes and do whatever it takes to serve their customers well. No matter what their product is, or what field they're in, they stay in constant contact with their customers to find out what they want.

Big thinkers focus on finding the highest-quality customers. They know that it's better to have four ideal customers than forty mediocre ones, because those four will generate referrals and help build the business, while mediocre customers can drain a business. And they know that *exceeding* their customers' expectations, not just meeting them, is the foundation of their success.

Big thinkers know that sales and marketing are the key. If you don't *sell* something, nothing happens.

BIG THINKERS TAKE ACTION

Big thinkers are not necessarily the smartest, most knowledgeable, or most skilled people in their field. What distinguishes big thinkers is that once a decision has been made, they have the courage to take action. There are plenty of brilliant and highly educated people who are nevertheless afraid to take action. Big thinkers know that the only antidote to fear is action, and that if you take action in the direction of your fear, no matter what it is, you will conquer it. Big thinkers take wholehearted action toward something they believe in.

Big thinkers know that it's all right to make mistakes, that mistakes are part of the learning curve and often the only way you learn. They know that the key is to learn from your mistakes, put them behind you, and keep moving forward.

Big thinkers are high-energy individuals who have an unusually strong work ethic. They understand that business success requires huge personal sacrifice, and they are not afraid to throw themselves fully into something twenty-four hours a day if that's what it takes to make it work. They know that investing their own effort heavily in the early days will pay high dividends, both financial and personal, in the long run.

Big thinkers give no time to procrastination, and they understand that this is exactly what holds most other people back from realizing their dreams. They see that most people say, "I'm going to take action *once I* put together the financing . . . or get that raise . . . or find the right person." Big thinkers refuse to let themselves go down that path. They know that the best time to take action is *right now*, when you think of it, because that's when you most *want* to do it. The only difference between those who are successful in business and most other people is that the successful ones *take action* instead of putting it off for a "better time." That better time never comes.

Big thinkers are tenacious. We've all heard the stories of immigrants from other shores who have come to North America with nothing in their pockets, and within a decade or two become amazingly successful. They arrive here with none of the advantages of education, networks, or connections, yet they become huge successes. How do they do it? Because they recognize the opportunity for what it is, they are willing to work tenaciously, they focus on the scope of the opportunity, and they block the possibility of failure out of their mind.

Big thinkers have no room in their brain for the concept of failure; it is simply not part of their vocabulary. The probability of failure in business is very high: 95 percent of businesses don't make it beyond their first five years. Big thinkers know these statistics—and ignore them.

BIG THINKERS KNOW HOW TO DELEGATE

When you first start out building a business, there is so much to do: production, design, legal, finance, sales, marketing, customer support, and on and on. As the business grows, it's easy to fall prey to the subversive notion that you still have to *do it all.* This is a critical error, often a fatal one.

Many businesspeople who start out well are not able to build on that success, because they never master the art of delegation. This is one of the biggest secrets of millionaires and billionaires in business: Surround yourself with the best people you can find, and then *get out of their way and let them do their job.* Not only that: Share the credit and the spotlight. Let the people you bring into the organization share in the glory. It reinforces their conviction and commitment to what they're doing.

Study the history of the world's most successful businesses, and you'll often find that the smartest thing the founders or top executives ever did was to bring in someone new to help with some crucial aspect or critical juncture of the enterprise. They learned how to get out of their *own* way. Big thinkers learn how to delegate as they grow, and how to build teams that bring together people of diverse and contrasting skills, abilities, and temperaments.

In fact, delegation is even more critical when you're the sole person in your business. You still have to know when to delegate a particular task to someone outside your business, and when to deal with it another time, so you can focus on your highest dollar-producing activity.

Big thinkers tend to go with their gut instinct—but they also are big advocates of the "gut check." They surround themselves with people whose opinions they trust, and they check their own sense of the deal or decision with that group.

HIRE IN OR HIRE OUT?

As your business grows, you'll often be faced with the option of delegating a task or area of responsibility to partners, executives, or other employees within your company, or to contract services or other independent forces outside your company. How do you choose whether to hire in or hire out? Every case is different, and there are many factors to consider, including the size of your business and your available resources. But here is a central guideline: Ask yourself whether this task or area is central to your business's value. Is it part of your corporate identity, a vital part of what you do?

Just as you have your own core strengths and unique abilities, so does your business. If your business needs a skill that you personally lack, you can hire someone with that skill, or even create an entire department within your business devoted to that area and put an executive in charge who plays at that area that you would have to work at. On the other hand, if there are critical tasks the business needs to perform, but doing them in-house would pull resources and focus away from your organization's core competencies, then outsourcing may be wiser than hiring. Common examples include such functions as accounting, manufacturing, and specialized marketing aspects (such as media, PR, or telemarketing), design, and so forth.

BIG THINKERS ASK FOR HELP

Businesses often reach a critical point where growth seems stalled, where we're hitting our heads on a financial ceiling we can't seem to get past. What is the obstacle that keeps us stuck at a certain level? This is the same question we explored back in chapter 7 when we talked about *limiting beliefs*. In other words, when our business plateaus, what's keeping it stuck there is often *us*. When that happens, it's time to ask for help.

Big thinkers know that asking for help can be a critical step in moving beyond their own limitations. They aren't afraid to ask for help when they need it, because they know that when we draw on other people's experiences, perspectives, and knowledge, we become larger ourselves.

Seeking help can occur in two ways, both of them critical to your success. First, you can bring in people to do tasks that you yourself are not as well equipped to perform—in other words, where *you know you need help*. But you can also enlist the services of people to help you in areas where *you don't yet know you need help*. The challenge here, of course, is that we're talking about getting help that you don't know you need. How do you ask for help in areas of weakness when you don't even know those areas exist?

The answer: You *assume* those areas exist. You don't need to have your areas of critical ignorance all mapped out. Just know that whatever they are, *you have them*, and ask for help in finding and addressing them.

A partner can fulfill this role, to some extent. For example, because the two of us are so different, we each tend to see the other's blind spots fairly quickly and often provide the what-you-don't-know-you-don't-know perspective for the other. However, the limitation of a partner is that he or she is part of your business. By definition, a partner lacks the kind of objectivity you'll find in someone who's looking at your business from the outside. That is exactly the objectivity that you get from a *mentor, coach,* or *mastermind group*.

TWO KINDS OF HELP

Help You Know You Need	Help You Don't Know You Need
partner	mentor
hiring employees	coach
delegating	mastermind group
outsourcing	partner (sometimes bartering)

People in this second category can greatly reduce your learning curve, and provide all sorts of resources to which you might never have had access otherwise. Far more important, they can help you see things you would never have seen on your own, and that will almost always result in your achieving far more than you could have ever achieved otherwise. We have seen a mentor, a coach, or a mastermind group make the difference between a business floundering or flourishing, between survival and failure. In fact, we believe that having a powerful mentor, coach, and/or mastermind group that is committed to your success is second in importance only to the ability to focus your own vision and control the thoughts in your brain.

BIG THINKERS HAVE MENTORS

Big thinkers look to mentors for advice. They understand that one key to success is to model themselves after somebody who has already done what they want to do.

They know that businesspeople often look to the wrong places for advice. For example, they seek counsel from accountants, college professors, lawyers, and other people who, while highly educated and very knowledgeable in their own field, may or may not have been successful businesspeople. If they have, then their opinions may be quite valuable. If their expertise is purely theoretical, be sure to take that into account.

Once they have achieved considerable success, big thinkers are willing and eager to be mentors themselves to others. You will have that urge, to share what you've learned when you're a successful veteran, too.

BIG THINKERS HAVE COACHES

If you've ever played a team sport you know that a coach is a person who is committed to your success, brings objectivity and outside perspective to your situation, is an expert at the game you are seeking to play, and has the willingness, the temperament, and the authority to hold you accountable to your goals, promises, and commitments. There was a time when the only people who had coaches were professional athletes. Over the past two decades, coaching has flourished in a wide range of applications, including the life coach and the business or executive coach.

In a typical coaching relationship, you and your coach will set up and maintain a regular schedule for conferring, often once a week, and you pay for the service. Depending on your coach, you may have access throughout the week as well, through conference calls, online resources, private calls, or other channels.

It is no exaggeration to say that everyone who is looking to create financial freedom and an extraordinary life through business needs a coach. We believe so strongly in the pivotal importance of having a strong coach that we both came out of retirement in 2005 to join forces and create a business focused on providing the finest business coaching to at least one million entrepreneurs, professionals, business owners, and other businesspeople. We asked a few of our clients to speak about what they have valued most from having a team of business coaches as part of their support system. Here's what they had to say.

"Having a coach has been invaluable in helping me focus on those things that are absolutely key to growing my business," says Fundamental Fitness's Suzanne Thomas. "Whenever I've had challenges I couldn't seem to solve, my coaches have been able to put their finger on what the issue was. When I get on the phone with them, they can identify an issue that might take me months to figure out on my own, and they typically nail it down in thirty seconds."

CASA's Rhonda Latreille talks about the value of simply having someone to turn to when things look bleak or challenging. "Being a business owner can be a very lonely place to be," says Rhonda. "Especially when you face problems and challenges and don't really know what to do or where to turn. When you wake up at two-thirty in the morning in a sweat, thinking, 'I don't know what to do to fix this,' where do you go?

"Knowing that I'm just one phone call away from getting advice and support from masters in business whose only agenda is my success has been a godsend. There have been numerous times when my coaches have gone out of their way to help me personally. This is something you simply won't get within the structure of your own business. Having access to that level and quality of support has been a remarkable experience."

BIG THINKERS USE MASTERMINDS

Many brilliant businesspeople have used the practice of masterminding to guide them in their lives and in their business decisions. The mastermind idea reflects a common practice among people in positions of power, authority, and decision making, as we see in a presidential cabinet or a corporate brain trust. Its popularity and success owes much to the emphasis placed on the "Master Mind" by Napoleon Hill in *Think and Grow Rich*.

The principle behind the mastermind is simple. As Hill puts it, "No two minds ever come together without, thereby, creating a third, invisible, intangible force which may be likened to a third mind." [10] Two brains are better than one—and five or six are even better.

A practical mastermind group might consist of as many as eight or nine people; for us, six seems to be ideal. We typically meet once a week for ninety minutes on the phone. We'll take five minutes in the beginning to come together, remind ourselves of our purpose, report on whatever has worked for us during the week since the last call, and have the leader of the call read aloud whatever agenda we've organized. (The call leader position typically rotates each week.) We then go around the "table," giving each member ten minutes or so to focus on his or her topics and ask the other members for suggestions, advice, or resources, and then we conclude with a five- or ten-minute wrap-up.

In choosing whom you'd like to invite to join your mastermind group, remember that you're looking for people who are all operating at a similar level of ability and commitment, yet who are also diverse. You're not looking for a bunch of "yes" people who all think the same way. You want people who each bring something unique to the table, people who can bring to your situation a perspective that you do not already have.

When you start out, it's helpful for each of you in the mastermind group to lay your agenda out on the table clearly for the others. What are your goals? What do you want to create in your business? What's

---

10. Napoleon Hill, *Think and Grow Rich* (Greenwich, CT: Fawcett Crest, 1960), p. 169.

really important to you? What are your strongest needs and most cherished values? The more you all share about yourselves, the faster things will move. In our experience, it typically takes three to four calls before the group gets into gear. Think of this as laying down the foundation; the sooner you do this, and the more carefully and thoroughly you do it, the sooner you can get to putting up the house.

HOW TO RUN A MASTERMIND GROUP

We have found that it is essential to create a clear agenda for each meeting ahead of time, and to designate someone as the timekeeper. When the timekeeper announces that a speaker's allotted time is up, then time is up. If the group opts by consensus to give the speaker a minute or two more to finish the thought, then that's fine, but otherwise, *time's up*. This helps keep the call moving.

As with any kind of brainstorming, it's easy to slip into making negative comments like, "That doesn't make any sense." Maintaining a productive atmosphere requires a commitment on each member's part always to speak with a positive orientation. One way to maintain this is to create the habit of simply asking yourself, when a comment occurs to you, "Does this serve the group?" If you happen to disagree with an idea you hear, or if you simply don't understand what's being said, ask clarifying questions.

The key to making your mastermind group effective is to play this game full out. Masterminding can be one of the most powerful things you've ever done, both for your business and for yourself. Bringing together a half dozen brains that collectively connect to the infinite intelligence of the quantum field opens up an amazing reservoir of resources. Thanks to connections we've made through mastermind groups, doors have opened for us that we would never have been able to open on our own.

THE VIRTUAL MASTERMIND

There is a second type of mastermind, the *virtual mastermind*, which you create by choosing great leaders and mentors from history and gather them into a group to which you turn for inspiration and guidance. At first glance, this might seem like nothing but a figment of the imagination. But imagination is a very powerful force. Our brains have the capacity to access the limitless resource of infinite intelligence, and creating your own virtual mastermind is a very powerful and extremely effective way to do exactly that.

John Assaraf's virtual mastermind group includes Mahatma Gandhi, Martin Luther King Jr., John F. Kennedy, and Andrew Carnegie. He chose each of these individuals for a specific set of reasons: Gandhi for his capacity to bring love and compassion to every situation; King for his conviction, passion, and commitment to achieving his vision; Kennedy for his poise, joie de vivre, sense of vision, unflagging can-do attitude, and capacity for leadership; and Carnegie for his philanthropic vision, his understanding of how universal laws operate in the sphere of human activity, and especially for his willingness to inspire and be a mentor to Napoleon Hill.

When John is working on creating a new event, developing a new strategy, or facing a new challenge, he takes some time to sit down in an empty boardroom, quiet his mind for a few minutes, and conjure up an image of each one of these four people as a way to focus his own mind and tap into the unified field of their intelligence. He begins a "discussion" with them by posing whatever issues he's facing as questions: "How would you do this? What would you do in this situation?" Then he lets himself be receptive to whatever guidance he senses. Every time he has consulted his virtual mastermind group, he has never failed to gain some insight that he would not have attained simply by thinking the situation through on his own.

BIG THINKERS SEEK MORE LIFE

There is one last point about how big thinkers think, and it may be the most important point of all: Big thinkers don't just want to create big businesses. They want to create a *big life*.

People sometimes have a conception of successful businesspeople as being obsessive, workaholic types who never stop to smell the flowers. That's not true of a big thinker. A big thinker doesn't just *stop* occasionally to smell the flowers. If you are truly thinking big, then you're making sure you're smelling flowers *every step of the way*.

Whatever it is that gives you joy, whatever makes your life feel full, be sure *that's* on your vision board. We want you to dream as big as you can and to make those dreams real, but they are *your* dreams to define, describe, and create. Your goals don't have to be all about fast cars and big houses. Your goals are important, but only because they are targets that help make the journey worthwhile. When we reach the end of our life, the only things we'll really have will be our experiences, our connections to other people, and our memories. They are the fabric of our life.

Big thinkers have a picture of success that includes balance. Big thinkers understand that there are multiple dimensions to life, and they want to enjoy *all* of them. As a result, even though they grow huge fortunes, big thinkers do not rely on money for their happiness. They know how to take great joy in the simple things in life, whether it's being with their children, going for a walk with their spouse, curling up by a fire with a great book, or sitting by the ocean and making castles in the sand.

Ultimately, success is really not about your business or financial goals; it's about your experience of life. The real purpose of building your dream business is to express and support the person you are in the process of becoming.

Conclusion

THE PATH

As we saw in our exploration of the brain, there is a part of us that loves growth because it seeks fuller expression, and there is another part of us that fights to maintain homeostasis. The aspect that seeks growth is our spiritual side. It is our larger "I," the part of us that seeks to reconnect with our origins in the quantum sea of pure consciousness. Then there is the organism, represented by the functions of our nonconscious brain, which seeks stasis in support of self-preservation. There is a natural and constant tension between these two aspects of ourselves, almost a tug-of-war. Yet this game is no contest. It has a predetermined outcome.

The truth is, stasis is an illusion. We're born, we live, we grow, and we cast off the bodily garments of this life; like fireworks arcing through the night sky, life arises and shines through the trajectory of our years before winking out and falling to the ground from which we arose. Shakespeare's character Prospero puts it beautifully: "We are such stuff as dreams are made on, and our little life is rounded with a sleep."[11] Our passing is inevitable, and we are here on this tiny planet for such a short time. The organism's heroic effort to keep us in homeostasis is understandable, but we know from the start that any homeostasis is

---

11. Shakespeare, *The Tempest*, act 4, scene 1.

temporary, just as no life is permanent. Energy has but one constant attribute: change. We are always growing or declining; there is no real status quo, only a temporary sense of respite from the waves of change.

Thoreau wrote, "The mass of men lead lives of quiet desperation,"[12] a poetic way of saying that when most people feel this tug-of-war, they simply let go of the rope and settle into self-preservation and acquiescence to mediocrity. But not you. You are a seeker of the exceptional, in pursuit of a life of financial freedom and personal fulfillment made available through an extraordinary business. You are one of those who seize the reins of change and hold on, determined to create a life of greatness, meaning, and impact. Your path is to feel that tug-of-war between change and stasis, growth and preservation, new horizons and the safety of the "average"—and allow it to pull you *into* the headlong pursuit of an ever-fuller expression of yourself and your vision. For our life may be temporary, but our visions are eternal.

That's what your dream business is all about.

We close *The Answer* with a question:

How will you spend your life?

When you think about the expression *spend your life*, you'll come to a sobering realization: Your life is something that you actually do *spend* every day, just as surely as if you were pulling out your wallet and peeling off hours like dollar bills as payment for each day's experiences and memories.

Every day, you are trading away the moments of your life for whatever it is you are creating and experiencing during those moments. What do *you* want to trade your life for? What is worth that trade? You get to choose; in fact, you *have* to. With every breath you take, you are already choosing what it is you're getting in exchange for the moments you spend: the people you're spending time with, the activities you're engaged in, the thoughts you're having, and the experiences you're allowing to happen.

---

12. Henry David Thoreau, *Walden*.

If you have chosen to spend that precious life in the pursuit of success in business, then don't let yourself settle for "good." Make that business a perfect expression of your values and purpose, the perfect expression of you. Make it the business of your dreams—and then make those dreams come true. Devote yourself to the pursuit of the exceptional.

You have at your disposal the most mind-boggling tools and resources imaginable. You have the zero-point field, the quantum ocean of infinite information, intelligence, and knowledge. You have the unstoppable and invariable power of universal law—the laws of Attraction, Gestation, Action, and Compensation.

You have the most powerful electromagnetic tuning device in the universe: the human brain, with its virtually unlimited capacity to tap, process, and articulate the infinite wisdom of the quantum universe. And you now also have the tools you need to create the thoughts, beliefs, and habits of mind to use that brain to create anything you desire.

You have the key steps it takes to envision your dream business, populate it with ideal customers, articulate its essential value and Unique Selling Proposition, and communicate that value with compelling messages through channels and media that will reach the people for whom they are ideally intended.

And you have the keys to creating the ideal support community to help you every step of the way, helping you meet the needs you know you have as well as the needs that still lie beyond the reach of your conscious brain. You know how big thinkers think, and you have all the tools you need to give voice and expression to your own big thoughts.

You have The Answer. Now, go use it! And as you do, let us know how you're doing. We'll be right there with you.

John Assaraf and Murray Smith

ACKNOWLEDGMENTS

A book, like any other creation or enterprise, starts as a seed and comes to full fruition only through the complex miracle of gestation and cultivation. We are awed and amazed at the people we have attracted to help us grow, water, weed, and nourish this project from start to finish. We came up with the acorn; the finished oak you hold in your hands owes an incalculable debt to all of them. Our deepest thanks go out to the following:

FROM JOHN AND MURRAY

To John David Mann, for your remarkable ability to grasp our thoughts, ideas, experiences, and intentions and transform them into words on the page.

To Peter Guzzardi and Peter Borland, our extraordinary editors, for your expertise, insight, and selfless dedication to the project.

To Judith Curr, president of Atria Books, for your vision and phenomenal grasp of what's possible when you put your mind to it.

To our peerless agent and friend Margret McBride, and to Donna DeGutis, Faye Atchison, and Anne Bomke at the Margret McBride Literary Agency—for your unflagging enthusiasm and unparalleled mastery of your craft.

To our team for believing in and being part of our vision to change the world one business owner at a time; you make what we do possible.

To Jennifer Tibbott, our executive liaison, for always keeping us on track and in line; you are a treasure of a human being and a superb employee.

To Jeff Perlis, Mike and Evva Fenison, Jason and Justin Abernathy—we thank you for your support and friendship in building One-Coach into the premier small-business-growth company in the world.

A special thanks to Adrian Ulsh, Jack Rued, and Tom Stacey for being instrumental in the creation of this book: We are forever grateful for your dedication and relentless commitment to excellence.

FROM JOHN

As always, to my children Keenan and Noah: You two are the best gift GOD has ever given me.

To my wife Maria: Your patience, kindness, and soft heart always melt me into blissful submission. You are the very best partner the Law of Attraction could ever have brought me.

To Walter Schneider: You continue to support me in so many ways as your younger brother. For this and for your unconditional love, I love you.

And to Murray, my business partner and best buddy: Without your constant and never-ending quest to make things better, neither our business nor this book would have turned out as well as they did.

FROM MURRAY

To my beautiful wife Lisa: My deepest appreciation for your dedication, love, and support in making all this possible.

To my children, Sheena, Tasjohnna, Sean, and Lauren, and to my grandchildren, Jeneya and Mariah: Thank you for always being my inspiration and passion; I love you with all my heart.

To my brother and sister, Steven Smith and Jennifer Golfetto, thank you for allowing me to hone my negotiating skills with you throughout our childhood.

To my parents, Sheila and Andrew Smith: I owe my love of entrepreneurship to you. I am who I am because of the way you raised me and the things you taught me: family, loyalty, tenacity, forgiveness, and love.

To my mentor, and dear friend, Michael Gold: I have learned so much from you that words cannot begin to describe how they have impacted my business and personal life. Thank you for being you—Mister Integrity.

To my business partner and best friend, Johnny (aka John Assaraf): You are a remarkable human being, always giving, caring, and loving. Allowing me to share this book with you is one of the highlights of my life. Allowing me to share life with you has been the kind of journey that most only dream of.

One of the biggest secrets to success that we've ever encountered is simply this: Surround yourself with the very best people you can find, and then get out of their way and let them soar. We are blessed to have been surrounded by a team of friends who soar so high they touch the sky. Thanks to you all.

Appendix 1

CUSTOMER SURVEY FORMS

CURRENT CUSTOMER SURVEY:
BUSINESS TO CONSUMER (B2C)

Interviewee _____

Business name _____

Address _____

City _____ State _____ Zip _____ Country _____

Phone _____ Email _____

Web address _____

1. Gender _____

2. Age _____

3. Income level_____

4. Marital status_____

5. Number of children_____

6. Education level _____

7. Job title_____

8. Geographic market _____

DECISION-MAKING ROLES

9. Who makes the final purchase decision to buy your products or services?

_____

10. Who influences the decision to buy your products or services?

_____

11. Who are the primary users of your products or services?

_____

PSYCHOGRAPHICS

Check the box next to all the traits that your survey interview reveals about this customer. Your industry may have specific traits not listed below; record these on the lines provided.

☐ Uses our services on a recurring basis.

☐ Selective about whom they do business with.

☐ Wants to be kept informed about problems/progress.

☐ Demands honesty.

☐ Is realistic and practical with regard to delivery expectations.

☐ Provides payment in full.

☐ Doesn't question invoice accuracy.

☐ Has been a long-term customer.

☐ Writes a testimonial when asked.

- [ ] Responds to our requests.
- [ ] Wants the latest innovations.
- [ ] Prefers annual service contract.
- [ ] Trusts our advice.
- [ ] Is easy to work with.
- [ ] Appreciates a job well done.
- [ ] Speaks highly of us and sends referrals.
- [ ] Uses us as their vendor of choice.
- [ ] Is cooperative, open, and not overly demanding.
- [ ] Is realistic and practical about expected results.
- [ ] _____
- [ ] _____
- [ ] _____
- [ ] _____
- [ ] _____

Rank the five traits that matter most to your customer, in order of the customer's preference.

1. _____
2. _____
3. _____
4. _____
5. _____

CURRENT CUSTOMER SURVEY
BUSINESS TO BUSINESS (B2B)

Interviewee name _____

Business name _____

Address _____

City _____ State _____ Zip _____ Country _____

Phone _____ Email _____

Web address _____

1. Number of employees_____

2. Headquarters location_____

3. Product or service type_____

4. Annual revenue _____

5. Size of branches _____

6. Location of branches _____

7. Year founded _____

8. Organizational structure_____

9. Geographic markets _____

DECISION-MAKING ROLES

10. Who makes the final purchase decision to buy your products or services?

_____

11. Who influences the decision to buy your products or services?

_____

12. Who are the primary users of your products or services?

_____

PSYCHOGRAPHICS

Check the box next to all the traits that your survey interview reveals about this customer. Your industry may have specific traits not listed below; record these on the lines provided.

☐ Uses our services on a recurring basis.

☐ Selective about whom they do business with.

☐ Wants to be kept informed about problems/progress.

☐ Demands honesty.

☐ Is realistic and practical with regard to delivery expectations.

☐ Provides payment in full.

☐ Doesn't question invoice accuracy.

☐ Has been a long-term customer.

☐ Writes a testimonial when asked.

☐ Responds to our requests.

☐ Wants the latest innovations.

☐ Prefers annual service contract.

☐ Trusts our advice.

☐ Is easy to work with.

☐ Appreciates a job well done.

☐ Speaks highly of us and sends referrals.

☐ Uses us as their vendor of choice.

☐ Is cooperative, open, and not overly demanding.

☐ Is realistic and practical about expected results.

☐ _____

☐ _____

☐ _____

☐ _____

☐ _____

Rank the five traits that matter most to your customer, in order of the customer's preference.

1. _____

2. _____

3. _____

4. _____

5. _____

Appendix 2

THE FIVE MAJOR INDUSTRIES: COMMON HOT BUTTONS

SERVICE INDUSTRY

Adult care facility

Airlines

Automotive services

Banking

Broadcasting, cable

Carpet cleaning

Commercial banking

Computer networking

Construction

Daycare

Diversified outsourcing

Education (schools)

Fencing contractor

Financial data services

Food service

Hair salon

Health care, medical facilities

Heating/cooling contractor
Homebuilders
Hotels, casinos, resorts
Insurance
Internet services and retailing
Investment services
IT services
Laundry services
Lawn care
Lodging and gaming
Mail, packaging, and freight delivery
Moving company
Oil and gas equipment services
Painting services
Payroll services
Pest control
Plumbing
Printer
Railroads
Real estate
Recreation and amusement
Restaurant—fine dining, fast food
Roofing contractor
Window cleaning

SERVICE INDUSTRY: COMMON CLIENT HOT BUTTONS

Fix it right
Fix it fast or on time; quick resolution
Honesty; don't charge me more, don't fix it unless it needs to be fixed
General customer service guarantee

Additional hot buttons may include:

Expected results
Options, variety
Selection

Quality, results match expectations

Educate about product or service

Additional products/services after the sale

No hassles

Make more money

Wants higher margins

Ease of change

Less hassle

Low risk

Evidence

Price

Validation

PROFESSIONAL INDUSTRY

Accountant

Advertising, marketing

Appraiser

Architect

Attorney

Biotech

Chiropractor

Consulting, coaching

Dentist

Education (teachers)

Engineering, construction

Entertainment (entrepreneur)

Health care services

Insurance agent

Investment advisor

Massage therapist

Nursing home

Nutritionist

Occupational therapist

Ophthalmologist

Optician

Orthodontist

Orthotherapist
Pediatrician
Photographer
Physician
Podiatrist
Real estate agent
Stockbroker
Travel agent
Veterinarian

PROFESSIONAL INDUSTRY: COMMON HOT BUTTONS

Expected results
Customer service
Price or affordability
Guarantee of results

Additional hot buttons may include:

Options, variety
Selection
Quality, results match expectations
Educate about product or service
Additional products/services after the sale
No hassles
Make more money
Wants higher margins
Ease of change
Less hassle
Low risk
Evidence
Validation

RETAIL INDUSTRY

Apparel and footwear
Auto parts

Automotive retail—dealer, parts, fuel

Bakery

Beverages

Building materials, glass (retail)

Chemicals (retail)

Computer hardware (retail)

Computer software (retail)

Electronics, electrical equipment

Energy (wholesale)

Fitness center, health club

Floor covering

Florist

Food—consumer products (retail)

Food and drug stores

Food production (retail)

Furniture (retail)

General merchandisers (retail)

Health care

Household durables (retail)

Household perishables (retail)

Industrial and analytic instruments (retail)

Insurance

Jeweler

Machinery (retail)

Motor vehicles and parts (retail)

Movies and home entertainment

Natural gas distribution (retail)

Network and other communications equipment (retail)

Office equipment/supplies

Packaging, containers

Pharmaceuticals

Printing

Publisher

RETAIL INDUSTRY: COMMON HOT BUTTONS

Product
Options, variety, and selection
Quality, results match expectations
Customer service
What you do in addition to the sale
Education, advice, and knowledge
Price
No hassles
Follow-through

Additional hot buttons may include:

Expected results
Additional products/services after the sale
Make more money
Wants higher margins
Ease of change
Low risk
Evidence
Validation

OPPORTUNITY/ENTREPRENEUR INDUSTRY

Broker
Chiropractor
Counselor (psychologist, psychiatric social worker, marriage and family
    therapist)
Cultural diversity consultant
Cyberspace specialist (using cyberspace for advertising or political organizing)
Developer
Direct marketing specialist
Environmental illness, allergist
Holistic health and nutrition specialist (health program coordinator,
    nutritionist)

Home care therapy consultant (speech therapist, occupational therapist, physical therapist)

Home-based businessperson

Independent contractor, consultant (master's degree preferred)

Insurance broker

Internet and online-service developer

Management information consultant

Manufacturer's representative

Massage therapist

Nutritionist

Personal safety and communication developer

Small business owner

Software developer for interactive learning and play

Special events consultant

OPPORTUNITY/ENTREPRENEUR INDUSTRY: COMMON HOT BUTTONS

Make money

Ease of changes

Evidence and proof

Proof of support

Additional hot buttons may include:

Expected results

Options, variety

Selection

Quality, results match expectations

Educate about product or service

Additional products/services after the sale

No hassles

Wants higher margins

Less hassle

Low risk

Price

Validation

WHOLESALE INDUSTRY

Aerospace and defense

Agribusiness

Alcohol and tobacco

Auto parts

Beverages

Building materials, glass

Chemicals

Coal mining

Computer hardware

Computer software

Electronics, electrical equipment

Food—consumer products

Food production

Forest and paper products

Furniture

General merchandisers

Health care

Household durables

Household perishables

Industrial and analytic instruments

Machinery

Metals

Mining, crude oil production

Motor vehicles and parts

Natural gas distribution

Network and other communications equipment

Office equipment

Oil and gas equipment

Packaging, containers

Petroleum refining

Pharmaceuticals

Publisher

WHOLESALE INDUSTRY: HOT BUTTONS

Make more money
Higher margins
Dealer-to-consumer marketing
Less hassle, ease of doing business with
Low risk

Additional hot buttons may include:

Expected results
Options, variety
Selection
Quality, results match expectations
Educate about product or service
Additional products/services after the sale
Ease of change
Evidence
Price
Validation

Appendix 3

DISTRIBUTION CHANNELS, MARKETING STRATEGIES, AND MARKETING TACTICS

DISTRIBUTION CHANNELS

Direct Sales

Direct sales includes any situation where you and your customer interact directly, without any intermediaries or agents. In a small business or sole proprietorship, this might mean that the business owner is personally interacting with each of her customers. In another common form of direct sales, the business will hire its own sales force to contact prospective customers and take them through the sales process. Direct mail is yet another common form of direct sales.

Sales Agents

This channel uses an outside force to connect with customers and prospective customers. There are many varieties of agents; examples include independent sales agents, wholesale, franchise, licensing, affiliates, and joint ventures.

Phone Sales

Some businesses use a sales force hired and trained exclusively to contact prospective customers and complete the sales process via the phone. This can be farmed out to an external telemarketing firm, or it can be managed in-house by creating a call center within the business.

Mail Order

In this model, the business communicates with prospects and customers through the mail and delivers its goods using a common carrier service. The most common examples of the mail-order channel are catalog companies, such as Lands' End, Victoria's Secret, and L.L.Bean.

Online

Starting as a virtual version of the catalog/mail-order model, the online channel has grown enormously because of its value to both the consumer and the merchant. Online sales offers the convenience of around-the-clock ordering and provides tremendous sophistication in how it delivers and collects information. Also, much of its operation can be automated, greatly reducing staffing needs. Well-known examples are eBay and Amazon.com.

Retail

Traditional brick-and-mortar retail outlets also provide a time-honored distribution channel for selling products to the public, from the smallest mom-and-pop store to the largest department store.

Events

Finally, some businesses reach their customers through live events, where prospects participate in a facilitated and rehearsed presentation.

MARKETING STRATEGIES

Advertising (television, radio, print)

Television advertising, which can include commercials, infomercials, or in-show placements, reaches the largest, most diverse market. Radio allows you to reach a more targeted group. Print is often the most affordable of the three. Media advertising is generally suited best to a long-term campaign.

Affiliate and Joint Venture

This strategy lets you leverage someone else's resources (such as a contact list or a website) to extend your reach. Because these arrangements are typically paid for on a pay-per-click or commission-per-sale basis, this is often a very affordable strategy.

Affinity Marketing

This is a method of promoting your brand's products or services to a carefully targeted niche audience. When using this strategy, it's crucial to take the time and care to thoroughly understand the needs and peculiarities of this specific niche, and to test the approach rigorously.

Barter

There are two types of barter: direct barter (sometimes called *contra*), where you trade your products or services with another product/service provider; and barter exchange, where you trade your products or services through a third-party broker or barter company. Barter can help you obtain needed goods or services when you have a limited budget; it can also facilitate the creation of partnerships that can lead to cross-promotional opportunities.

Catalog Marketing

The Internet has not killed catalogs! In fact, many companies have found that printed catalogs actually help drive online sales. A study by the United States Postal Service reports that consumers who receive catalogs in the mail are more than twice as likely to make an online purchase from that company.

Direct Marketing

The most common direct marketing vehicle is direct postal mail, but it can include other vehicles, such as email, telephone, and door-to-door. While print advertising can cast a wider net, direct mail allows you to more precisely target your audience.

Event Marketing

This strategy revolves around a carefully planned and meticulously executed event to reach your target market. Examples include promotional bus tours, sporting events (including charity runs and marathons), block parties, in-store promotions, giveaway events, and "happenings" at malls. You can produce an event yourself or participate as a sponsor (e.g., sponsoring a team at a sporting event).

Frequent Buyer Programs

Businesses often develop frequent buyer programs to reward customer loyalty with free products or services, discounts, reward points that can be traded for goods and services, and so forth. Customer loyalty can be a key component in directing marketing efforts.

Internet

Internet marketing has grown into a huge and diverse collection of strategies, including online promotion, pay-per-click advertising, reciprocal linking, search engine optimization, paid search, podcasting, blogging, opt-in email, and other methods. Far from being limited to online businesses, Internet marketing is also a valuable element in the marketing efforts of many traditional brick-and-mortar businesses.

Outdoor Media

Unlike TV, radio, or print advertising, outdoor media cannot be turned off or thrown away. Billboards are the best-known outdoor marketing medium; other examples include mall displays, buses, taxis, airports, rail stations, and movie theaters. An innovative new form of outdoor media is building illumination, where an image is projected onto a building. Outdoor media is a specialty within the advertising industry, and you'll be most likely to get your best results by using an agency that focuses strictly on this type of media.

Point of Purchase (POP) and Point of Sale (POS)

These refer to the placement of your marketing message right at the location where the product or service can be purchased. The most common example is in a retail store, where high-margin "impulse buy" items are placed next to the cash register.

Place-Based Media

This relatively recent strategy delivers marketing messages outside typical distribution channels. Examples of place-based media include television screens in grocery store checkout lines; interactive kiosks in shopping malls or retail stores; in-store radio commercials; coupon dispensers in retail stores (in which a motion detector triggers an audio message about the product when a customer walks past); and airplanes towing advertising signs.

Promotions and Cross-Promotions

A promotion is a focused, short-term effort to introduce a new product or service or to promote, publicize, or improve its position in the marketplace. Promotions tend to be highly targeted and time-bound. In a cross-promotion, you leverage your product or service to promote another, such as the "buyers who bought X also bought Y" promotions you see on the Internet. You can cross-promote among your own products or collaborate with other providers to reap the benefits of your joint target markets.

Public Relations (PR)

Small businesses often overlook public relations, seeing it as either cost-prohibitive or inapplicable. However, PR can be an effective way for businesses of any size to establish visibility and credibility.

Referrals

Word of mouth is the most powerful way to sell. A referral program is simply an organized arrangement for offering incentives to customers or other businesses for referring business to you.

Signage

Signage refers to any displayed words, symbols, or other images designed to advertise your business, from storefront signs and countertop placards to banners at events or trade shows. For companies that rely on drive-by or walk-in traffic, signage may be their most important business identifier.

MARKETING TACTICS

800 phone number
900 phone number
Ad tracking
AdSense by Google
AdWords by Google
Animation
Articles
Auctions
Audio marketing
Autoresponders
Award recognition
Back-end marketing
Banner ads
Birthday reminders
Blogging

Bonus offers
Business cards
Case studies
Conference calls
Consulting
Contests
Discussion groups
Download page
eBay
eBooks
Email
Endorsements
E-zines
Feedback forms
Follow-up marketing
Forums and newsgroups
Freebies
Funnel marketing
Guarantees
Info products
Interviews
Keywords
List building
Mailing lists
Membership sites
Minicourses
Mini-eBooks
Minisites
Network marketing
News feeds
Newsletters
Niche marketing
Pay-per-whatever
Peer-to-peer relationships
Permission-based marketing
Pop-overs
Pop-unders

Pop-ups

Postcards

Postscript (P.S.)

Preselling

Price reduction

Pricing

Private label

Public speaking

Questions

Radio (Internet)

Reports

Sales letters

Scarcity

Screen savers

Search engine optimization

Seminars

Signs

Surveys

Sweepstakes

Talk shows

Teleconferencing

Teleseminars

Testimonials

Thank-you pages

Tips

Troubleshooting

Tutorials

TV (Internet)

Unsubscribe message

Upsell

Videos

Viral marketing

Voice mail

Web pages

Website design

Welcome or confirmation message

Yellow Pages

Appendix 4

THE FIVE MAJOR INDUSTRIES: COMMON DISTRIBUTION CHANNELS AND MARKETING STRATEGIES

SERVICE INDUSTRY: COMMON DISTRIBUTION CHANNELS

Direct sales
Online
Retail

SERVICE INDUSTRY: COMMON MARKETING STRATEGIES

Advertising (TV, radio, print)
Affiliate and joint venture programs
Affinity marketing
Barter
Competition
Continuity programs
Cross-promotions
Customer loyalty
Database marketing

Innovation

Internet

Multimedia

Outdoor media

Point of purchase and point of sale

Promotions

Referrals

Signage

PROFESSIONAL INDUSTRY: COMMON DISTRIBUTION CHANNELS

Direct sales

Online

PROFESSIONAL INDUSTRY: COMMON MARKETING STRATEGIES

Advertising (TV, radio, print)

Affiliate and joint venture programs

Affinity marketing

Barter

Competition

Continuity programs

Cross-promotions

Customer loyalty

Database marketing

Event marketing

Innovation

Internet

Multimedia

Point of purchase and point of sale

Promotions

Public relations

Referrals

Signage

RETAIL INDUSTRY: COMMON DISTRIBUTION CHANNELS

Direct sales
Events
Mail order
Online
Phone sales
Retail

RETAIL INDUSTRY: COMMON MARKETING STRATEGIES

Advertising (TV, radio, print)
Affiliate and joint venture programs
Affinity marketing
Barter
Catalog
Competition
Continuity programs
Cross-promotions
Customer loyalty
Database marketing
Event marketing
Innovation
Interactive media
Internet
Media buying
Multimedia
Outdoor media
Point of purchase and point of sale
Pricing
Promotions
Public relations
Referrals
Signage

OPPORTUNITY/ENTREPRENEUR INDUSTRY:
COMMON DISTRIBUTION CHANNELS

Direct sales
Events
Online
Phone sales

OPPORTUNITY/ENTREPRENEUR INDUSTRY:
COMMON MARKETING STRATEGIES

Advertising (TV, radio, print)
Affiliate and joint venture programs
Affinity marketing
Barter
Catalog
Competition
Continuity programs
Cross-promotions
Customer loyalty
Database marketing
Event marketing
Innovation
Interactive media
Internet
Multimedia
Point of purchase and point of sale
Pricing
Promotions
Public relations
Referrals

WHOLESALE INDUSTRY: COMMON DISTRIBUTION CHANNELS

Direct sales
Events
Mail order

Mall centers
Online
Retail
Wholesale

WHOLESALE INDUSTRY: COMMON MARKETING STRATEGIES

Advertising (TV, radio, print)
Affiliate and joint venture programs
Affinity marketing
Barter
Catalog
Competition
Continuity programs
Cross-promotions
Customer loyalty
Database marketing
Event marketing
Innovation
Interactive media
Internet
Media buying
Multimedia
Outdoor media
Point of purchase and point of sale
Pricing
Promotions
Public relations
Referrals
Signage

RESOURCES

NEUROTECHNOLOGY

The Answer—Neural Reconditioning Companion CD: www.the
  powertoachieve.com
John Assaraf Vision Board software: www.johnassaraf.com/visionboard

FORMS

Online versions of the various forms mentioned in chapters 1 to 8 can
  be found at: www.JohnAssaraf.com/forms.
Forms from Murray Smith and those mentioned in chapters 9 to 15
  can be found at: www.GetTheAnswer.com/forms.

RECOMMENDED BOOKS: BUSINESS

Benton, D. A. *How to Think Like a CEO: The 22 Vital Traits You Need
  to Be the Person at the Top*. New York: Warner Books, 1996.
Buckingham, Marcus, and Donald O. Clifton, Ph.D. *Now, Discover
  Your Strengths*. New York: Free Press, 2001.
Canfield, Jack. *The Success Principles: How to Get from Where You Are
  to Where You Want to Be*. With Janet Spitzer. New York: Harper-
  Collins, 2005.

Demartini, Dr. John F. *How to Make One Hell of a Profit and Still Go to Heaven.* Carlsbad, CA: Hay House, Inc., 2004.

Godin, Seth. *Purple Cow: Transform Your Business by Being Remarkable.* New York: Portfolio, 2003.

Hagelin, John, Ph.D. *Manual for a Perfect Government: How to Harness the Laws of Nature to Bring Maximum Success to Governmental Administration.* Fairfield, IA: Maharishi University of Management Press, 1998.

Hall, Doug. *Jump Start Your Business Brain: Scientific Ideas and Advice That Will Immediately Double Your Business Success Rate.* Cincinnati: Emmis Books, 2005.

Kim, W. Chan, and Renée Mauborgne. *Blue Ocean Strategy: How to Create Uncontested Market Space and Make the Competition Irrelevant.* Boston: Harvard Business School Press, 2005.

Staples, Dr. Walter. *Think Like a Winner.* North Hollywood, CA: Wilshire Book Company, 1993.

Thomson, David G. *Blueprint to a Billion: 7 Essentials to Achieve Exponential Growth.* Hoboken, NJ: John Wiley & Sons, Inc., 2006.

RECOMMENDED BOOKS: OTHER

Amen, Daniel G., M.D. *Change Your Brain, Change Your Life: The Breakthrough Program for Conquering Anxiety, Depression, Obsessiveness, Anger, and Impulsiveness.* New York: Times Books, 1998.

Benson, Herbert, M.D., and William Proctor. *The Breakout Principle: How to Activate the Natural Trigger That Maximizes Creativity, Athletic Performance, Productivity, and Personal Well-Being.* New York: Scribner, 2003.

Browning, Geil, Ph.D. *EMERGENETICS®: Tap into the New Science of Success.* New York: HarperCollins, 2006.

Bryson, Bill. *A Short History of Nearly Everything.* Toronto: Doubleday Canada, 2003.

Byrne, Rhonda. *The Secret.* New York: Atria Books/Beyond Words, 2006.

Childre, Doc, and Howard Martin. *The HeartMath Solution: The Institute of HeartMath's Revolutionary Program for Engaging the Power of the Heart's Intelligence*. With Donna Beech. New York: Harper-Collins, 1999.

Demartini, Dr. John F. *The Breakthrough Experience: A Revolutionary Approach to Personal Transformation*. Carlsbad, CA: Hay House, Inc., 2002.

Emoto, Masaru. *The Hidden Messages in Water*. New York: Atria, 2001.

Friedman, Thomas L. *The World Is Flat: A Brief History of the Twenty-first Century*. New York: Farrar, Straus & Giroux, 2005.

Kaku, Michio, and Jennifer Thompson. *Beyond Einstein: The Cosmic Quest for the Theory of the Universe*. New York: Anchor Books, 1995.

Laszlo, Ervin. *Science and the Akashic Field: An Integral Theory of Everything*. Rochester, VT: Inner Traditions, 2004.

Lipton, Bruce, Ph.D. *The Biology of Belief: Unleashing the Power of Consciousness, Matter and Miracles*. Santa Rosa, CA: Mountain of Love, 2005.

McTaggart, Lynne. *The Field: The Quest for the Secret Force of the Universe*. New York: HarperCollins, 2002.

Nørretranders, Tor. *The User Illusion: Cutting Consciousness Down to Size*. New York: Viking, 1998.

Pearce, Joseph Chilton. *The Biology of Transcendence: A Blueprint of the Human Spirit*. Rochester, VT: Park Street Press, 2002.

Pert, Candace P., Ph.D. *Molecules of Emotion: The Science Behind Mind-Body Medicine*. New York: Simon & Schuster, 1997.

Pritchett, Price. *You^2: A High-Velocity Formula for Multiplying Your Personal Effectiveness in Quantum Leaps*. Dallas: Pritchett & Associates, Inc., 1994.

Scheele, Paul R. *Natural Brilliance: Overcome Any Challenge . . . At Will*. Wayzate, MN: Learning Strategies, Inc., 2000.

Thomas, Peter. *Never Fight with a Pig: A Survial Guide for Entrepreneurs*. Toronto: Macmillan, 1991.